Modern Jewish Mythologies

edited by
Glenda Abramson

Hebrew Union College Press
Cincinnati

Library of Congress Cataloging-in Publication Data

Modern Jewish mythologies / edited by Glenda Abramson
p. cm.

Includes bibliographical references.
ISBN 0-87820-216-1

1. Jews—Intellectual life—20th century.
2. Jews—Identity.

I. Abramson, Glenda.

DS113.M58 1999   99-26975
305.892'4—dc21   CIP

Contents

Preface

In our time, as in earlier periods, our understanding of reality is constituted not only by facts but by the ways in which we approach and understand these facts. Among the major influences upon our responses to reality are myths of various kinds: historical, religious, scientific, and national narratives that replace the sacred myths of the past. In Jewish culture and history, the presence of shaping myths is generally accepted. Their role in modern Jewish consciousness has been discussed in the past, albeit fragmentarily. Now there is a need to explore discoveries regarding myths in the contemporary Jewish world, to demonstrate their function and dynamic effect in Jewish cultural, social, political, and psychological life.

Throughout this volume, scholars offer many definitions of the term "myth," the most basic perception being that they are emotionally-charged beliefs represented by a society. These beliefs both construct and reveal that society's view of the world. Each of the scholars has taken a myth—or belief—of the modern Jewish world, or of a specific Jewish community, and examined it within its historical or social context. For example, Jonathan Webber explores what is claimed to be a deep cultural belief among contemporary Western Jews: that of memory as an essentially Jewish value, remembrance as a Jewish moral duty, *zakhor* as a statement of the Jewish identity to be declared to the world at large. According to Webber, the stated desire to remember is to be taken as a statement of belief about what constitutes the nature of the central Jewish purpose or mission. Yet the idea that Jews form and have always formed their identity as a people of remembrancers does not derive from the empirical facts: it is a contemporary Jewish myth.

Webber further argues that there is no such thing as one Jewish historical consciousness and that historical memory does not just appear, in his words, "from mid-air." Instead, it is usually the self-conscious product of some institutional source (museum, survivors' organization, academic institution or department) that aims to deliver a particular rendering of its historical past. Out of this chaos of competing institutional histories, he continues, something of a consensus has been emerging in the public Jewish mind concerning the need to protect the memory of the Holocaust from trivialization and banalization. Despite the outpouring of Holocaust representations in an ever-increasing flood of books, exhibitions, films and conferences, the meaning of this historical event remains elusive. The phenomenon of Holocaust remembrance has begun to develop many of the signs of a new secular religion.

Modern Jewish myths, like those of other cultures, are no longer expressed exclusively through sacred literature but in the cinema and theater, in modern literary texts, in historical memory and personal narrative, and through modernized archetypes. The work of the only folklorist in the volume, Eli Yassif's paper opens with a definition of the term "myth." According to Yassif, most anthropologists and historians would agree to define myths as "sacred narratives": stories told by a society that construct their view of the world and that chart their social norms and institutions. However, when dealing with "modern mythologies," as this volume does, the term "sacred" should be replaced by "secular."

In Yassif's opinion, one element central to any discussion of myth as folklore is traditionality. Rather than being the creation of individuals, myth is created by society and transmitted from generation to generation by oral or written means. In his paper, Yassif attempts to fill in the gaps between traditionality and modernity by presenting the ancient Jewish myth of the Golem, the homunculus, and its development into a central symbol of modern Jewish life. The myth of the Golem presents an exemplary test case for the exploration of cultural continuity from the pre-monotheistic myths and beliefs to modern technological culture. It expresses the profound changes that have occurred in Jewish life and thought. The theme is expressed throughout different media, including literature and cinema—all of which proves its versatility. In his Introduction to the volume, Yassif discusses traditional approaches to the study of myth, stressing in particular the relationship between text and ritual.

Within the parameters defined by Eli Yassif in both of his essays, each paper in this volume presents a different approach to myth and a different application of the term to the events, peoples, experiences, institutions, or texts it examines. Both David Cesarani and Anita Shapira demonstrate the underlying assumption of the majority of scholars in this volume, that the process of creating myth is related one way or another to attempts by social and ethnic groups, and by women, to shape their collective memory; changes in the myth through time reflect changes in the self-image of a given society or group and its basic values. As a case study, Cesarani has used the oral and written testimonies of Jewish immigrants from eastern Europe to Britain. Anita Shapira has chosen an episode in the Israeli War of Independence, 1948: a battle on the plain of Latrun between a newly-formed Israeli brigade and units of the Arab Legion, which ended in an Israeli rout. The mythical components of the Latrun narrative have served changing social groups, but have never lost their vitality. Latrun exemplifies the mythopoeic dynamic: how a myth crystallizes around a certain basic kernel of fact, and then constructs and molds the collective memory according to the changing patterns of national identity.

Relevant to the shaping of collective memory is the self-identification generated by extraordinary circumstances. The South African Jewish community has, from its early development in the late nineteenth century, been a vibrant and identified one, comparatively free of both antisemitism and the necessity for comformity to the wider culture. Since the demise of apartheid, questions about the Jewish community's historical attitude to the ruling Afrikaner hierarchy and right-wing National Party and the communal and individual Jewish stance in relation to apartheid have been increasingly debated. From within the growing discussion, Milton Shain and Sally Frankental interrogate the widely-held view that during this period South African Jewry operated on a higher moral plane than most other white South Africans.

Some of the most potent modern myths are those of national foundation. Many modern Jewish myths have their source in Zionism and the creation of the State of Israel, whose founding myths were an important element of the "invention" of a national tradition. They immediately established a precedence of state and community over the individual. Hebrew fiction and drama of the *yishuv* and the early years of the State were distinguished by their retelling of "national" events. In Yael Zerubavel's words, Hebrew writers and educators turned Jewish history into "legends" that would inspire the Hebrew youth. Whereas history provided the legitimizing basis for the Zionist national revival, Hebrew literature contributed to the emergence of new forms of commemorating the past, and reinforced their significance.[1]

Many of Israel's founding myths, for example that of the sabra hero, rested on strong factual foundations, for social imagination is constitutive of social reality[2] and myths follow from authentic history. The male "Hebrew" hero of the 1940s and 50s represented a generation that belonged explicitly to a certain chapter of modern Jewish history, that of Zionism and the foundation of Israel. This persona became an enduring archetype that ultimately attracted the opprobrium of the writers who saw him as "monolithic in his political existence."[3] The early national Zionist cinema set up this Israeli male as a super-persona and the center of gravity in the Zionist myth. However, this cinema was not able to ignore the differences of class, sex, and race this persona had been intended to obliterate. Nurith Gertz argues that, since the 1960s, these differences have been increasingly revealed in films that dwell on the diaspora-Jewish past, the Arab past of the country, and the female image: elements repressed by the the unifying myth of the Hebrew male.

Because of its preoccupation with political ideology and the male hero, feminism and gender politics have not occupied a prominent place in Israeli literature until recently. Dan Urian's paper, which examines the place of women in Israeli theater and drama, focuses on two broadly feminist Israeli plays of the 1990s. Both rewrite the biblical story of Sarah from a feminist point of view. In much of the dramatic repertoire, female characters have been depicted from a masculine viewpoint and consequently the few plays that succeed as "feminist theater" are highly significant. *Womb for Rent* (1990), written by Shulamith Lapid, weaves the biography of one of Israel's most prominent actresses, Hannah Marron, into the dramatic text. Plays by the Theater Company of Jerusalem (TCJ), illustrate the demand for "a new Judaism" by women who question their inferior status as embodied in the Torah. For example, the TCJ's *Sarah* (1993) argues for a different Judaism, which privileges the place of women.

One of the fundamental ideas of the Haskalah was the conviction that Western Jewry could find redemption only by an increased adoption of modern, Western cultural values. Later, the natural relationship of the Muslims of Palestine to the land and to their own past was seen as offering a model for déraciné Jews deformed by the abnormalities of diaspora existence. This perception suggested that new models of redemption were possible for the Western Jews. Tudor Parfitt's survey explores Western and Israeli perceptions of the Yemenite Jews, and he argues that these perceptions were often suited to the discourse on "orientalism."

Sylvie-Anne Goldberg discusses Jewish relationships with regard to death, changes in perceptions of communal institutions, and the evolving role of the *hevrah kaddisha* in Prague, and Matthew Olshan offers an analysis of Kafka's animal fables as parables for the Jewish response to tradition, the inability of Jews either to embrace or reject it.

This volume could not have come about but for the generosity of the Oxford Centre for Hebrew and Jewish Studies, which made it possible for scholars to meet and discuss the intricacies of modern Jewish mythology. It would also not have been possible without the guiding presence of Eli Yassif, who has been equally generous in sharing his ideas and profound knowledge of the subject. My grateful thanks, too, to Barbara Selya of the Hebrew Union College Press for her patience, her careful attention to the text, and her valuable suggestions, the results of which considerably enhanced this book.

Glenda Abramson
Oxford, July 1999

1. See Yael Zerubavel, *Recovered Roots. Collective Memory and the Making of Israeli National Tradition* (London and Chicago: The Chicago University Press, 1955), pp. 79, 83.

2. See Myron Aronoff, "Myths, Symbols and Rituals of the Emerging State" in Laurence J. Silberstein, ed., *New Perspectives on Israeli History* (New York and London: New York University Press, 1991), p. 176.

3. Moshe Shamir, quoted by Avraham Oz in "Chasing the Subject: The Tragic as Trope and Genre and the Politics of Israeli Drama," *Contemporary Theatre Review* 3,2 (1995): 141.

Introduction:
Modern Jewish Culture as a
System of Myths

Limits of Definition

When the *Encyclopedia Judaica* was published in 1972, its editors, as well as the public for which it was intended, saw in it the synopsis of Jewish knowledge from the time of the *Wissenschaft des Judentums* in the nineteenth century. This compendium of scholarship attempted to consolidate the achievements of Jewish studies over approximately two hundred years. It is rather interesting to begin a survey of myth in Jewish culture from this standard source, as a starting point for the conventional, agreed point of view.

The entry "Myth, Mythology" covers about one and a half columns and, after a very short, rather conservative introductory note about myth and ritual, is dedicated to "Myth and Mythology in the Bible."[1] This apparently suggests that from biblical times until 1972, the year the *Encyclopedia Judaica* was published, there has been no myth in Jewish culture, and that myth has not been important within the development of the culture. The entry was written by the "Editorial Staff of the Encyclopedia," as were all secondary, less important entries. In contrast, a previous entry, "Kabbalah," occupies 164 columns and was written by one of the greatest scholars of the age, Gershom Scholem.[2]

My intention is not to criticize the *Encyclopedia Judaica*, but only to point to the relatively low status and importance of the concept of myth in the study of Judaism during the 1960s (the actual time of the *Encyclopedia's* compilation). This attitude, it seems, emerges from its general definition and understanding of the concept. According to the *Encyclopedia Judaica*,

A myth is a story about the universe that is considered sacred. Such a story deals with the great moments of man's life: birth, initiation, and death, referring them to events that took place in "mythical time." The myth is often recited during a dramatic representation of the event it narrates (e.g., the Enuma Elish was recited at the Babylonian New Year festival). . . . Myths can be classified according to their subjects, as: theogonic, cosmogonic, anthropogonic, soteriological, and eschatological, myths of paradise, myths of flood, hero myths, etc.[3]

If such is the definition of myth, it is not difficult to understand why the entry in the *Encyclopedia* is limited to the Bible alone, for cosmological myths of this type are to be found predominantly in the Bible.[4] If this is so, the creation of myths began in the Bible, and ended there.

The definition of myth and the ways it is understood determine its application to different cultures and periods. This is not a new observation, but it is exceptionally complicated. It is no exaggeration to say that there are very few other cultural concepts that have been defined in so many ways. In fact, it can be said that "everyone has his own myth," from the major thinkers who developed complicated philosophical systems regarding myth, to its everyday use by journalists, politicians, and ordinary people.[5] For this reason it is possible for the "Editorial Staff" of the *Encyclopedia Judaica* to choose its own definition of myth and, being consistent, limit Jewish myth to the Bible.

In a culture like ours, where there is almost no area in which the term is not somehow applicable—religion, politics, psychology, literature, economy, history, and even the army and science—there is no reason for limiting the definition of myth to its classical applications. The definition should be changed according to the place of myth in reality, not vice versa, that is, making the myth fit the definition.

I do not intend to add yet another definition to the dozens already existing, or to add another methodological discussion about the differences between the various philosophical, religious, anthropological or semiological systems dealing with myth. All this has been done.[6] It seems better to turn to the concrete study of myth, to the analysis and interpretation of specific myths or systems of myths rather than the theory, and to enlarge the basis of data before the theoretical system collapses upon itself. It seems that since the 1950s, when Roland Barthes opened the way for an entirely new body of data to be studied as myth—from the face of Greta

Garbo to the recent Citroen car—the theoretical corpus has continued to expand, almost consuming itself, without a serious attempt to adapt itself to changing reality.

Sacred History, Discourse, and Ritual

Technically we may approach the concept of myth through two main methods, derived from the systems of two thinkers of the 1950s. One is the Rumanian exile Mircea Eliade, and the other, the French semiologist Roland Barthes. Eliade developed in broad terms the classical approach to myth, that is, myth as "sacred history":

> Myth narrates a sacred history; it relates an event that took place in primordial Time, the fabled time of the "beginnings". In other words, myth tells how, through the deeds of Supernatural Beings, reality came into existence.[7]

It is clear that most of what we usually call myth in recent culture cannot be defined in this way. Though Eliade is willing to accept that even in the modern world some myths of the "return to origins" exist—those myths that are the basis of modern nationalism, the myth of social equality in Communism, the myth of the hero—he considers all these as "survivals and camouflages of myths," rather than real myths.[8] Although this understanding of myth limited Eliade's direct influence on the study of modern mythology, his authoritative scholarship in world religions exerted a strong influence upon the field.

The second system, which turned the concept of myth upside down, was that of Roland Barthes. In his well-known essay "Myth Today" he suggested:

> . . . since myth is a type of speech, everything can be a myth, provided it is conveyed by a discourse. Myth is not defined by the object of its message, but by the way in which it utters this message: there are formal limits to myth, there are no 'substantial' ones. Everything, then, can be a myth? Yes, I believe this, for the universe is infinitely fertile in suggestions.[9]

Thus myth is a type of discourse that belongs to the wider field of semiology. It is a sign whose application and meaning are introduced through discourse. It is understandable that this approach to myth opened up a wide range of possibilities for the use of the term not only in the fields of religion, folklore, and parallel fields (such as the study of the Bible), but in almost all areas of life and culture, encompassing even the most naive and banal—for example, a boxing competition or eating a steak—as Barthes demonstrated in his *Mythologies*.

Another seminal difference between these two approaches is the ritual component. The debates surrounding the myth-ritual hypothesis have been among the most intense and renowned in the history of myth studies.[10] The fact that in Eliade's definition ritual has a central role, while in Barthes's approach it has no place at all, is characteristic of that debate. The denial of the connection between the "textual element" (the myth) and the performance act has been typical of the approach to myth in the second half of the twentieth century. However, after moving from the naive concepts of the myth-ritual conception, a different, more careful understanding became apparent.

Two prominent anthropologists were responsible for the change. The first was Klyde Kluckhohn who, already in 1942, suggested a different, careful, and complex hypothesis. He rejected the idea that myth is derived from ritual or vice versa, even though he believed in the close association of the two while each is able to appear, independently of the other. He concluded, "The myth is a system of word symbols, whereas ritual is a system of object and act symbols. Both are symbolic processes for dealing with the same type of situation in the same effective mode."[11]

About twenty-five years later, in an influential entry in the *International Encyclopedia of the Social Sciences*, Victor Turner continued this line of thought. He suggested applying the concept of "rites of passage" to the definition of myth: "myths as liminal phenomenon . . . [emerge when] a whole social group is in ritual transition," and so myths become "symbols of liminality."[12] Those liminal situations are characterized simultaneously by two cultural phenomena: myths and rituals, and so the functional relationship between the two cannot be ignored. Kluckhohn and Turner offered an important hypothesis on the complex relationship between myth and ritual, without which many central phenomena of Jewish modern culture could not be understood.

It becomes clear that even in modern culture, both in traditional religious ceremonies and in civil religion—for example, national or academic ceremonies—there is a clear relationship between mythical texts and repetitive actions societies perform in connection with them. These relationships are not direct and mechanical as previously thought, but more complex and multi-dimensional. Nevertheless they are undeniable. Even that famous salute of the black French soldier to the French flag, which for Barthes symbolized the myth of French imperialism,[13] is an unconcealed ritual act, inseparable from the "mythical text."

Myth, Ritual, and Religion in Modern Jewish Culture

I would like to illustrate this complex relationship of myth and ritual in modern Jewish culture with two examples, one involving only Israelis, the other, Jews throughout the world.

The story of Masada is one of the best known and discussed myths in Israeli culture. Although the story itself was told for the first time by Flavius Josephus, for almost 1900 years it did not arouse the interest of traditional Jewish culture.[14] Only in the early 1930s, when the rock and fortress in the Judean desert were rediscovered by youth movements, paramilitary units, and political groups in pre-state Israel, did it begin to occupy a central place in public discourse. From that time on, these groups made regular pilgrimages to Masada. After a long and tiring journey in the desert they climbed the steep rock face, gave patriotic sermons, and presented performances that were ritualistic in character. Since 1948, army units have made regular, formal journeys to the fortress, where they collectively confirmed their national vows and received their personal weapons—symbols of the independence of the state.[15] These ceremonies were of salient ritualistic character. They included a textual vow that mentioned the warriors of Masada of two thousand years ago; military parades, and the distribution of weapons—a typical mixture of mythical text and ritual action. It seems impossible to explain one of the most important modern myths without this inevitable relationship between the text—the Masada story—and the ritual, which endows the text with formal structures that ensure its existence in the society's collective memory.[16]

However, while the myth and ritual of Masada developed almost spontaneously as part of internal contemporary developments,[17] the myth of

Hanukkah originated outside native Israeli reality, in the religious tradition. Many halakhot and customs have been created since the composition of rabbinic legal literature. These halakhot defined Hanukkah's ritual character: what to do and how to do it, when and where the Hanukkah candles are to be lit, how and from which materials they should be made, who should light them and what texts—blessings and prayers—are to be recited while doing so. We note two types of myths in modern Jewish culture: those that were created almost out of nothing, independent of previous religious traditions; and those that are a continuation of religious tradition, transformed into modern myths after substantial changes. The Masada myth is a typical example of the first; Hanukkah, of the second.

Hanukkah candles were lit in Talmudic times, as they are now, but there is a world of difference between the two ritual acts. In rabbinic literature it is stated that the Hasmoneans could not use the candelabrum in the Temple since the Greeks had defiled it. They therefore took seven iron spits, covered them with zinc, and used them as a candelabrum (Scholium to *Megillat Ta'anit*). Another *baraita* ascribes the eight-day celebration of Hanukkah to the kindling of the Temple candelabrum. It states that on entering the Temple, the Hasmoneans discovered that the Greeks had blemished all the oil except for one cruse, which contained enough oil to keep the candelabrum burning for one day. However, a miracle occurred and it was kindled for eight days. A commemorative festival lasting eight days was instituted for future generations (Scholium to *Megillat Ta'anit*; Babylonian Talmud, Shabbat 21b).[18]

However, the candles assume new significance in Israeli civil religion: they have come to symbolize the struggle for independence, the uprising of the Jewish people against its oppressors, and the last military victory of a Jewish army until the IDF's recent victories. The blessing *Al ha-nissim* ("on the miracles") and the traditional liturgical song *Ma'oz tzur* follow the lighting of the candles in the Israeli Hanukkah ritual, as they always did in Jewish religious tradition. Immediately afterward, however, the Hanukkah songs that have become inseparable from the Israeli Hannukah are sung. The song *Anu nos'im lapidim* ("we carry torches") expresses the victory of light over darkness, the Jews against their oppressors, the struggle for independence. *Banu hoshekh legaresh* ("we came to banish darkness") expresses national solidarity and the need for unity in the face of great challenges; *Ner katan* ("a little candle"), and *Sevivon sov-sov-sov* ("dreidel, spin around"), the love for the land of Israel. These values and concepts were never part of the story of Hanukkah, but an outcome of new life in Israel. It is no coincidence that all these new ritual-like songs have no relation to the religious tradition or giving thanks to God "for his miracles, in those days, [and] in our own time," as is said in the blessing on the candles.

Another important component of the modern Hanukkah ritual is the eating of jelly doughnuts. The folk-etymology of this custom is the same Temple miracle, for the Hanukkah doughnuts are fried in oil. Although this is a new festival custom,[19] today it is an inseparable part of the Hanukkah ritual in Israel, second only to the lighting of the candles. The dynamic force of the Hanukkah myth in real life will be understood through the following event, in which the "new" component of the myth is central:

At Hanukkah, 1996, as in the past, the Chabad (Lubavich) Hasidim in Israel went to the Knesset to serve its members jelly doughnuts. However, a Labor MK barred the door to one of the committee conference rooms against them. The religious MKs and members of Likud were taken aback, for the Hasidim were performing a good deed, carrying out a religious precept! A compromise was reached only when one of the Likud members stepped out, took the package from the Hasidim, and brought the doughnuts in himself.

All this furor over a jelly doughnut can only be understood in the context of the last elections. The Lubavich movement was the most aggressive supporter of the right wing, contributing many millions of dollars, mobilizing thousands of activists, and chartering planes to bring Hasidim with Israeli citizenship to Israel to vote for Benjamin Netanyahu. As a result, the left in Israel no longer sees the Lubavich as a spiritual and religious movement, whose members are allowed to visit the Knesset, army camps, and schools, but as a political movement.[20] It was clear to all that more than jelly lay within this traditional holiday treat. It had become the symbol of the great divide: the Lubavich Hasidim sought to "feed" the Knesset— representative of the sovereignty of the State of Israel—with their "traditions." Labor members, representatives of the secular left, claimed that the sugar-dusted exterior of this seemingly innocent confection encompassed a clear political message: West Bank settlements, Israeli expansionism, and religious fundamentalism, as opposed to the classical, humanistic Jewish heritage.

But the context is even more complicated. The myth upon which the sanctity of Hanukkah was based is the oil-miracle story, not the revolt against the great Greek empire, or the war and heroic victory, and not even the establishment of the last independent Jewish state for two thousand years.[21] An example of the difference of attitude towards the celebration of Hanukkah between secular and ultra-Orthodox communities is seen in the explicit words of one of the spiritual leaders of the ultra-Orthodox, Yitzhak Breuer (1982):

> The Hellenizers loved their people and their land in their own
> fashion. . . . They loved the land but loathed the Land of Torah;
> loved the people but despised the people of the Torah; loved Greek
> licentiousness but hated the burden of Torah. . . . It is not for the
> Jewish State that the Hasmoneans fought but for the people of the
> Torah. They did battle against the kingdom of evil when it threat-
> ened the People of the Torah with destruction. . . . They also fought
> against the wicked among their own people . . . This was a kul-
> turkampf. . . . Greek culture triumphed over the whole world, and
> only the Torah culture was able to withstand it.[22]

With their offering of fried doughnuts to the Knesset the Lubavich Hasidim are indicating that the essence of the State of Israel is not the political entity represented by the Knesset, or the army, or any of the other symbols of the independent state. Rather, this small doughnut represents the heavenly miracle expressed in the Scriptures. Beyond the political conflict, this debate indicates the *kulturkampf* played out every day in Israel: are we "a nation like all the other nations," or are we the bearers of the divine message on earth?

Hanukkah is not only an Israeli festival but one belonging to all Jewish communities, and it is celebrated publicly by the largest Jewish community outside Israel—that of the United States. If we do not take into account the ultra-Orthodox communities in the United States, for whom the festival has the same meaning and ritual as among the very religious in Israel (we have to remember that the Lubavich movement is prominent in America), the meaning of Hanukkah in the American–Jewish community is entirely different. The calendar proximity of Hanukkah to Christmas is very important. Preparations for Christmas begin weeks before the actual festival—the buying of Christmas trees, their ornamentation, the long preoccupation with personal gifts and preparations for the holiday meals and vacations, constitute a peak in the annual cultural cycle in the United States. On the face of it, the American Jews have no place in this central component of American culture. This is why Hanukkah has become one of the most important Jewish holidays in the United States, transcending its place in the traditional Jewish calendar. The complicated cultural process that led to this phenomenon can be defined as integration-differentiation. The Hanukkah festival enables the American-Jewish community to participate fully in the preparations before the actual holiday, preparations that are psychologically more important than the holiday itself. The centrality of lights in the Hanukkah ritual, and their similarity to the illumination of Christmas trees in the houses and streets, enables members of the Jewish community to share other components as well, like the ornaments, presents, meals, and vacations. This is an exemplary process of integration within mainstream American society, as part of a central social ritual. But Hanukkah is not Christmas; its sources, language, and meaning are different. So, by emphasizing the differences, the Jewish community gives prominence to its cultural uniqueness. Through its different elements (Hanukkah lamp instead of Christmas tree, Hanukkah songs instead of Christmas carols, the stories of the Hasmonean wars instead of the birth of Christ), they sharpen the cultural and social differentiation between Hanukkah and the mainstream festival of American society.[23]

In the United States, as in Israel, the ancient myth of Hanukkah plays an important role in the struggle for cultural identification and discourse with other communities. The integration of this ancient myth in the collective memory of the community in both centers of Jewish life has been achieved through ritual. Some rituals were part of an older tradition and transmitted along with it (the candles, the liturgies, the playing with dreidels), and some were created in contemporary Jewish life (eating jelly doughnuts, Hanukkah folk-songs, buying personal gifts, ornamenting the house).

Major trends in the study of myth have revealed that the religious component is essential for understanding myth. The definition of myth as "sacred history" is characteristic of the acknowledgment of this component.

In many societies, and according to certain philosophical trends, religion and myth are almost synonymous. Some students of myth believe that the significance of labeling a culture as "myth" is a form of alienation, of defining it as the culture of "the other."[24] It is possible therefore to consider the definition of religion as "myth" as the means by which those who reject a particular religion alienate themselves from it by regarding its followers as "others."

In modern Jewish history, this same process was part of the struggle of the Haskalah (Enlightenment) movement in the nineteenth century to reevaluate religiosity within Jewish society and promote a move towards modernity. They used the classical symbols of the cosmological fight between darkness and light. The forces of light—the Jewish Enlightenment—battle against the forces of darkness—the religious traditions labeled as superstitions—and try to expel them. The overt use of such terms as "the battle of the light against darkness" as a description of the struggle of the Jewish Enlightenment casts the movement and its goals in mythological terms. Similar struggles between the forces of light and darkness were the basis of ancient religions (for example, Gnosticism, which had a great influence on Judaism and Christianity), and is important evidence of the mythological foundation of religion.[25] However, it is clear that when the *maskilim* described their struggle in these terms they did not refer only to their metaphoric significance, but to the full force of traditional myth.

The connection between myth and religion is clearly expressed in the actual life of contemporary Israel. One characteristic example was the matter of the jelly doughnuts, where the ancient myth of the Hanukkah miracle was transformed into the debate between the Israeli religious community and its opponents. Another example is the ritual of pilgrimage to the saints' tombs. The custom of travelling to these holy sites for the purpose of contacting saints from biblical, talmudic, and medieval times, or religious authorities from later generations is evidence for a mythical component within modern life. Here the ritual perspective of myth becomes obvious: the veneration of saints is cyclical, takes place at fixed times, and includes ritual acts such as the lighting of candles, pouring of olive oil on the tomb, and reciting prayers created especially for the occasion.

What is the significance of the ritual pilgrimage to the saints' tombs? As with every myth, as we have seen, it is a statement, a type of social communication. The believers come to encounter the myth in reality, in the midst of modern life. An important component of their journey is the connection between life and death. Contrary to the modern, scientific approach that takes death as a finality with nothing following it, the pilgrimage to the saints is a strong statement for the myth of the afterlife, the ability and even necessity to establish communication with the dead.

The purpose is not only communication, but concrete benefit. The dead saints can act on behalf of the living and have the power to affect health and family, wealth and love. In other words, the complicated ritual of pilgrimage to the saints suggests that the most important elements in life are not in one's own hands, but are ordained in another, otherwordly, reality. The dead who are buried in these tombs (fictional graves, in many cases) represent the active forces in Jewish religious history, approved by the pilgrimages: biblical history, talmudic law, medieval mysticism, or the Hasidic religiosity of later times. Hands caressing the tomb, or people lying on it, indicate the physical response to the force symbolized by the saint. Ultra-Orthodox Jews from New York and Europe, Sephardi Jews from all over the world, particularly Canada and South America, regularly travel to the Holy Land on these pilgrimages, which constitute a Jewish, rather than an Israeli, phenomenon. In the Christian world, pilgrims also seek their own myths. These efforts are being intensified with the approach of the millennium, especially in sacred centers such as Nazareth and Bethlehem.

Jewish History as a System of Myths

Modern Jewish history is in a typical state of liminality. This is characterized by the transition from the traditional structures of Jewish society to modern reality, from conditions of exile to the majority of the Jews living in an independent state, from the inhuman conditions in many parts of eastern Europe and the Mediterranean countries to civil rights in the West. The definition of myth as expressing liminal states (Turner), when there is a need to redefine human condition (Baeten), fully suits the condition of Jews in our time.

The history of modern Jewry almost parallels the map of its myths. They include the myths of "out of the Ghetto" and the "battle of light against darkness" of the Haskalah; the myths of "Holocaust and heroism," which are the culmination of all *kiddush ha-shem* martyrology; the myths of "return to the Holy Land" and the "conquest of the land" *(kibbush ha-'aretz)*;[26] the myth of the "new Jew—the Sabra,"[27] who contrasts sharply with the "diaspora Jew," the bookish weakling; the myths of "security," which is placed in Israel above and beyond any other value; and, in the largest and strongest Jewish community outside of Israel, the myth of success: the poor east European immigrant arrives in the New World and with diligence, hard work, and much "Jewish wisdom," becomes a rich and respected citizen.

Jewish culture of the past few generations may be considered to be a complicated net of its myths. These express the deepest beliefs and conflicts of Jewish society and the most vital forces that have given it its present shape. It is important to emphasize, however, especially in a period of demythologization such as ours, that by delineating each of the phenomena mentioned as myths, my intention is not to characterize them as fictional and deny their "factuality." In the cultural study of myth, this is not a relevant question. By labeling them as "myths," I only mean that these phenomena have become powerful forces in Jewish history.

Only from this point of view can we label the Holocaust as myth: this is an event in the past whose narrative was founded as part of the collective memory of Jewish society, which returns to it ritually again and again through the marking of Holocaust Day, visits to the concentration camps and Holocaust museums, and the presentation of compulsory courses in schools. It is an event that has decisive power over people's lives and ideas. From this point of view, the "myth of the Holocaust" is one of those modern Jewish myths without which it is impossible to understand modern Jewish history, and especially to identify those underground forces that have made Jewish life in the modern world what it is.

1. *Encyclopedia Judaica* (Jerusalem, 1972), vol. 12, cols. 729–30.

2. Ibid., vol. 10, cols. 489–653.

3. *Encyclopedia Judaica,* vol. 12, col. 729.

4. And in some midrashic texts of the Middle-Ages (as *Pirkei de-Rabbi Eliezer*), and differently in the Kabbalah. See Gershom Scholem, "Kabbalah and Myth," in his *Elements of the Kabbalah and Its Symbolism* (Jerusalem, 1976), pp. 86–112 [Hebrew].

5. Elizabeth M. Baeten, *The Magic Mirror: Myth's Abiding Power* (Albany, 1996), pp. 35–36, presents some of these common uses of the term "myth."

6. See, for example, Baeten, ibid., who deals with the systems of Cassirer, Barthes, Eliade, and Hillman; Ivan Strenski, *Four Theories of Myth in Twentieth Century History* (Iowa 1987), who deals with Cas-

sirer, Malinowski, Lévi-Strauss, and Eliade; M. Detienne, *The Creation of Mythology* (Chicago, 1986) [in French, 1981], and William G. Doty, *Mythography: The Study of Myths and Rituals* (Tuscaloosa, 1986), who gathers more than fifty different definitions of the concept.

7. Mircea Eliade, *Myth and Reality*, trans. from the French by William R. Trask (New York, 1963), p. 5; and idem., *Myths, Rites, Symbols: A Mircea Eliade Reader*, eds. Wendell C. Beane and William G. Doty (New York, 1975), vol. 1, pp. 2–4.

8. Eliade, *Myth and Reality*, pp. 181–93.

9. Roland Barthes, *Mythologies*, selected and translated from the French by Annette Lavers (London, 1972 [1957]), p. 109.

10. Joseph Fontenrose, *The Ritual Theory of Myth* (Berkeley, 1971); Catherine Bell, *Ritual: Perspectives and Dimensions* (New York and Oxford, 1997), pp. 3–22, and the large bibliography suggested there.

11. Klyde Kluckhohn, "Myth and Rituals: A General Theory," *Harvard Theological Review* 35(1942): 45–79, quoted from p. 58.

12. Victor W. Turner, "Myth and Symbol," *International Encyclopedia of the Social Sciences*, ed. David L. Sills, 1968, vol. 10, pp. 576–82 (quotation from p. 576).

13. Barthes, *Mythologies*, pp. 116–17.

14. Flavius Josephus, *The Wars of the Jews with the Romans*, chaps 2.17.2–9; 4.7.2; 7.8.2–7.9.2. In the tenth-century Jewish chronicle of the Second Temple period, the *Josippon*, the story is taken from Josephus and changed (*The Josippon*, ed. with an introduction, commentary, and notes by David Flusser [Jerusalem, 1978], vol. I. pp. 423–31), but it still had almost no influence on Jewish culture until the Jewish settlement in Palestine.

15. These developments are described in detail in Yael Zerubavel, *Recovered Roots: Collective Memory and the Making of Israeli National Tradition* (Chicago, 1995), pp. 60–78, 114–37; Nachman Ben-Yehuda, *The Masada Myth: Collective Memory and Mythmaking in Israel* (Madison, Wisconsin, 1995). In his bibliography, Ben-Yehuda lists the many published studies on the myth.

16. Yael Zerubavel, "New Beginning, Old Past: The Collective Memory of Pioneering in Israeli Culture," in Laurence J. Silberstein, ed., *New Perspectives on Israeli History* (New York, 1991), pp. 193–215.

17. These are listed in Ben-Yehuda, *The Masada Myth*, pp. xix–xxi; Zerubavel, *Recovered Roots*, pp. 192–213.

18. Moshe David Herr, "Hanukkah," in *Encyclopedia Judaica* (Jerusalem, 1972), vol. 7, pp.1280–88; Solomon Grayzel, "Hanukkah and Its History," in Emily Solis-Cohen, *Hanukka: The Feast of Lights* (Philadephia, 1955), pp. 17-48; and translation of the main sources into English, pp. 119–46.

19. As late as 1938, Hayyim Schauss in his popular *The Jewish Festivals: History and Observance* (New York, 1938), pp. 234–36, does not mention this at all among the holiday customs. In the popular Hebrew anthology by Z. Ariel, *Sepher ha-ḥag veha-mo'ed* [The Holiday Book] (Tel-Aviv, 1961), pp. 141, 157–161, different kinds of foods specific to Hanukkah are mentioned, but jelly doughnuts are not among them.

20. On the spiritual and institutional development of this Hasidic movement, see Naftali Loewenthal, *Communicating the Infinite: The Emergence of the Habad School* (Chicago and London, 1990). On the recent extreme developments, Aviezer Ravitzky, "The Contemporary Lubavitch Hasidic Movement: Between Conservatism and Messianism," in Martin E. Marty and R. Scott Appelby, eds., *Accounting For Fundamentalisms* (Chicago and London, 1994): 303–27; Menachem Friedman, "Habad as Messianic Fundamentalism: From Local Particularism to Universal Jewish Mission," in ibid., 328–60; William Shaffir, "When Prophecy is not Validated: Explaining the Unexplained in a Messianic Campaign," in *The Jewish Journal of Sociology* 37 (1997): 119–36.

21. About the importance of this festival for the ideology of the Zionist movement, see Eliezer

Don-Yehiya, "Hanukkah and the Myth of the Maccabees in Zionist Ideology and Israeli Society," in *The Jewish Journal of Sociology* 34 (1992): 5–24; and preceding him, but with a naive approach, Hortense Levy Amram, "The Maccabean Spirit in Zionism," in Solis-Cohen Jr., *Hannuka—The Feast of Lights*, pp. 49–58. See Schauss, *The Jewish Festivals*, pp. 229–30, about protests against the miraculous interpretation that began as early as the seventeenth century.

22. Moriah, *Jerusalem* 1982: 89, quoted from Don-Yehiya, "Hanukkah and the Myth of the Maccabees," p. 13.

23. On these and other aspects of Hanukkah acculturation in the United States see Ruth Rubin, "Chanukkah," *New York Folklore Quarterly* 9(1953): 255–60; Abraham G. Duker, *Emerging Cultural Patterns in American Jewish Life*, New York 1954.

24. Baeten, pp. 36–38.

25. See Paul Ricoeur, *The Symbolism of Evil*, trans. Emerson Buchanan, Boston 1969, esp. pp. 161–74.

26. Tamar Katriel and Aliza Shenhar, "Tower and Stockade: Dialogic Narration in Israeli Settlement Ethos," *The Quarterly Journal of Speech* 76(1990): 359–80.

27. Oz Almog, *The Sabra: A Profile* (Tel Aviv, 1997) [Hebrew].

Social Memory, History, and British Jewish Identity

The writing of Jewish history is a peculiar feature of Jewish modernity. Jewish historiography dates from the 1820s at the earliest and does not find institutionalized expression until the 1920s. Cecil Roth, the first professionally trained and employed Jewish historian in Britain, was appointed to a readership in Post-Biblical Hebrew Studies at Oxford only in 1939. Since then, the study of Jewish history has burgeoned for curious reasons. Yosef Yerushalmi remarks, "The modern effort to reconstruct the Jewish past begins at a time that witnesses a sharp break in the continuity of Jewish living and hence also an ever-growing decay of Jewish group memory. In this sense, if for no other, history becomes what it had never been before—the faith of fallen Jews."[1]

Yerushalmi ascribes the development of modern Jewish history writing to two forces. First, the Haskalah (Jewish Enlightenment) imported into Jewish studies the categories of thought current in general scholarship. By applying scientific methods to the study of the Jewish past, the *maskilim* (enlighteners) intended to display the willingness and capacity of Jews to assimilate contemporary cultural standards. Second, the Haskalah was used to push forward the adjustment of Jewish beliefs and rituals to the temper of the times. The earliest practitioners of the *Wissenschaft des Judentums,* such as Leopold Zunz, were also proponents of religious reform and used Jewish studies to demonstrate precedents for their agenda.[2]

The very impetus that the writing of Jewish history received from acculturation and modernization was inimical to cultivating the past for the purposes of guarding popular memory or generating group cohesion. Yerushalmi notes that "only in the modern era do we find, for the first time, a Jewish history divorced from Jewish collective memory and in crucial respects, thoroughly at odds with it." Jewish historians seem to write about everything other than that which Jews cherish as their past. When scholars do turn their attention to historical nostrums, it is apparently only in order to demolish them.[3] Consequently a gulf has opened up between memory and history. Yerushalmi laments that "many Jews today are in search of a past, but they patently do not want the past that is offered by the historians."[4] So we have arrived at a perplexing juncture. More than ever before, history is necessary to Jews as a reservoir of meaning in Jewish life and an element of their identity. But the historians are deemed the least able to supply this need. As Yerushalmi observes: "Jews have fully re-entered the mainstream of history, and yet their perception of how they got where they are is most often more mythical than real."[5]

This paper will examine some of the myths that have guided the lives and informed the identities of British Jews. But before embarking on another "demolition job," it is necessary to qualify the dichotomy that Yerushalmi draws between history and memory, and to point to a lacuna in his analysis. Historiography is not immune to myth-making. Indeed, since personal testimony (either directly recorded or in the form of memoirs) is one source of historical research, there is always a tendency for history to replicate myth. One constituent of the myth-making process that Yerushalmi overlooks is the ethnicity of those whose past is being recalled or chronicled and their interaction with other ethnic groups.

The relationship between memory, history, and ethnicity has been perceptively analyzed by John Bodnar, the distinguished American historian of immigration. Bodnar draws a distinction between "official history" and "vernacular history." The former is generated by leadership élites serving the state, local authorities, and the full constellation of social, including ethnic, groups. Since they have a vested interest in manufacturing social unity and consent for the status quo, their intrepretation of the past serves this end. "Vernacular history," by contrast, emerges from below, from the experience of everyday realities. When it finds articulation by spokespersons—Gramsci's "organic intellectuals"—or popular leaders, it is often at variance with the version fostered by those in power. Bodnar argues that "public memory" is a depiction of the past that mediates between the two and broadly satisfies both.[6]

When turning to the construction of ethnic memory in the U.S., Bodnar notes that the pressure for Americanization being exerted by the state could not be ignored by the leadership of minority ethnic communities. At the same time, ethnic élites were engaged in dialogue with their own constituencies to formulate an acceptable past that would meet their interests and satisfy the demands of the immigrant memorialists. The result was the celebration of adaptation and success, combined with nostalgia for the old country. Communal leaders, as well as rank and file, could agree that "the past most relevant for the present and worthy of celebration was one that included the values and institutions of the dominant society to which they were inextricably tied, as well as those of a more distant past that could both provide inspiration for ordinary individuals and fulfill longings to honour personal ancestors."[7]

Ethnic memory is thus shaped to harmonize with the history of the majority and to echo its values. Historians of their own ethnic groups invariably select from the past of their own communities that which appeals most to the dominant forces in society. History and memory then interact to create the filters through which succeeding generations interpret their experiences. The weakness of Yerushalmi's otherwise brilliant meditation on Jewish memory is his insistence on a monolithic transmission process and an oversimplified dichotomy between memory and history. As this paper will show, memory is no less vulnerable to social change than is history. Ethnicity plays a key role in the constant process of reinterpreting the past.

In the specific case of British Jews, the Jewish Historical Society of England, founded in 1893, was the progenitor of "official history" within the Jewish milieu. It set out to legitimate the presence of the Jews in Britain by demonstrating their utility to the state and their enthusiastic adoption of British culture. The society's relentless chronicling of Jewish enterprise and upward social mobility, from the readmission in 1656 to the Victorian era, was in part defensive. Yet the society also articulated the "collective memory" of the Jewish elite, recording and celebrating its rise to respectability. Until the 1970s the *Transactions of the JHSE* almost entirely excluded the history of east European immigration since the 1880s and the immigrant experience.[8] This was left to a subterranean "vernacular history" that bubbled beneath the official version. It was the orally transmitted and occasionally recorded history of uncomfortable immigration, painful settlement, hardship and struggle, often culminating in tragedy or failure. It was a narrative that encompassed the popular culture of the Jews, the experience of labor, crime, social protest, and the memories of children and women.

In the "official history," the immigrant experience was marginalized; but it was not entirely ignored. As the embodiment of Anglo-Jewish "popular memory," it bore the traces of contested accounts of the past. The celebration of success to some extent acknowledged the existence of a social substratum, present and past. By harping on the humble origins of Jewish worthies, the "official history" tacitly, albeit within a Smilesian genre, paid some heed to the poor and the immigrant masses.

However, this meager recognition of the immigrant experience was unsatisfactory and unsustainable. From the 1960s, historians beyond the ambit of the "official" chroniclers began to examine the Jewish immigrant past. Oral history, in particular, enabled historians to recover the experiences of growing up, the roles that family members played, struggles in the workplace, the extent of political radicalism, and the mute business of getting by.[9]

The Manchester Studies Unit, under the guidance of Bill Williams, made the first concerted attempt to garner the "vernacular history" of the immigrants and their children.[10] In October 1980, the Jewish Historical Society organized a conference on the Jewish East End.[11] Other initiatives followed, including the establishment of the Manchester Jewish Museum and the Museum of the Jewish East End. During the 1980s, a number of personal and collective oral history research projects were set in motion, such as the interviews with former refugees conducted by the Birmingham Jewish History Research Group, and the work of the Jewish Women in London Group. By the end of the decade, an impressive body of publications that recorded the previously submerged history of ordinary Jews in London and other British cities had appeared.[12]

Much of the theoretical underpinning and the impetus for the extension of oral history into British Jewish history came from the work of British historians involved with the History Workshop, including Raphael Samuel, Jerry White, and Bill Williams.[13] Another important influence was Paul Thompson, whose book *The Voice of the Past* appeared in 1978. However, Thompson was soon challenged by Richard Johnson and Patrick Wright, leading members of the Popular Memory Group at the Birmingham University Centre for Cultural Studies, who drew on the sophisticated use of oral history developed by Luisa Passerini in Italy. Passerini stressed how memories "draw upon general cultural repertoires, features of language and codes of expression which help to determine what may be said, how and to what effect." For her, memory is socially produced: what is bequeathed to the present is shaped by social relations. In addition, it is influenced by myths of the past prevailing at the time remembered events occurred, and accretions of history since then.[14]

The work of John Bodnar and Luisa Passerini obliges us to rethink the treatment of "vernacular history" in British Jewish historiography. It is no longer plausible to hold that oral history is some privileged species of historical truth, unmediated by scribes or vested interests. "Collective memory" or "social memory" is no less a construction than any other way of recalling the past. It too is governed by societal influences and rhetorical devices.[15]

Does the oral history of British Jews in the 1970s and 1980s give us direct access to a neglected past—a slice of British Jewish history ignored by the hagiographers who served the Cousinhood? Or does it merely record versions of the past refracted by and interleaved with myths of modern Jewish history? And how far is Jewish "popular memory" the product of complex interactions between sections of the Jewish population and between the Jews and British society? Finally, how does this help us to understand the identity of modern British Jews? As Agnes Heller has argued, what is recalled today from the past constitutes an element of everyday life and finds its place in the consciousness, the identity, of individuals and groups. As such, it shapes interpretations of the present and impacts upon the future as that which is remembered as having happened.[16]

In the autobiographical accounts of emigration from eastern Europe to Britain, (as recorded by the immigrants themselves or transcribed by their children), four main reasons are recurrently given as triggers for departure: pogroms, religious persecution, poverty, and the fear of military service. Jack Caplan, born in Glasgow in 1926, records: "My parents were immigrants from Lithuania . . . who, like thousands of other victims of anti-Semitism were compelled to flee from the pogroms, the burnings, the killings, and the rapings permitted and encouraged by the corrupt Russians."[17] This theme is echoed by Evelyn Cowan, writing of her childhood spent in the Gorbals in the 1920s. She recalls that her mother and father were typical of the immigrants who "arrived in Scotland at the turn of the century on the run from pogroms or long military service in their native Russia, Poland, or Lithuania."[18]

In the first volume of his memoir trilogy, Ralph Glasser, born in the

Gorbals in 1909, remembers "poignant anecdotes from 'der haim'—the ghetto of origin—constantly overheard, seared into the brain: of casual pogroms with their cold Danteesque brutality, routine rapes, floggings, merciless discrimination, extortion both financial and sexual."[19]

Harry Blacker, born in Bethnal Green in 1910, sums up the two most common reasons for emigration in his affectionate account of the "Mittel East" or East End of London. "Most of the inhabitants of the Mittel East left the land of their birth under pressure of poverty or pogroms."[20] In the brief family history that opens his autobiography, Israel Sieff does not fail to mention the pogroms that supposedly drove his father from his birthplace in a village near Kovno in Lithuania. Indeed, he maintains that the anti-Jewish violence so scarred his father that he was perpetually frightened. "Even in England, in Leeds, the pogroms were fresh in his mind."[21]

Yet there were no pogroms in Lithuania, not even during the period of revolutionary upheaval in 1904 and 1905. According to Lloyd Gartner, "Emigration did not begin on account of pogroms and would certainly have attained its massive dimensions even without the official anti-Semitism of the Russian Government."[22] Vivian Lipman baldly states that "immigration came mainly from Lithuania and White Russia, areas hardly affected, except indirectly, by pogroms."[23] This reason for Jewish emigration from eastern Europe is part of a myth of origins. But why did the immigrants tell such vivid tales and pass them on to their children in such a way that they became the mental furnishings of their identity as Jews in Britain?

One explanation is to be found in the public debate over the mass immigration of Jews from eastern Europe. From the time of the great protest meeting in the Mansion House, London, in February 1882, the Anglo-Jewish leadership explained that the Tsarist Government was driving Jews out of the country by a combination of religious intolerance, political repression, and economic victimization. The immigrants were characterized as "refugees," and it was said to be "asylum" that they sought in Britain. This formula was designed to appeal to liberal opinion, but also to mask the underlying economic opportunism that fueled the steady stream of emigration that had been underway since the 1860s. As Eugene Black has commented, "Western Jewish leaders in every country came to say, some even to believe, that Russian political misbehavior was the principal cause for Jewish immigration. Politics became a convenient explanation, and the myth that equality for Jews would keep them in the East was born. Convenience, however, did not render it less of a myth."[24]

Use of the "asylum" formula was hardened into orthodoxy by the political controversy over Jewish immigration that began in the mid-1880s and culminated in the passage of the Aliens Act of 1905. The restrictionist argument had the support of popular opinion in several urban localities, especially East London, and of large sections of the British labor movement. It also had the support of the Conservative Party. But these groups faced extensive opposition. Sections of the labor movement were wedded to the free movement of goods and labor, while socialist fraternity impelled them to view the plight of Jews in Tsarist Russia with sympathy.

The Liberal Party was committed to free trade and was deeply attached to the principle of asylum.[25] Indeed, until the late nineteenth century the notion of asylum was integral to Britain's self-image as a liberal country. So it was a powerful weapon in the hands of those resisting immigration controls.[26]

Asylum was such a potent idea that the Conservative Government felt obliged to enshrine it in the 1905 Aliens Act. Genuine refugees, defined as persons "seeking admission to this country solely to avoid persecution or punishment on religious or political grounds or for an offence of a political character, or persecution, involving danger of imprisonment or danger to life or limb on account of religious belief," were excluded from its purview.[27] The position of asylum seekers was further strengthened by the end of Conservative rule and the election of a Liberal Government in 1906. The new Home Secretary, Herbert Gladstone, instructed immigration officers and immigration boards to give the benefit of the doubt to immigrants who claimed refugee status and came from areas where pogroms had occurred.[28]

It was thus in the interests of both Anglo-Jewry and the immigrants to characterize the flow of migration as a flight from persecution. For the immigrants at the point of arrival, the stated reasons for their migration could make the difference between admission to Britain and instant deportation. Life histories reflect this pressure to interpret the immediate past in Russia in a certain way. The debate over immigration and the operation of the Aliens Act were responsible for standardizing accounts of migration and settlement and helped to generate a myth of origins. The ubiquity and power of this myth is apparent in accounts that make no sense other than as myths with a social function.

For example, *Take a Basket* is the memoir of Gloria Mound who, with her family, founded a Jewish delicatessen in Wembley (that my family used to frequent). On the first page she writes, "My grandfather, Maurice Drybent, was a hairdresser who came from Galicia to escape the pogroms like so many of his co-religionists at the end of the century." In fact, there were no pogroms in Galicia. It was part of the Austrian Empire and from 1867 onwards the Jews were equal citizens.[29]

Elaine Blond writes of her father, Michael Marks—the founder of Marks and Spencer—who was born in Slonim in 1864, that "as a teenager [he] was caught up in the terrors of the pogroms." This is unlikely, since there were no pogroms in Slonim while her father was in his teens. Her brother-in-law, Israel Sieff, in his memoirs struggles with this discrepancy. He resolves it by suggesting that "Michael Marks must have been one of the very first Polish Jews of the new diaspora precipitated by the assassination of Alexander II in 1881. What little we know indicates that he had left by 1882, when he was nineteen years old." To make matters even more awkward, he travelled to England because he had a brother who was already in London. Either both were remarkably quick off their marks or the pogroms were an element woven into their story later on.[30]

The conflict between actuality and expectation was responsible for the blurring of reasons so typically found in oral histories. Morris Serlin epitomizes this tendency when he recalls, "Of course—you know the story, there was no life there—apart from the pogroms and everything else, you just couldn't make a living. So they all of them with one or two exceptions . . . came over and started up cabinet making and small joiners . . . ."[31] Serlin's father emigrated from Poland, and it is unlikely that he ever experienced a pogrom. Of course, fear of attack was just as effective a force in driving Jews to leave the Russian Empire as actual physical assault. Yet there is a significant difference between the two, as current immigration and asylum regulations make us painfully aware.

At this point it is also necessary to question the ubiquity of military service. According to Elaine Blond, "Like thousands of his compatriots who were made the scapegoat for Russia's chronic economic and social ills, the best he [her father] had to hope for was a future as an army conscript." Israel Sieff explains that his father, Ephraim, emigrated from Lithuania to evade military service in the Russian army. Ephraim had first left home and crossed the border into East Prussia, settling in Koenigsberg. He was expelled from there along with other alien Poles in 1886, but refused to return permanently to Lithuania and face the army.[32] Cyril Spector, born in 1921 in Bethnal Green, never forgot what his father suffered for his religion. The son of a rabbi in Ekaterinoslav in Ukraine, the elder Spector "decided to marry and leave the country to escape the awful humiliations he was receiving in the forces because he was a Jew."[33]

Yet historians of the late-Tsarist army have demonstrated that you had to be either very poor or very stupid to be conscripted. At times when the Russian Empire was at war, such as the late 1870s and in 1904–1905, there was greater pressure on the draft. But outside of these periods, the Russian army was ramshackle, its recruitment officers corrupt, and service was easily avoided by means of bribery.[34] Moreover, the poorest, who were most likely to end up in the army, were the group least prone to migrate.[35]

However, as with the appeal for asylum, the alibi of conscription was finely tuned to the sensibilities of a liberal-minded English audience. Since the seventeenth century, the English had been famed for their loathing of standing armies and conscription. Contempt for military service and the militaristic ethos prevalent in continental countries was a significant component of the smugness that the English felt about their own country and a source of sympathy for those fleeing to its shores.[36] Thanks to the activity of London-based Russian political exiles such as Alexander Herzen (who wrote evocatively on the evils of the cantonal system), conscription had been entered on the charge sheet against Tsarism. It remained prominent, notwithstanding the fact that by the 1880s the practice of conscripting Jews for twenty-five years of service, along with other subjects of the Tsar, had long been scrapped.

Ironically, the notion that Jews gleefully evaded military service returned to haunt them. During the Boer War, the British Jewish leadership was at pains to encourage volunteering and bruited the martial tradition to be found amongst the descendents of the Maccabeans. It was around this time that Hanukkah became a militarized event in the calendar of British Jews. From the late 1890s to the First World War, annual Hanukkah parades and synagogue services, at which Jewish servicemen were proudly put on display, were held. During the First World War, when British Jews were regularly accused of evading armed service (and in the case of those born in Russia, the charge was not without foundation), the identity of the Jew as someone with an aversion to the military became an embarrassment that had to be countered by active pro-war propaganda and promotion of the stereotype of the Jew as biblical warrior.[37]

Another function of the myth of origins was to make manifest the Jews' patriotism and love of their new country. Charles Poulson, born in Stepney in 1911, carried with him from childhood the reasons his mother and father had left Russia. "We knew very well the long, frightening story of our parents, of what they had suffered in this cause under the Tsar before they came to England and freedom. And these tales of murder, pogrom, harassment, and cruelty borne made us proud of them—glad to be British, the loyal subjects of King George the Fifth, and part of what our elders were beginning to call 'Anglo-Jewry.'"[38]

Having recited the litany of indignities to which Russian Jews like his parents were subjected, Jack Caplan adds, "They found a land of peace, a land of beauty with mountains and lakes and a wonderful people to match—the Scots. If ever a prize will be given to a nation for its tolerance, its compassion, its humanity and understanding, and the claim to be one of the world's most civilized nations—then Scotland is assured of the presentation of gold."[39] Although his own account, like so many others, also charts years of struggle and frequent experiences of brutal antisemitism in his adopted country, the template of Russian history was always there to steer the narrative away from ungracious and seemingly ungrateful expressions of resentment or anger.[40]

A similar function can be detected in another standard element of accounts of migration and settlement in Britain: that of the accidental immigrant. Emanuel Litvinoff, born in the East End in 1915, informs readers of his memoir, *Journey through a Small Planet*, that his parents, who set off from Ukraine in 1914, "were part of a vast migration of Jews fleeing Tsarist oppression to the dream of America." They only got as far as England because they were tricked by an unscrupulous ticket agent. The Captain on the boat shooed them off with the words: "Anybody but a miserly lot of Jew-spawn would know the money they'd paid wouldn't cover the fare of a decent river ferry, never mind passage to New York."[41]

This tragicomic landfall is to be expected in Litvinoff's conscious espousal of the "shlemiel," but what is to be made of the equivalent tale told by a member of a millionare family? David Clore, brother of the more famous Charles, told David Clutterbuck, biographer of *The Man and His Millions*, that their father "always used to tell me that he and my mother arrived penniless on the wharf at Liverpool. He had only 4d in his pocket. Like a lot of emigrants he thought they were going to the United States."[42]

Historians of the mass migration have certainly uncovered many examples of ticket fraud. It was so widespread that in the 1900s Jewish agencies were set up specifically to counter it. Nevertheless, over one and a half million Jews managed to make it from eastern Europe to the U.S. without being cheated out of their dream. Of these, four hundred to five hundred thousand broke their journey for some length of time in Britain, voluntarily or otherwise, but succeeded in leaving. Indeed, the practice of the shipping lines put a premium on travelling to America in two stages, via British ports. It was economically rational to travel first to Britain and work to earn the rest of the money for the onward journey. Since immigrants had the option of on-migration or staying, the notion that large numbers of those who remained did so involuntarily, due to fraud, is extremely dubious.[43]

But this is to miss the point. Whether or not large numbers of emigrants from Russia were really cheated by unscrupulous ticket agents, a myth of accidental arrival has been installed in Anglo-Jewish "popular memory." Harold Pollins has commented, "One sometimes gets the impression that the Anglo-Jewish community was built up of those who did not get to America—the standard folklore tales are of those who got to Britain but were cheated out of their money and could not proceed; or thought they were already in New York."[44] Why should Jewish individuals and entire communities cultivate a self-denigratory myth of origins so pervasive that it includes Jack Caplan's parents, who arrived in Hull when they were aiming for New York, as well as those of Israel Sieff?[45]

To begin with, the myth of accidental arrival was another alibi for those who migrated for opportunistic migration. It was hard enough to carp at the arrival of a "refugee," let alone one who found himself stripped penniless by a land-shark upon his arrival. On another level it was a sensitive reflection of the disdain for money-making that was assuming an important place in English culture. Martin Wiener has argued persuasively that from the 1870s on, a powerful reaction to industrial capitalism was underway. As Wiener and Bryan Cheyette have shown, it was becoming increasingly

25

common for immigrants and "aliens" to be construed as the bearers of a hateful capitalistic spirit that threatened an idealized England typified by a rural life-style and preindustrial values.[46]

This was not merely a literary fantasy. The identification of Jewish immigrants with the spirit of capitalism was made explicit by influential social commentators such as Beatrice Potter and J. A. Hobson. Their characterization of the Jewish immigrant worker as "homo economicus" in turn reinforced the resentment felt by some sections of the labor movement, which accused the Jews of undercutting English labor.[47] To counteract this, anything that could be used to depict the immigrants as hapless and unenterprising was woven into the narrative of their arrival.

Over time, such myths became part of the social fabric of immigrant communities. Telling and retelling them was a way of creating and transmitting group memories, establishing and preserving a sense of community and identity. Emanuel Litvinoff, recalling the East End courtyards of his youth, gives a lovely vignette of this process in action.

> People spoke of Warsaw, Kishinev, Kiev, Kharkov, Odessa as if they were neighbouring suburbs. And the old women kept the old folk ways alive . . . So drowsily we absorbed our racial memories—stories of foreign lands we would never see with our own eyes, of wonder rabbis and terrible Cossacks spearing Jewish babies with their lances, of families cowering in cellars as mobs battered at the doors shouting "Kill the Jews and Save Russia."

In like manner, Arthur Franklin's amateur epic poem, "Times Remembered," recalls "the hot summer evenings when everyone sat out on the pavements to long after midnight cursing the butcher . . . We could hear the stories of the Hame, the Russo-Japanese war—Pogroms—Escapes over the border. Hiding from the Cossacks—a fire on them—Father's arrival from Plotsk. . . ."[48]

These scenes marvellously encapsulate the formation of "social memory" and the ambivalences inherent in it. Their function was to preserve group memories, while, at the same time, they also serve to reaffirm the motives for deserting the old ways.

Nor did memory evolve in a cultural vacuum, conveying some authentic and unadulterated Jewish experience. The spinners of many an immigrant tale, like Olga Franklin's father, had read Yiddish versions of Dickens, Zola, or Zangwill.[49] Frequently they absorbed established literary tropes into their own life histories, a tendency that was accentuated by the appearance of the great English and American sagas of immigrant life such as Abe Cahan's *The Rise of David Levinsky* (1917) and Simon Blumenfeld's *Phineas Khan. Portrait of an Immigrant* (1937).

Memory is highly plastic and molded as much by social relations as by the prevailing political and cultural ethos. For this reason certain memoirs do not shy away from admitting to an economic motive for migration. These divide roughly into those with a socialist undergirding and those that celebrate capitalism and the achievements of individualism.

Communist Party activist Joe Jacobs, born in Whitechapel in 1913, recalls a district populated by Jews "fleeing from impossible economic conditions to say nothing of the pogroms and anti-Semitic persecutions which most of them had experienced." Military service only added to their woes.[50] In Glasser's memoir, a socialist's clear-sighted appreciation of the economic impulse behind migration is interwoven with the more customary reasons: "For Jews the motive was escape from oppression, and economic only because of the hope that almost anything in the west could be better."[51]

Elaine Blond is keen to celebrate her father's success, yet finds herself constrained by the apologetic conventions of British-Jewish memory. The resulting ambivalence is telling. She writes:

> Even allowing for the appalling reality of the city ghettos experienced by most immigrants, a one-way ticket to New York was clearly favoured as the best chance to make good. So attractive was it that some of the more unscrupulous sailing masters were not above conning their passengers into paying for an Atlantic passage when their intention was never to venture beyond the North Sea. It is even possible that Michael was caught out in this way since in my younger days there was talk in my family of his landing in Britain by mistake.

She was unsatisfied with this inadvertence and comments, "My guess is that he cut his suit to fit his cloth. Britain was the nearest country untarnished by violent antisemitism, the shortest and cheapest journey on offer."[52]

By contrast, Lord Young of Graffham, Trade Secretary in Mrs. Thatcher's second government, is unequivocal and entirely unapologetic about his antecedents. He states boldly in his memoirs that his grandparents came from Russia to Britain in order to seek a better life, and succeeded. It may be significant that David Young was born in 1932, much later than the other memoirists quoted so far, and grew to maturity in a different climate. More likely the "Thatcherite" ethic prevalent in the late-1980s when he was writing (and which many commentators at the time saw as an expression of the mythologized Jewish historical experience) did not necessitate any excuses for seeking economic advancement.[53]

While Lord Young may differ from other British Jews in his analysis of what caused Jewish immigration, he is at one with them on its outcome. The "popular memory" of British Jews has been structured around the "upward social mobility" of the immigrants or their children. But it is a largely fictive version of the past and fails to represent the development of British Jewish society with any accuracy.[54] Furthermore, it is associated with another myth: the alleged correlation between increasing affluence and declining Jewish consciousness. In contemporary British Jewry it is virtually axiomatic that parents and grandparents were more Jewishly literate or observant than their descendants. The alleged earlier lifestyle is contrasted unfavorably with that of Jewish people today, often with the intention of denigrating modern, nontraditional expressions of Jewishness. Not only is this bad history, it is bad policy. It rests on a failure to appreciate the subtle evolution of Judaism and Jewish identity in Britain over the last seventy years.

Jewish society in Britain from the 1920s to the 1940s was characterized by rapid social, spatial, cultural and ideological diversification. All the social mores that were commonly identified as "Jewish" were on the wane or mutating. Jewish religious observance and literacy were in steep decline. Does this mean that these Jews were becoming less Jewish or was their Jewishness expressed differently from that of their parents and grandparents?

The interwar years saw the remaking of the British Jewish working class, but not its disappearance. British-born Jews moved out of the immigrant trades and the districts where the immigrants had settled and adopted different occupations and lifestyles. Very often this represented a sideways social movement with only the illusion of upward social mobility. The interwar Jewish population remained predominantly working- or lower middle-class, in humble white-collar or unskilled clerical occupations. Large numbers became hairdressers, barbers, taxi drivers, or self-employed in the retail trades or the markets. Relatively few broke into the professions. As compared to their children born in the 1950s and 1960s, these Jews were less well-educated and only superficially middle-class.[55]

As the Jewish population decanted from the inner city areas of settlement into inner and outer suburbs, family structure altered. The extended families that characterized inner city existence were sundered by the out-migration of the younger members. Ribbon settlements replaced vertically stacked ones. The intimacy of community and the "Jewish family," which was held to be characteristic of Jewish life, was in eclipse.[56]

At the same time, Jewish religious observance, Jewish culture, and Jewish secular ideologies were in flux. Reform and Liberal Judaism were well established and offered an alternative to mainstream Orthodoxy. More strictly Orthodox communities were equally well-rooted. Yiddish culture, while in gradual decline, still possessed vitality. Alongside it there was an Anglo-Jewish cultural effervesence in academic studies and popular literature. Simultaneously, competing political ideologies fought for the allegiance of British Jews. These included the Victorian tradition of assimilation and emancipation; Jewish nationalism in both its secular and religious versions; socialism and communism, both of which had enormous appeal to young Jews and substantial followings.[57]

Certain trends were particularly important regarding traditional ways of being Jewish. Throughout this period the proportion of Jewish children in *cheder* and *talmud torah* was in decline, especially in inner city communities where the enrollment dwindled even more than the decrease in the size of the Jewish population. The slack was not fully taken up in new areas of settlement. The majority of Jews growing up in the 1920s, 30s, and 40s were exposed to some form of Jewish education: *cheder*, supplementary schooling or *talmud torah*. *Shul*-going was common; bar-mitzvah was an established and joyfully extravagant business. However, the overwhelming evidence from memoirs and oral history suggests that religious education was a negative experience. Hebrew was soon forgotten. Jews could still follow services, but the prayers lost their meaning.

There was very little serious study of Jewish texts after bar-mitzvah. A large amount of anecdotal and statistical material points to evidence of non-observance. More and more Jews traded or worked on the sabbath, especially in the newer areas of employment such as market-trading, retailing, hairdressing, and taxi-driving. In other words, Jewish religious education had been only partially successful in inculcating Judaism, instilling a positive sense of Jewishness, or ensuring obedience to Jewish law.[58]

Secular, even anti-religious ideologies, had a greater appeal. Poverty and the rise of fascism led many young British-born Jews to align with the Communists, the Labour Party or other socialist groups. In the East End of London, Marxism and socialism were the dominant Jewish ideologies and had virtually driven out Zionism. Much of what remained of Jewish nationalism was actually a compromise with leftism, notably in the form of the Poale Zion and the Hehalutz movements. Zionism was most firmly rooted in the suburbs amongst the children of the immigrants or immigrants themselves who had "made good" before and during the First World War. It was a predominantly secular movement, although the Mizrachi Zionists were a substantial group. The largest and most important social organizations in the suburban communities were B'nai B'rith and the Jewish friendly societies. These nonsectarian, secular bodies embraced a high percentage of adult employed Jews.[59]

Yet Jewish identity was perpetuated; Jews continued to marry other Jews and to raise families with a sense of being Jewish. How was this achieved? According to oral and written life histories, Jewish youth clubs were a major influence. The boys' and girls' clubs, the Association for Jewish Youth, the Jewish Lads' and Girls' Brigades, and the Zionist youth movements offered young Jews what they wanted and needed, and consequently aroused tremendous affection alongside fierce loyalty. A similar impression is given by the recollections of those who were active on the left. It is an exaggeration to say that the left was dominated by Jews, but the proportion of Jews active in the Communist Party, the Labour Party, trade unions, and other socialist groups was considerable in relation to the total membership of these organizations and, perhaps more pertinently, with respect to the size of the Jewish population.[60]

Becoming and being Jewish in this period could mean joining a Habonim group or a Communist Party cell as much as attending a *talmud torah*. Sometimes the two would overlap. But the most effective and enduring form of socialization as a Jew was arguably the former, which was more fun. Above all, it was concordant with the values of the wider society and dovetailed with a variety of other activities that were identifiably Jewish.

While Jewish education faltered, the interwar years saw a revolution in Jewish leisure-time occupations, with the young engaging in recreations alien to the expectations and practices of their immigrant parents. Whole areas of sport in the interwar years were dominated by Jews. Boxing was the most notable. In the cities with major Jewish populations, attending a fight would commonly involve seeing two Jewish boxers with Jewish managers and trainers fight in a Jewish-owned venue before a predominantly Jewish audience. Gambling attracted such large numbers of Jews that in certain areas Jewish argot was the lingua franca of the race-tracks. To a lesser extent the same was true of table-tennis and other sports.[61]

For youthful East End Jews, dancing "up west" became a routine Friday and Saturday night adventure. It had its equivalent in Manchester at the Ritz and the Rivoli. Rambling became a craze between the wars and attracted hundreds of inner-city Jews, many of whom went out in Jewish rambling clubs. Swaths of the British coast were colonized by Jewish boarding houses and boasted large Jewish populations in the summertime. Jews engaged in crime and fought in street gangs as Jews, too. In some districts of Manchester there were well-established Jewish gangs. Similarly, the East End of London was well known for its Jewish criminal fraternity, of whom Jack Spot was the leading member until well into the 1950s.[62]

Four more elements reinforced distinctively Jewish forms of social behavior and social networks: language, neighborhood, work, and anti-semitism. Personal relations between Jews were cemented by and articulated through the private argot of street Yiddish. This enabled Jews to communicate in confidence and, just as important, allowed them to identify themselves to each other and to outsiders as Jews.[63] The process of socialization as a Jew was bounded within and maintained by Jewish neighborhoods. A sense of place was integral to a sense of being Jewish. Where Jews came from differentiated them, both within the Jewish world and in the world at large. What Jews did to earn their living and where they did it could be equally definitive. A person engaged in tailoring, furniture making, hairdressing, market trades, wholesale trading, taxi-driving, or real estate in the cities where most Jews lived was more than likely to be Jewish. The mutual self-definition engendered by occupational clustering was reinforced by Jewish trade unions, Jewish friendly societies, and certain unions or professional associations in which Jews predominated.

There was one other defining factor in addition to how Jews sounded, where they lived, what they did for a living and the way they relaxed: the shared experience of antisemitism. Whether it was exclusion from council housing because their parents were non-British born or exclusion from a suburban golf club, the effect was the same. The cultural dominance of Christianity and institutional and informal discrimination all made Jews aware of being Jewish, if only in a negative sense. The results of this heightened self-consciousness, however, could be positive. Jewish pride, fostered by parents, has been one of the most effective influences on children, providing a basis upon which to build a strong Jewish identity.

The process of socialization through the common experience of prejudice received reinforcement from outside of Britain. The ascendency of the Nazis, the Jewish refugee crisis, the rise of domestic fascism in the mid-1930s, and the Spanish Civil War were causes against which Jews defined themselves—not only as Jews, but also as leftists or democrats. While Jewishness could be marginalized or compartmentalized in relation to these struggles, the Second World War and the Nazi onslaught against Europe's Jews were unique shaping experiences for all Jews who lived through them.

In British Jewry in the 1990s the ways of becoming and being Jewish are not dissimilar. Yet communal leaders charged with ensuring "Jewish continuity" insist on trying to inculcate a narrowly-defined Judaism that is at odds with the everyday experience of most Jews. The leadership prescribes that continuity is a matter of biological transmission rather than socialization. Huge emphasis is placed on endogamy rather than on the construction of Jewish social milieux or the utilization of Jewish space and ethnic neighborhoods. In fact, communal organizations seem bent on destroying the natural habitat of Jewish youth and the street culture in places like Edgeware and Hampstead, which nurture an Israeli-style Jewish identity.

Thanks to the myths of Jewish history and the fallacies of "popular memory," British Jews are the prisoners of a dessicated, materialistic triumphalism on the one hand and a habit of spiritual self-denigration on the other. Yosef Yerushalmi warned, "Myth and memory condition action

...There are some that lead astray and must be redefined. Others are dangerous and must be exposed."[64] To fulfill the task set out for them by Yerushalmi, British Jewish historians must rescue Jews from a memory that has been warped by the stresses of ethnicity and set in its place a history that clearly and accurately describes the lineaments of Jewish survival in Britain.

1. Yosef Yerushalmi, *Zakhor: Jewish History and Jewish Memory* (New York: Schocken, 1989), p.86.

2. Ibid. pp. 82–85.

3. Ibid. pp. 93–94.

4. Ibid. p.94.

5. Ibid. pp. 99–100.

6. John Bodnar, *Remaking America: Public Memory, Commemoration, and Patriotism in the Twentieth Century* (Princeton: Princeton University Press, 1992), pp. 13–20. Bodnar was, of course, greatly influenced by Maurice Halbwachs, *The Collective Memory*, first published in 1950.

7. Ibid., pp. 48–49 and pp. 41–77 passim.

8. The exceptions were Peter Elman, "The Beginnings of the Jewish Trades Union Movement in England" (delivered July 1948), *Transactions of the Jewish Historical Society of England (TJHSE)* 17 (1951–52): 53–62; Joseph Leftwich, "Israel Zangwill" (delivered March 1952), *TJHSE* 18 (1953–55): 77–88; Leonard Schapiro, "The Russian Background of the Anglo-American Jewish Immigration" (delivered June 1961), *TJHSE* 20 (1959–61): 215–31.

9. In 1980, in the Foreword to Jerry White's *Rothschild Buildings* (London: Routledge, 1980), Raphael Samuel could still write that "Jewish history in Britain, insofar as it exists, is heavily institutional in bias and entirely celebratory in tone, recording the progress of the 'community' in terms of political status and professional and commercial success." p.x. For the matrix of the new social history of British Jews, see Richard Johnson, "Culture and the Historians," in John Clarke, Chas Critcher and Richard Johnson, eds, *Working Class Culture: Studies in History and Theory* (London: Hutchinson, 1979), pp. 64–68.

10. For example, Bill Williams, "The Jewish Immigrant in Manchester: The Contribution of Oral History," *Oral History* 7 (1979).

11. Aubrey Newman, ed., *The Jewish East End 1840–1939* (Leicester: Leicester University Press, 1981), p. vii.

12. Zoe Josephs, *Survivors: Jewish Refugees in Birmingham 1933–1945* (Oldbury: Birmingham Jewish Historical Society, 1988); Jewish Women in London Group, *Generations of Memories: Voices of Jewish Women* (London: Women's Press, 1989).

13. Raphael Samuel, "Local History and Oral history," *History Workshop* (1976), pp. 191–208; Jerry White, *Rothschild Buildings*.

14. Johnson et al, eds, *Making Histories: Studies in History-Writing and Politics* (London: Hutchinson, 1982), pp. 205–52; Luisa Passerini, *Fascism in Popular memory. The Cultural Experience of the Turin Working Class* (Cambridge: Cambridge University Press, 1988), originally published in Italian in 1984.

15. James Fentress and Chris Wickman, *Social Memory* (Oxford: Blackwell, 1993), p. 88.

16. Agnes Heller, *A Theory of History* (London: Routledge, 1982), chaps. 1–3.

17. Jack Caplan, *Memories of the Gorbals* (Edinburgh: Pentland Press, 1991), p. 89.

18. Evelyn Cowan, *Spring Remembered: A Scottish Jewish Childhood* (New York: Taplinger Publishing Company, 1974), p. 18.

19. Ralph Glasser, *Growing Up in the Gorbals* (London: Pan, 1986), p. 17. Glasser's father was from Lithuania and came to Scotland in 1902; it is therefore doubtful that he ever witnessed a pogrom personally.

20. Harry Blacker, *Just Like It Was: Memoirs of the Middle East* (London: Valentine Mitchell, 1974).

21. Israel Sieff, *The Memoirs of Israel Sieff* (London: Weidenfeld and Nicolson, 1970), pp. 9–11 and pp. 22–23.

22. See John Klier and Shlomo Lambrozo, eds., *Pogroms* (Cambridge: Cambridge University Press, 1992); Lloyd Gartner, *The Jewish Immigrant in England, 1870–1914* (London: Simon Publications, 1960), p. 41.

23. Vivian Lipman, *A History of the Jews in Britain Since 1858* (Leicester: Leicester University Press, 1990), p. 44.

24. Eugene Black, *The Social Politics of Anglo-Jewry 1880–1920* (Oxford: Blackwell, 1988), pp. 245–46.

25. Bernard Gainer, *The Alien Invasion* (London: Heinemann, 1972).

26. Bernard Porter, *The Refugee Question in Mid-Victorian Politics* (Cambridge: Cambridge University Press, 1979).

27. J. M. Evans, *Immigration Law* (London, 1976), p. 9 and p. 44 n. 43. Also, Ann Dummet and Andrew Nichol, *Subjects, Citizens, Aliens and Others* (London: Weidenfeld and Nicolson, 1990), pp. 103–12.

28. Ibid., p. 9.

29. Gloria Mound, *Take a Basket* (London: privately published, 1980), p. 1.

30. Elaine Blond with Barry Turner, *Marks of Distinction: The Memoirs of Elaine Blond* (London: Vallentine and Mitchell, 1988), pp. 1–2, p. 9; cf. Sieff, *Memoirs*, p. 5. Mrs. Ray Hille recalls that she arrived with her father from Slonim in 1905, having crossed the border "frightened by fire and guns." Interview, January 22, 1986, Tape 53, London Museum of Jewish Life.

31. Interview with Morris Serlin, b. 1922 in London, Tape 71, London Museum of Jewish Life.

32. Blond, with Turner, *Marks of Distinction,* p. 9; Sieff, *Memoirs of Israel Sieff*, pp. 9–11.

33. Cyril Spector, *Volla Volla Jew Boy* (London: Centreprise, 1988), p. 3.

34. Norman Stone, *The Eastern Front* (London: Penguin, 1998), chaps. 1–2.

35. John Bodnar, *The Transplanted* (Bloomington: Indiana University Press, 1985), pp. 13–23.

36. Bernard Porter, "Bureau and Barrack: Early Victorian Attitudes towards the Continent," *Victorian Studies* 26,1 (1982): 407–33.

37. David Cesarani, "An Embattled Minority: The Jews in Britain During the First World War," in Tony Kushner and Kenneth Lunn (eds.), *The Politics of Marginality* (London: Cass, 1990), pp. 65–66.

38. Charles Poulson, *Scenes . . . from a Stepney Youth* (London: THAP Books, 1988), p. 16.

39. Caplan, *Memories*, p. 89.

40. Israel Sieff mentions that his father endured several nasty antisemitic incidents in his new home, but still writes that England had "given him freedom and self-respect," *Memoirs*, cf. pp. 23–24 and 28.

41. Emanuel Litvinoff, *Journey Through a Small Planet* (London: Michael Joseph, 1972), p. 28. See also Olga Franklin, *Steppes to Fleet Street* (London: Gollancz, 1968), p. 10.

42. David Clutterbuck and Marion Devine, *Clore: The Man and His Millions* (London: Weidenfeld and Nicolson, 1987), p. 4.

43. Gartner, *The Jewish Immigrant*, pp. 34–36,; idem., "North Atlantic Jewry" in *Migration and Settlement* (JHSE, 1970), p. 121; Lipman, *A History of the Jews in Britain*, p. 47; Black, *Social Politics*, p. 249.

44. Harold Pollins, *Hopeful Travellers: Jewish Migrants and Settlers in Nineteenth Century Britain*. London Museum of Jewish Life, Research Papers No. 2 (London: London Museum of Jewish Life, 1987), p. 25.

45. Caplan, *Memories*, p. 89; Sieff, *Memoirs*, p. 10.

46. Jamie Camplin, *The Rise of the Plutocrats: Wealth and Power in Edwardian England* (London: Constable, 1978), pp. 141–58, 170–90, 193–218; Martin J. Wiener, *English Culture and the Decline of the Industrial Spirit, 1850–1980* (Cambridge: Cambridge University Press, 1981), pp. 30–31, 60 and passim; Bryan Cheyette, "Jewish Stereotyping and English Literature 1875–1920: Towards a Political Analysis," in Tony Kushner and Kenneth Lunn, eds., *Traditions of Intolerance* (Manchester: Manchester University Press, 1989), pp. 12–32.

47. Gainer, *The Alien Invasion*, pp. 84–90; Colin Holmes, *Anti-Semitism in British Society 1876–1939* (London: Edwin Arnold, 1979), pp. 15–20; idem., "J. A. Hobson and the Jews," in Colin Holmes ed. *Immigrants and Minorities in British Society* (London, 1978), pp. 130–50; Joseph Buckman, *Immigrants and the Class Struggle* (Manchester: Manchester University Press, 1983), pp. 2–5.

48. Emanuel Litvinoff, *Journey Through a Small Planet*, p. 30; Arthur Franklin, *Times Remembered* (London: privately published, July 1984) (copy in Museum of London Jewish Life), pp. 10–11.

49. Franklin, *Steppes to Fleet Street*, p. 24.

50. Joe Jacobs, "Out of the Ghetto: My Youth in the East End," in *Fascism and Communism 1913–1939* (London: Janet Simon, 1978), p. 11.

51. Glasser, *Growing Up in the Gorbals*, p. 17.

52. Blond with Turner, *Marks of Distinction*, p. 2. Another case of ambivalence is indicated by a curious grammatical turn. David Clutterbuck and Marion Devine write that Charles Clore's father "quickly succumbed to the entrepreneurial spirit." Clutterbuck and Devine, *Clore*, p. 5. It is notable that in Maurice Corina's biography of Sir John Cohen, *"Pile it High and Sell it Cheap." The Authorised Biography of Sir John Cohen, Founder of Tesco* (London: Wiedenfeld and Nicolson, 1971), origins are hardly mentioned at all although there is a good deal on the "rise" of the Cohens.

53. David Young, *The Enterprise Years* (London: Weidenfeld and Nicolson, 1990), pp. 3–5.

54. Tony Kushner, "The End of the Anglo-Jewish Progress Show: Representations of the Jewish East End, 1887–1987," in Tony Kushner, ed., *The Jewish Heritage in British History* (London: Cass, 1992), pp. 78–105. Cf. Sherry Gorelick, *City College and the Jewish Poor: Education in New York, 1880–1924* (New Jersey, 1981), pp. 1–9 for an American critique of the "myth of progress."

55. For a contemporary view, see Henrietta Adler, "Jewish Life and Labour in East London," in Sir H. Llwellyn Smith, ed., *The New Survey of London Life and Labour*, vol. 6, *Survey of Social Conditions* (London: King and Son, 1934), pp. 283–87. It is also possible to extrapolate backwards from the surveys of suburban residents: Ernest Krausz, "Occupational and Social Advancement in Anglo-Jewry," *Jewish Journal of Sociology (JJS)* 4,1 (1962): 82–100; Ernest Krausz, "The Edgeware Survey: Occupation and Social Class," *JJS* 11,1, (1969): 75–95, esp. pp. 84–88; S.J. Prais and M. Schmool, "The Social Class Structure of Anglo-Jewry, 1961," *JJS* 27,1 (1975): 5–16. Cf. J.W. Carrier, "A Jewish Proletariat," in Murray Mindlin and Chaim Bermant, eds., *Explorations: an Annual on Jewish Themes* (London: Weidenfeld and Nicolson, 1967), pp. 120–40.

56. See Alan Jackson, *Semi-Detached London* (London: Wild Swan), 1991, pp. 49, 221.

57. Geoffrey Alderman, *Modern British Jewry* (Oxford: Oxford University Press, 1992), chap. 6.

58. David Cesarani, "The East End of Simon Blumenfeld's Jew Boy," *London Journal* 13,1 (1987/88): 46–53. See, for example, William Goldman, *East End My Cradle* (London: Robson, 1988) [first published in 1940]; Bernard Kops, *The World is a Wedding* (London: McGibbon and Kee, 1963); Morris Beckman, *Hackney Crucible* (London: Cass, 1995); Arnold Wesker, *As Much as I Dare: An Autobiography* (London: Century, 1993).

59. David Cesarani, "The Transformation of Communal Authority in Anglo-Jewry, 1914–1940," in David Cesarani, ed., *The Making of Modern Anglo-Jewry* (Oxford: Blackwell, 1990), pp. 115–40; Elaine Smith, "Jewish Responses to Political Anti-Semitism and Fascism in the East End of London,

1920–1939," in Kushner and Lunn, *Traditions of Intolerance*, pp. 53–71; Henry Srebrnik, *London Jews and British Communism, 1935–1945* (London: Vallentine Mitchell, 1995).

60. For anecdotal evidence, see the memoirs, cited above, by Glasser, Spector, Poulson, Litvinoff, and Jacobs. On the J.L.B., see Sharman Kadish, *A Good Jew and a Good Englishman: The Jewish Lads' and Girls' Brigade, 1895–1995* (London: Vallentine Mitchell, 1995).

61. On the boxing scene, for example, see John Harding with Jack Kid Berg, *Jack Kid Berg: The Whitechapel Windmill* (London: Robson, 1989); David Cesarani, "A Funny Thing Happened on the Way to the Suburbs: Social Change in Anglo-Jewry Between the Wars, 1914–1945," *Jewish Culture and History*, 1, 2(1998), pp 5–26 charts the transformation in general.

62. On Benny Rothman, see *The Independent*, March 21, 1992 and *The Guardian*, March 10, 1994. Jewish-run boarding houses took pages of advertisements in the *Jewish Chronicle* in advance of, and during, the annual holiday seasons. For accounts of Jews and the crime scene in London, see Raphael Samuel, *East End Underworld* (London: Routledge, 1981), pp. 178–86, and on Manchester, Bill Williams, *Manchester Jewry: A Pictorial History 1788–1988* (Manchester: Archive Publications, 1988), pp. 81–82.

63. Eddie Conway, "Wej Patter: A Selective Glossary," unpublished paper, 1990.

64. Yerushalmi, *Zakhor*, pp. 99–100.

Myth and Identity:
The Case of Latrun, 1948

In the history of nations, a special place is reserved for what has been termed the "myth of foundation." By their nature, wars of independence that lead to the creation of a new social and political entity are prone to mythologization. Because the myths of the creation of a state are a fundamental component of a national identity, their character and essence are shaped by the subsequent changes that national identity undergoes. Thus the transformations of the myth over time reflect shifts in the self-image of the society, its basic values, and the manner in which it relates to itself and to others.

These dynamic features of mythopoesis are also manifest in the myths connected with the War of Independence of the State of Israel. The first narrative of the War of Independence was created by two generations of participants: that of the fathers, who defined Zionist ideology, and that of the sons, the warriors who had won victory on the battlefield, securing patrimony. That primal narrative contains several key components:

1. The notion of *eyn breirah,* "no choice": The war was unwanted, forced upon the Jews by the intransigent Arabs. This was the basic legitimization for viewing the conflict as unavoidable, a war of self-defense. The concept of "no choice" had another implication as well: the Jews, unprepared for the war, were compelled to fight from a position of weakness. But they had "no choice." Exigency exacted action.

2. The central role of the generation born in Palestine in achieving ultimate victory. It was the native "sons of Palestine," especially members of the Palmach, who bore the brunt of confrontation, particularly in the first critical phases of combat. After the war, the figure of the sabra emerged as a paragon and as the aspiration and

the goal of formal and informal education. That figure was accepted as a normative paradigm by the majority of the society.

3. Israel as the sanctuary of the "surviving remnant" *(she'erit ha-pleitah)* of European Jewry. From Zionism's inception, the establishment of the Jewish state had been identified with the ideal of a safe haven for persecuted Jews. For that reason, the ingathering of the exiles, and especially the bringing of the survivors from the refugee camps in Europe and Cyprus to Israel during the course of the war, became a key component in the saga of the birth of the nation, the meaning and justification of the entire tumultuous sequence of events.

4. The role of David Ben-Gurion in the victory: The myth of Ben-Gurion as the father of the nation was forged in the wake of the War of Independence. His leadership, vision, historical foresight, resolute determination, and readiness to challenge the powerful and lead his people with a mighty arm to the Promised Land became accepted tenets that only few dared to contradict.

One of the chief myths of the War of Independence is the myth of Latrun. It is my intention here to sketch the changes that have taken place in attitudes toward this event and its presentation and re-presentation over the course of the years. How did this battle become a focus of attention for different groups, each perceiving it as a way to achieve and legitimize a participant role in the War of Independence, that primal matrix experience shaping Israeli society? The question of Israeli identity and its permutations is central to the salience of this myth.

The Chronicle of Events

Latrun was a small Arab village. Located nearby was a large, fortified police station, overlooking the plain of Ayalon, a famous battleground from the days of antiquity, located halfway between the coastal plain and Jerusalem. During the Mandate, a vital road between Tel Aviv and Jerusalem passed through Latrun, in effect the only road linking Jerusalem with the rest of the Jewish settlement—the yishuv—in Palestine.

After the Arabs rejected the UN General Assembly decision on November 29, 1947 to partition Palestine into two states, one Jewish, one Arab, the Arabs swung into action against the Jews. Most of their attacks were concentrated on traffic moving between Jewish settlements. In February and March of 1948, the Arab offensive reached its peak, and Jerusalem was in effect cut off from the coastal plain. Following the British pullout on May 15, a number of units of the Arab Legion, under British command, seized the police station building on May 17. From then on, they had a commanding view of the road and prevented all traffic from moving between Jerusalem and the coastal plain. In the course of the War of Independence, a total of six battles were fought over control of Latrun, all of which ended in failure. During the course of the fighting, an alternative road was opened up to Jerusalem, southwest of Latrun. That new artery carried traffic to Jerusalem up to 1967. In the six battles, a total of 168 Israelis lost their lives.[1]

The myth of Latrun centers on the first battle that raged during the night of May 24–25, continuing into the next day. The High Command had received alarming cries of distress from Jerusalem: it appeared that the city would be unable to hold out for more than another week or two at the most. Ben-Gurion ordered Yigael Yadin, operations officer and deputy chief of staff, to concentrate troop strength in order to breach a road to Jerusalem, come what may.[2] The only reserve force at the disposal of the general staff was a contingent being formed precisely at that time, the Seventh Brigade.

The Seventh Brigade did not yet exist as a fighting unit. Most of its officers, headed by Shlomo Shamir, had served in the Second World War in the British Army. The junior officers came from the Haganah. But the preponderant majority of the soldiers were green recruits who had been dispatched straight from the recruitment centers. Among them were some 140 new immigrants who had arrived on May 14 from Europe and been given hasty training in the handling of weapons. The soldiers and officers were unfamiliar with each other. To strengthen the new unit, the 32nd Battalion from the Alexandroni Brigade was brought in. Made up of young men raised in Palestine, it ranked among the most experienced battalions in the Jewish defense forces at the time.

But that move did not solve the fundamental problem facing the Seventh: equipment had just begun to arrive in Palestine. The machine guns were still packed in protective Vaseline, and the soldiers did not know how to fire them. All soldiers had been issued rifles, but not everyone was wearing a uniform. Only about a quarter of the 32nd Battalion had water canteens, and even fewer of the 72nd Battalion of the Seventh Brigade (which would bear the brunt of the fighting along with the 32nd) had them. None of the soldiers was familiar with his personal equipment. In short, the brigade had no time to consolidate itself militarily and organize itself in terms of command structure.[3]

Ben-Gurion ordered the army to attack the Latrun police station the night of May 23–24. With much effort, Yadin and Shamir succeeded in persuading him to delay the attack 24 hours in view of the chaotic conditions in the Seventh Brigade. A bitter dispute erupted between Ben-Gurion and Yadin, who wished to postpone the whole operation; Ben-Gurion refused, forcing Yadin to accept his decision.[4]

The attack commenced the night of May 24–25. Two companies from the 32nd Battalion—A and B Company, about 180 men—as well as companies B and C of the 72nd Battalion, some 217 fighting men all told, set out to launch the attack. B Company of the 72nd Battalion was made up largely of new immigrants (approximately 65–70 men).[5] The second company consisted of other recruits. According to the plan, the battle was supposed to commence at about midnight. But it started several hours later. Dawn came shortly after the attack was under way. B Company of the 32nd Battalion (Alexandroni) was caught and pinned down in extremely heavy crossfire. It absorbed heavy losses, and by the end of the day, had ceased to exist: casualties were 48 dead, 46 wounded (most, lightly); with six men taken prisoner.[6] The 72nd Battalion lost 23 men, 15 of them from B Company. Forty-seven were wounded, most not seriously. Eight of the dead were new immigrants, all from B Company.[7]

The weather that May day was oppressive, a withering *ḥamsin*. The combatants suffered enormously from the heat and dryness. A number of soldiers fainted from lack of water and heat-stroke; others showed signs of extreme apathy and fatigue, to the point where they lost their will to survive. Here there was no difference between the newcomers and the native sons of Palestine.

The trauma of defeat and hasty retreat was aggravated by the fact that they had to leave behind dead and even wounded, most of whom were later killed by irregular Arab forces. Seventy-one or seventy-two men died in battle that day. In the first few days after the battle—until it became clear that some of the missing were in hospital or had returned to their homes—there was a pervading impression that an even worse catastrophe had occurred.

The Battle of Latrun: the Ben-Gurion and Shamir Version

In the struggle over the image of the battle of Latrun in national memory, the first view was created by Ben Gurion and his men. The line of explanation of the "official version" was worked out by Ben-Gurion, who claimed that the battle for Latrun had been a success. That interpretation was formulated about a month after the events, and Ben-Gurion espoused it on a number of occasions. The first time he set out this version was during a debate with Yadin before the Commission of Five (a commission of ministers set up to investigate Ben-Gurion's allegations regarding a political revolt in the army general staff). In response to Yadin's claim that "the operation had ended in a terrible catastrophe," Ben-Gurion responded (July 3, 1948): "In my view, it was a great victory, although it did not come cheap."[8]

The most serious endeavor to propagate the "official version" of the battle for Latrun was made by Yisrael Ber in 1955. Lt. Col. Ber had been one of Yigael Yadin's two subordinates in the planning department of the general staff during the War of Independence. At that time, he joined in Yadin's vehement criticism of Ben-Gurion's intervention in connection with the Seventh Brigade in Latrun. But over the next seven years, he changed his tune, becoming one of the most adept explicators of Ben-Gurion's version of events.

Ber depicted the events at Latrun as parts of a heroic epic—occurrences that take place at the birth of nations or during a historical breakthrough. He formulated the essential conclusion to be drawn as the "dialectical law operative in warfare": while the tactical achievements at the beginning of the war on the Jerusalem front did not guarantee the security of the city and protect the access route to it, the three tactical failures in Latrun nonetheless did secure the supply route to Jerusalem (opening up of the Burma Road) and led to the diversion of forces of the Arab Legion away from Jerusalem. According to Ber, the dialectical inversion (defeat that is, in effect, victory) derived from the secret of strategic understanding of the situation by the supreme commander, Ben-Gurion, who was able to identify the key elements and to subordinate the necessarily limited tactical considerations of the army command to this broader perspective. Acknowledging the deficiencies and faults of the command, the brigade, tactics, and equipment, Ber attributed them all to the specific situation: the birth of a state and the concomitant emergence of a fighting force from the underground.[9]

Ben-Gurion adhered to this version all his life. Speaking about the Latrun campaign after the events, he once again underscored the suffering of Jerusalem under siege and bombardment during the month of battle after May 15, and noted:

> We set up a new brigade then—the Seventh. It was made up of immigrants from Cyprus who had just come to Israel [another myth in circulation: actually, there were no immigrants whatsoever from Cyprus that month—A.S.]. . . . Not a single battalion of that brigade was trained, and based on the established rules of warfare, it should have been forbidden to send them to the front. But Jerusalem was in mortal danger, there was no choice . . . Latrun was not conquered—but Jerusalem was saved.[10]

The elements of "Jerusalem in danger," "no choice," and "defeat that is victory" transformed the battle for Latrun into a myth, imbuing the bloodletting there with transcendent meaning and value.

The Battle of Latrun: Two Antipodal Elite Versions of the Myth

Why do certain events become the focus of intense public attention, to the point where they are mythicized, while others are forgotten and buried under the refuse of history? As I see it, in the case of the battle of Latrun, the genesis of the myth can be traced to the power struggle between two leading elites for which this battle became a focal point: Ben-Gurion and the veterans of the British army versus the leaders of the Haganah and Palmach.

Tensions between these two elites erupted in connection with the organization and structuring of the army and later spilled over into the struggle over the shaping of the collective memory of the War of Independence. In Latrun, it found a powerful focus and symbol. The complete and unwavering loyalty of the veterans of the British army to Ben-Gurion, and his open preference for them over seasoned veterans of the Haganah and Palmach, were two fundamental motifs in the dramatic construction of the memory of Latrun. Those enraged by Ben-Gurion's preferences regarded Latrun as decisive proof of his evident misjudgment.

The "official version" of Ben-Gurion and the veterans of the British army disregarded the operative and tactical details of the campaign, fore-grounding instead the strategic conception and the role of the events at Latrun in the rescue of Jerusalem. The "other version," espoused by Yadin and men of the Haganah and Palmach, concentrated on the particulars of the operation's implementation. Yadin's basic argument was that the brigade had been sent to a defeat that was predestined, inevitable, expected from the start. Defeat and failure were the only options, because the unit was unprepared for combat. At the heart of the Yadin version were an array of disturbing details: the defective equipment of the soldiers and their lack of familiarity with it, the absence of water canteens; the delay in launching the attack, the absence of intelligence, and so on. Against the claim of *ein breirah* ("no choice"), the dissenters raised the allegation of "criminal negligence." Against the glorification of the dead and the value of their sacrifice, they set the antipodal claim: namely that these losses had been useless, that these men had "died in vain."

In the framework of this dispute, the question regarding the participation of recent immigrants in the battle was broached for the first time. In his testimony before the Commission of Five, Yadin described the state of the Seventh Brigade on the eve of battle. He noted that the men "were all green recruits." He recounted the events:

A battalion that had been given three days of basic training was sent into battle, and men were killed, the safety-latches on their rifles still locked. . . they went straight from the boat to the recruitment center. There were more casualties that day than in any previous operation.[11]

The emphasis of Yadin on the inexperienced nature of the battalion, the fact that it was made up of new immigrants, the extent of the casualties—these points were meant to underscore his fundamental contention that

the brigade had not been combat-ready, and that Ben-Gurion's intervention violated all the rules of military logic.

The press at the time reported sparingly on the battle at Latrun. Only
between the lines was it possible to discern that there were new immigrants in the ranks of the recently-formed brigade. Yet rumors about Latrun soon began to circulate both in the army and the general public.
References to the battle appeared in Uri Avneri's book, *Bi-sedot peleshet*
("In the Fields of Philistia"), in correspondence between members of the
Palmach, and in letters to the editor in the press.[12] Because the ruling elite
had control over access to the media, the "other version" was forced to
utilize alternative channels: rumor and word of mouth in campfire con-
versations, in the tents of the soldiers, and at get-togethers of former combatants.

Belles-lettres played a significant role in communicating the message,
since literature was not affected by the censorship or limitations to which
men in the military were subject. In one of the best-known theatrical
pieces of the era, *Be-arvot ha-negev* ("In the wastes of the Negev"), the author Yigal Mossinsohn has one of the protagonists exclaim:

> I was in Latrun! I don't know if that name, Latrun, means very
> much to you. But man, that was hell on earth, Latrun! And there
> as well, I had recruits from abroad. Not only weren't there enough
> weapons. There weren't any water canteens either. And then the
> *ḥamsin,* and flies and insects—the men fainted in the field, fainted
> and died out there in the field . . . and the order handed down
> was pitiless: to go on! Go on at any price! To open up the route
> to Jerusalem—otherwise Jewish Jerusalem would be obliterated!
> And I'll never forget one of the new immigrants who was lying
> there on the ground, in the throes of death. He'd asked to speak
> with me, his officer. The smile of a dying man! He said to me:
> "Better, here! It's better here! Take care of my mother." Then he
> died. Nobody knows where his mother is. To go through every-
> thing—and then to be killed in Eretz Yisrael![13]

There were two essential features in the rumors that were propagated: the
extent of the casualties suffered, and the large percentage of new immigrants among them. As the story spread, these two elements were increas-

ingly stressed. What gave these rumors credibility was the fact that the majority of the soldiers who fell in Latrun were not given a proper burial until after the war, in a special operation carried out by Rabbi Goren in cooperation with the Jordanians. Stories about unidentified dead were common in that situation.[14]

As long as Ben-Gurion continued to serve as "Prime Minister and Defense Minister," the criticism of Latrun was restricted to hearsay and fiction. But after he left office, and particularly in the wake of the Six Day War, when public interest in military operations increased sharply and respect for the taboo of secrecy declined, the dispute erupted onto the pages of the press, where it has remained ever since.[15]

The themes of the heavy losses suffered at Latrun and the large number of new immigrants among the many dead expanded, ramified, and assumed mammoth proportions. However, in the more serious discussions in the press and in historiographical literature that had begun to appear (in particular, in Aryeh Itschaki's book, *Latrun*, which, despite its inaccuracies and controversial assertions, is based on primary sources), there was basic agreement on the number of fatalities. All investigations had arrived at the figure of 71 to 73 dead, as indicated above; there was also consensus that the number of new immigrants among them was quite limited—eight.

One might have expected that given this agreement, the facts regarding the exact number of casualties would no longer have been a matter of controversy. But that is not what happened. Simultaneously with these publications, other totally different statistics appeared in the established press and were not dismissed. Writing in the daily *Ha'aretz* about the memorial monument at Latrun, Haviv Kena'an stated that during the War of Independence, 430 soldiers of the Israeli armed forces had been killed in action in the Ayalon plain (by comparison, Itschaki's figures were 168 slain in the six attacks on Latrun).[16] In a letter to the editor in response, Barukh Nadel amplified even further: he contended that the number of those killed was roughly double the figure given by Kena'an. He claimed that in the first battle for Latrun, to which "survivors of the Holocaust" were sent, "armed with rifles they did not know how to fire . . . some 500 men had died in battle in one day alone."[17]

In the 1980s, a number of articles appeared in the national press emphasizing the established and agreed-upon facts regarding battlefield losses. Nonetheless, these frequent references to the actual extent of the fatalities did not penetrate into the collective memory. In a debate in the Knesset on November 18, 1985, Knesset member Uzi Landau touched on the battle at Latrun, citing a staggering casualty figure—2,000 dead. After others responded that that was a gross exaggeration, given the fact that the number of fatalities for the entire war was 6,000, Landau backtracked. He was ready to accept a compromise figure of 1,000 dead at Latrun, but no fewer. In the wake of these exchanges on the floor of the Knesset, accurate facts were again published in the papers, but the public image of the number of dead at Latrun remained a mythologized quantity.[18]

Latrun: The Myth of the Immigrants of the War of Independence

From the mid-1970s on, behind the lattice of the two existing versions, another story of the battle at Latrun began to germinate. It presented the battle—and through the prism of that confrontation, the War of Independence as a whole—as it had come to be depicted over the years in the memory of those who had remained on the periphery of collective remembrance: the new immigrants.

In the mid-1970s, several processes transformed the Israeli self-image and modified emphases in national identity. While the Six Day War and its immediate aftermath brought the symbol of the strong and heroic sabra (native-born Israeli) to its crowning point, the Yom Kippur War not only diminished the aura around Moshe Dayan, the ultimate personification of the sabra, but also raised questions about the validity of generally accepted truths in Israeli society. From the welter of anxieties generated by the war, powerful images of the Holocaust arose. From this watershed on, the Holocaust became an element of abiding presence in the collective memory of Israel. Israeli history was no longer presented as a tale where all was light, success, and heroic victory. It was also the story of those who had failed, a chronicle of the weak. The Holocaust survivor assumed new significance in national memory and consciousness.

This process of revision gained momentum with the ascendance of Menachem Begin to power. While previous governments had largely been the heirs of the elites of the pre-state yishuv, Begin belonged only marginally to the yishuv. His government gave expression and a new sense of empowerment to everyone who felt disadvantaged or discriminated against when it came to his or her place in the old patterns of national memory: Oriental Jews, new immigrants, the Irgun. The emergence of new elites was accompanied by the construction of a new narrative of the past. That narrative was principally based on testimony by the living and nourished by the claim that existing documentation did not accord them their proper place in history.

Soon Latrun became the central myth of Holocaust survivors who participated in the War of Independence. What elements in the Latrun complex functioned to transform it into the lodestone for their frustrations in the 1948 war on the one hand, and the focus for their integration into the collective memory of the war, on the other? As mentioned, the leitmotif of new immigrants had accompanied the Latrun story from its inception. There was a kernel of fact here: the participation of a company from the 72nd Battalion, most of whose men were new immigrants who had just arrived in Israel. And there was a basis for myth: the fact that dead were left behind on the battlefield; the confusion and uncertainty during withdrawal and defeat. It appears that there was no other battle during that war in which the role of the new immigrants was so central to the story of events. For that reason, when the survivors became interested in their place in the history of the War of Independence, Latrun lent itself as a natural focus for mythologization.

In the first years after the war, the immigrants wanted only to make sure that the collective memory would give them credit where due and record the importance of their contribution to that battle. They were insulted by the widespread notion that their lack of experience was one of the supposed factors underlying the defeat—a notion that had fostered a negative image of the immigrants in Israeli public opinion. One immigrant stated: "It's simply not true that the immigrants fell apart right away, that they didn't demonstrate any fighting spirit." He did not criticize the fact that immigrants were sent into the line of fire: "There was no one else." And he had no complaints about their lack of equipment: "There simply were no canteens. And nobody hid the ammunition. There just wasn't any." This particular immigrant did not look back in anger. Rather, he regarded the confrontation at Latrun from the perspective of a man who had found his place in the system and viewed his own past as an integral part of that fabric of national belonging.[19]

Together with this desire to be included in the saga of heroism at Latrun, another approach represented Latrun as the focus for the disappointments and bitterness of the new immigrants. "I was Sent Straight to La-trun" was the title of an article on the immigrant recruits, a piece for which 1948 immigrant soldiers had been interviewed, depicting those past days in the light of the present.[20]

In these interviews, Latrun emerged as a drama of alienation and es-trangement; the immigrants sent into battle were strangers in a strange land. They set out in the dark of night, not knowing where they were being taken. They did not know where to pull back to, what route to fol-low. They came as lonely, solitary individuals, sole survivors of their fami-lies or communities. They knew no one, and no one showed them affec-tion or care. They were not even allowed to contact relatives—if they had any. They were baffled by the Hebrew in which they were addressed. No-body briefed them on what they should do or why they were embarking upon this attack. And when dawn came, they found themselves under a murderous hail of fire, abandoned, aghast.

The strange sun blazed down on their heads, and the horrible heat sapped their last ounce of strength. The bites of the mosquitoes drove them to distraction. They cried out in Yiddish, "Wasser, wasser," but on that bitter day, no one paid them any heed. Latrun symbolized everything that was strange and difficult and alienating in the course of absorption. The impersonal way in which they were treated, the obliteration of their previous identities, the disregard of their recent suffering, the arrogant at-titude of the natives—all these contributed to their disappointment with a Jewish state that had not given them a sense of belonging, of having come home.[21]

This then was the pattern of memory of the War of Independence as it was stamped in the remembrance of a segment of the Holocaust survivors. For them, coming to Israel provided, simultaneously, a catharsis of libera-tion and the genesis of new traumata. The demand, overt or covert, to as-similate to the dominant culture, manners, and social norms in Israel as a precondition for absorption was accepted by the majority of the immi-grants without protest. Over the course of many years, they internalized those patterns to the best of their ability. Only after they had completed the lengthy process and become an integral part of Israeli society—only after those same norms they had tried so hard to embrace in their youth began to crumble with the decline of the elite of the yishuv—only then did long suppressed feelings of alienation and estrangement re-emerge into the field of consciousness.

Releasing those feelings from the hidden recesses of their memory, immigrants found the harrowing outlines of their own wretchedness in the images of Latrun that had already taken root in collective memory. They appropriated the story recounted until then by the veterans, and it became their own claim to glory. Their purpose was neither to destroy the foundations of the basic myth of the establishment of the state, nor to challenge its existence, but rather to claim their own participation in it. In the historical documentation, they had hitherto been depicted as marginal and secondary, the object of action by others; now they demanded their rightful place of honor.

Latrun: the Myth Demolishing Israeli Identity

Simultaneous with the development of the immigrants' version of the Latrun myth, writers and poets also latched onto the story of Latrun, transforming it into a kind of battering ram for deconstructing one of the basic mythologems of the state: Israel as the ingatherer of the exiles, the sanctuary for *she'erit ha-pleitah*.

The first poet to deal with the Latrun affair was Natan Alterman. In his poem *Be-terem or* ("Before light"), he recounts the story of the Seventh Brigade, asking why the ones sent to face the fire of battle were specifically refugees from Europe who had survived the war—this while most of the members of the yishuv went on with their regular lives. In the final analysis, however, Alterman integrated the disaster of the Seventh Brigade into the broader epic of the birth of the nation, in this way making his peace post factum with the events.[22]

Some 25 years later, Aryeh Sivan recalls the memory of "the immigrant soldiers who died in the fields of Latrun in the course of Operation Bin-Nun" (*Ma'ariv*, May 8, 1981). The experience of the Holocaust, which in Alterman's poem is hidden, is presented here in an overt form, exposed. Sivan's battle for Latrun takes place in a closed world, devoid of historical context, bereft of explanation—and patently without justification. The poem is meant to immortalize the unknown and nameless—in contrast to the native sons, whose place in memory is secure. Although there is no di-

rect accusation in his poem, it highlights the absurdity of these lonely survivors being sent to their death.

The best known and most provocative of the poems dealing with Latrun is *Peter ha-gadol* ("Peter the Great") by Gabi Daniel (Binyamin
Hrushovsky):

> Peter the Great paved Petersburg.
> In the swamps of the north
> On the bones of peasants.
> David Ben-Gurion
> paved
> the way to the Burma Road, that road
> the route to the road leading to the capital, Jerusalem,
> on the bones of boys from the Holocaust.[23]

This poem presents a reversal of the myth of the ingathering of the exiles,
undermining the dichotomy of "Holocaust and rebirth" (*sho'ah u-
tekumah*). The survivors are presented as passive; their voices are not heard;
they have no desire of their own. The others, the Israelis, instrumentalize
them as objects.

The only ones sacrificed are the new immigrants. The Burma Road
was paved on their bones alone. There is no trace here of the elements of
human error, weariness, "no choice," tragedy, and breakthrough. What remains is the arrogant arbitrariness that strips the individual of his freedom
of choice and humanness, turning him into a tiny cog in the grand ma-
chinery of historical events.

What was internalized as self-evident by Binyamin Hrushovsky (now
Harshav), the young immigrant who carved out a place for himself and
found anchors to identify with in Israeli culture and society, is rejected by
the adult poet. No longer able to identify with the Israeli reality of the
1980s, he returns to earlier vistas of his childhood memories and a cultural
identity that had been suppressed. It seems that for most immigrants, voic-
ing these accusations and venting their anger tended to strengthen their
Israeli identity and reshape it in a new form. In the case of Hrushovsky, it
was a moral justification to break his ties with it.

The undermining of Israeli identity was even more pronounced in the
case of Matti Meged—chief editor of the Palmach leaflet, one of the edi-

tors of the *Sefer ha-palmaḥ,* and a member of the yishuv elite. Meged set out to deconstruct the memory of those days, protesting in this way against present-day Israeli realities. For him, the events at Latrun became a point of encounter between the living and the dead, the assimilators and the assimilated, morality and history, past and present, fact and fiction, memory and reality.

Meged's version of Latrun first emerged after the Six-Day War, when Dominique Lapierre and Larry Collins interviewed him for their book *O, Jerusalem.*[24] He told the interviewers how, as a staff officer of the Haganah in Europe, he had accompanied illegal immigrants on the ship "Khalanit" to Israel's shores. He arrived with them in Haifa immediately after the proclamation of statehood (May 15, 1948); then, at the port, a black Olds sedan waited for him and took him directly to meet with Ben-Gurion. The "old man" expressed interest in the immigrants and asked about their military training. He then informed the astonished Meged that the immigrants were to be sent immediately into battle.

According to Meged, he protested to Ben-Gurion about his decision, but Ben-Gurion responded by saying that there was no choice. Within 72 hours of their arrival, Meged went on, the new immigrants had been dispatched to the front at Latrun, and Meged was with them. Not knowing how to use their weapons, whose safety-latches were locked, they were like frightened animals. Under the heavy fire at Latrun, a young man whom Meged knew from among the immigrants, gasping his dying breath, whispered in Meged's ear: "We've failed you." An abbreviated version of Meged's story was later included in Michael Bar-Zohar's *Ben-Gurion.*[25]

No one raised doubts about the credibility of Meged's story or the messages it contained, since it differed little from the accounts and rumors that had circulated in the tents of the Palmach in the wake of the Latrun battle. Moreover, the controversy with Ben-Gurion, the details of the combat at Latrun, such as the lack of experience among the immigrants under fire, the conversation on the battlefield with the dying immigrant—all this was part of a literary narrative that was familiar in the discursive context of Latrun. As mentioned before, Yigal Mossinsohn had made similar use of this narrative in his popular play *Be-arvot ha-negev,* transforming it in the process into part of the collective memory of Latrun.[26]

The storm erupted in 1987 when Meged visited his native Israel from his home in exile, New York. Interviewed in *Ha'aretz*, he repeated the narrative. This time, however, Latrun was not used simply to invoke an attack on Ben-Gurion within the legitimate and accepted framework of the "other version" of events. Rather, it was now a symbol of and proof for the need for radical revision: nothing that had taken place in the early days of the state had really occurred the way it had been presented and constructed. The message of the present to the past is evident in almost every line: "There was something grotesque there right from the beginning, but in all honesty, it took me quite a good many years to comprehend that." Meged is conscious of the sea change that has taken place in his memory: "My past is evaporating, and nothing remains of it."

For Meged, Latrun plays a key role in the process of the vaporization of the past. In the interview, he goes on at great length to describe his meeting with Ben-Gurion, his protest against Ben-Gurion's intention to send the immigrants into dangerous combat, his complaint to Yigal Allon, the Palmach commander, and his joining, à la Korczak, the group of his disciples who went off to battle. Meged claims that he had heard Shlomo Shamir (commander of the Seventh Brigade) proclaim: "We're no longer an underground! We don't have to operate now at night. We'll go in broad daylight!" This was followed by the description of the battle at Latrun, and the moving final words of the dying immigrant.[27]

What, back in 1972, had been a kind of collective tall tale, documenting the standard version that had circulated in the tents of the Palmach regarding the events at Latrun, now became a pointed indictment of the whole system of relations between Israel and the diaspora, the concept of the redeemers and the redeemed, and the arrogance and callousness of the army command contrasted with the purity of sacrifice of the green immigrant recruits. Meged's assault was aimed at the entire edifice of the Israeli establishment and did not distinguish between the Palmach and Ben-Gurion.

The extraordinary element in the story was that Mati Meged, as far as was known, had not been a member of the Haganah general staff in Europe; nor had he come to Israel in May 1948. The ship "Khalanit" did not dock in Haifa until July 1948. The immigrants who embarked from it did take part in combat in the War of Independence, but not at Latrun. The story of his meeting with Ben-Gurion and the conversation that ensued, the meeting with Yigal Allon, the quote from Shamir, his description of combat at Latrun and the heartrending variant of "dulce et decorum est pro patria mori" in the form of the dying immigrant in Latrun and his last words—all these elements were simply fictional. In a letter to *Ha'aretz*, the poet Haim Gouri stated outright that everything Meged had recounted about the events was fabrication, pure and simple. Shlomo Shamir also let it be known in the press that Meged had not taken part in the battle at Latrun.[28]

In Meged's reply to responses by the poets Natan Zakh and Haim Gouri, facts are intermixed with fiction, memory with history, the past with the present. While Gouri attempted to distinguish between criticism of Latrun based on reality and that rooted in fiction and invention, Meged and Zakh refused to recognize the absoluteness of that distinction. Does the past shape the present, or is it the other way around? Is the recollection of events as some person recalls them less valid than the picture delineated by documents and testimony?

Meged admitted that in the interview with Tamar Maroz in *Ha'aretz*, he made reference to a novel he was working on, and "was not careful enough in drawing the line between the 'hero' of the novel and myself." However, to his mind, that does not invalidate the internal truth expressed in the interview: the attempt to locate the roots of the contemporary malaise afflicting the State of Israel in events of the past. To the present day, he contends, the slogan of *eyn breirah* continues to cloak and whitewash "all the unnecessary failures, the callous indifference to unnecessary victims, and even criminal acts." As to whether he was or was not actually in Latrun, Meged asserted: "I was not meticulous with regard to details, and I don't remember many details precisely any more. But I was there and experienced what I recounted. *No documents from archives or other evidence can disprove that truth*. Yet that's really not what's important. [emphasis added, A.S.]"[29]

Meged questions the version of history as interpreted by the established tools of the discipline. In its place he juxtaposes the personal internalization of historical events, similar to the documentary drama that mixes fact and fiction, yet presents the internal truth of the events as understood by the author. The pattern of events as fashioned in the imagination of the individual is a recollection of the events as they were ideally supposed to have happened. "These past thirty-five years, I've been carrying around that story inside me, as if I'd really been there," as Gouri quoted a remark made by Meged.[30]

Just as the creation of a common identity requires the invention of a common past, the dismantling of that same identity demands the jettison- ing of a shared memory. Meged's liberation from Israeli identity was bound up with his breaking free from memories of the past. In the Israel of the 1980s, such an attempt at dismantling of identity met with mixed feelings. Though criticism of the founding myth of the state was accepted and even fashionable at the time, the majority of the public was not pre- pared to let go of it completely. The version of Latrun used to deconstruct the myth of the ingathering of the exiles ultimately remained confined to a small group within the intelligentsia whose scathing critique of Israeli society was broad, cutting, and unambiguously political.

Latrun exemplifies the mythopoeic dynamic and demonstrates how a myth crystallizes around a certain basic kernel of fact, and then constructs and molds collective memory. The ideology behind the myth changes with time, and the social groups that are aided and empowered by it also shift. Yet the symbol that has been created does not lose its centrality and salience. Collective memory seizes upon symbols like that of Latrun as a kind of peg to hang onto. In the battle for national identity, "identity- defining functions of memory" acquire enormous significance. In those shifting currents, a changing Israeli subidentity found its symbolic moor- ing in the myth of Latrun.

The variant versions of events at Latrun raised fundamental questions about the central mythologems of the War of Independence: "no choice," the superiority of Ben-Gurion's leadership, the sabra as an ideal Israeli model, and the State of Israel as the haven of the survivors. These ques- tions did not challenge the basic legitimacy of the state, but made it possi- ble for differing conceptions of Israeli identity to gain competing legiti- macy. Nearly fifty years after the establishment of the state, the foundation myth of its creation is undergoing adjustment, being recalibrated to a changing reality. In commenting on the deconstructive fashion of "smash- ing the myths" of the War of Independence, S. Yizhar characterized the re- lation between the present and the past: "All maturation is an examination of the beginnings. And any examination is both in order to learn, in order to separate from the past, and to justify that separation."[31]

In its variant as the myth of the participation and sacrifice of the new immigrants in the War of Independence, Latrun continues to gather potency: anyone who wishes to be a part of it will relate himself in some way or other to the battles that raged on the killing-fields at Latrun. Recently, the official organ of the Israeli Air Force published an account of the arrival of forty immigrants from India to Israel by plane via Cyprus. As the story goes, they arrived in Israel from Cyprus on the eve of the establishment of the state. Naturally, they were sent to Latrun. According to the author, twenty-eight of them lost their lives on the battlefield there over the course of three weeks; another eight were wounded. And just as in legends, where one is not supposed to look for any hard facts, the article notes that the lists of names of those Indian immigrants were also destroyed in the battle . . .[32]

The myth of Latrun lives on . . .

Translated by William Templer

1. The most comprehensive work about Jerusalem in the 1948 War is Itshak Levy, *Tisha Kabin* (Tel Aviv: Ma'arakhot, 1986).

2. Levy, pp. 263–64.

3. Arieh Itzchaki, *Latrun. Ha-ma'arakha ba-derekh li-yerushalayim* (Keter, 1982), pp. 197–202; Shlomo Shamir, *Be-khol mekhir—li-yerushalayim* (Tel Aviv: Ma'arakhot, 1994), pp. 41–122, 265–66, 524.

4. Anita Shapira, "The Minutes of the Committee of Five," in *Mi-pitur ha-rama ad peruk ha-palmaḥ* (Israel, 1985), pp. 110–11.

5. Itzchaki, pp. 203–4.

6. Itzchaki, p. 226.

7. Shlomo Shamir, *Be-khol mekhir—li-yerushalyim*, p. 485. Shamir checked the personal files of all the combatants of the Seventh Brigade in the Israeli Army Archives. He concluded that there were no casualties that were unidentified in this battle.

8. Shapira, p. 111.

9. Yisrael Ber, *Kravot Latrun* (Tel Aviv: Ma'arakhon, November, 1955), pp. 7–44.

10. David Ben-Gurion, *Yerushalayim ba-milḥama: Tzava u-vitakhon* (Tel Aviv: Ba-Ma'arakhah), p. 154.

11. Shapira, pp. 110–11.

12. Uri Avneri, *Bi-sedot peleshet 1949* (A.L. [Special Edition], 1975), p. 100.

13. Yigal Mossinsohn, *Be-arvot ha-negev* (Or-Am, 1989), pp. 38–39.

14. Letter of Rabbi Goren to Shlomo Shamir, June 4, 1951. Shamir, p. 483.

15. See, for example, Zeev Shiff, *Ha'aretz*, March 13, 1964; Yair Evron, *Ma'ariv*, May 15, 1964; Rafael Bashan, *Ma'ariv*, May 14, 1967; Uri Oren, *Yediot Aḥaronot*, June 7, 1968 and June 14, 1968.

16. Haviv Kena'an, "Ha-krav he-hadash al Latrun," *Ha-aretz*, August 10, 1973.

17. Barukh Nadal, "Haznahat halale Latrun," *Ha'aretz*, August 19, 1973.

18. The Knesset Minutes. Sessions no. 138–140 of the 11th Knesset, November 18–20, 1985.

19. Nurit Baretzki, "Oleh ḥadash magia le-Haifa," *Ma'ariv*, April 15, 1975.

20. Tehila Ofer, "Nishlakhti yashar le-Latrun," *Ma'ariv*, May 10, 1978.

21. This approach was strongly emphasized in a TV documentary, "Shever be-anan." Broadcasted in

June 1989, it presented interviews with newcomers of 1948. See also Hana Yablonka, "Klitatah u-be'ayot hishtalvutah shel she'erit hapletah ba-ḥevrah ha-yisraelit ha-mithavah" (Unpublished dissertation, Hebrew University 1990), pp. 113–19.

22. Natan Alterman, "Be-terem or," in *Ir Ha-yona* (Hakibbutz Hameuchad, 1978), pp. 97–102.

23. Gabi Daniel, "Shirim bamerhav," *Yigra* no. 2, 1985/86.

24. Larry Collins and Dominque Lapierre, *O Jerusalem* (London: Weidenfeld and Nicolson, 1972).

25. Michael Bar Zohar, *Ben-Gurion* (Tel Aviv: Am Oved, 1977), p. 763.

26. See above, n. 13.

27. Tamar Meroz, "Sheon ha-hol," *Ha'aretz*, January 9, 1987.

28. Gouri's letter was published in *Ha'aretz*, January 16, 1987; Shamir's letter was published in *Ha'aretz*, February 3, 1987.

29. Mati Meged, "Re'ayon ve-shivro," *Ha'aretz*, February 4, 1987.

30. Hayyim Gouri, "Ha-kazav ve-hatif'eret," *Davar*, February 6, 1987.

31. S. Yizhar, "Aḥarei ha-tzaharayim shel ha-mitosim," *Yediot Aḥaronot*, May 7, 1991.

32. Dan Sela, "Mivza Picnic," *Israeli Air Force Journal* 92 (August 1993): 31–33.

"Community with a Conscience": Myth or Reality?

The often-made contention that the past is constructed not as fact but as myth to serve the interests of a particular community may still sound radical to some, but it cannot (and should not) stupefy most historians.

> [Alon Confino, "Collective Memory and Cultural History: Problems of Method." *American Historical Review* 102,5: 1387]

At an international conference held at the University of Cape Town in 1996,[1] a passionate indictment of South African Jewry during the apartheid regime was propounded by Claudia Braude, one of the participants. Noting in particular the silence of the rabbis, she depicted an inward-looking Jewish community, blind to the realities of the wider society of which it was a part. After substantial discussion, including a spirited defense of the establishment from the floor, Ezra Mendelsohn, a distinguished Hebrew University scholar of eastern European Jewry and Jewish political behavior, posed a fundamental question to Braude and to the gathering: What could the Jews have done?

As a scholar of minority politics in eastern Europe, Mendelsohn was fully aware of the constraints, opportunities, and dangers that Jews have always faced as a minority within broader polities. This outsider, unencumbered by the kind of existential reflection and guilt so familiar to many South African Jews, clearly understood Jewish feelings of vulnerability, especially in the wake of the Holocaust. Cognizant of Jewish history, he appreciated the limitations on activism by a group numbering 118,200 at its height in 1970, or 3.1 per cent of the white population at that time.[2]

In this brief exchange, three important perspectives on the South African Jewish community's responses to apartheid had been articulated: an uncompromising indictment of Jewish moral failure, a defense of the establishment, and a sensitive understanding of the community's dilemmas. A very different position was expressed in post-conference discussion by a non-Jewish academic who had witnessed the exchange. For Ken Hughes, a noted polymath from the University of Cape Town, the Jewish community had always been particularly visible in its opposition to apartheid. He had always been impressed by disproportionate Jewish involvement in unionist, liberal, and radical activities: as union organizers, as members of the National Union of South African Students (NUSAS), in parliamentary and extra-parliamentary politics, in legal defense, and even in violent opposition to the state.

The Making of a Myth

It would seem that Hughes's proposition can be empirically validated. Long before the inauguration of the apartheid government in 1948, east European Jews had been active in trade unions, and in 1918 a Yiddish-speaking branch of the International Socialist League, a forerunner of the South African Communist Party (SACP), was established. Ever since, Jews have been notable among the prominent whites in the SACP. The Jewish left also engaged in the struggle against burgeoning fascism and anti-semitism in the 1930s. A wide range of Jewish individuals—such as Ray Alexander, I. Israelstam, I. Kessler, Fanny Klenerman, and Solly Sachs—rooted in Bundism and Marxist principles, devoted enormous energy to the upliftment of South African workers, regardless of race, color or creed. Others, such as Morris Alexander, Morris Kentridge, and Bertha Solomon, participated in mainstream parliamentary politics and were noted advocates on behalf of the underdog.

The implementation of "Grand Apartheid" under National Party rule generated a range of responses in which Jews were often prominent: some as members of the Liberal Party (until its dissolution in 1968), others as members of the centrist United Party (UP), and still others as members of the SACP. Helen Suzman, prominent among those who broke away from the UP to form the Progressive Party,[3] gained international recognition as a champion of the oppressed. Jews were conspicuous in that party, both as supporters and as activists. Indeed, the phenomenon of a Jew standing for the National Party in the early 1970s was perceived in the public domain as deviant and thus newsworthy. In the eyes of many Jews, support at that time for the National Party, with its racist principles, was seen as a scandalous betrayal of the lessons of Jewish history and morality. The liberal humane tradition was also exemplified in legal activities and defense: individuals such as Sidney Kentridge, Israel Maisels, Arthur Suzman, Arthur Chaskalson were (and are) household names known for their pursuit of social justice.

Beyond mainstream politics, Jewish activists such as Ruth First, Dennis Goldberg, Arthur Goldreich, Baruch Hirson, Sam Kahn, Albie Sachs, Joe Slovo, Harold Wolpe, and others were prepared to confront the state directly. More than half of the twenty-three whites involved in the Treason Trial of the 1950s, and all five whites apprehended in the "Rivonia Arrests" of 1963 were Jewish.[4] Indeed, an inventory of the South African left demonstrates a disproportionate presence of Jews. Given this record, it is hardly surprising that in his major study Gideon Shimoni characterized South African Jewry as a "community with a conscience."[5] No less a person than Nelson Mandela effectively endorsed this view when he noted in his autobiography that he "found the Jews to be more broad-minded than most whites on issues of race and politics."[6] He suggested that Jews are relatively tolerant because "they themselves have historically been victims of prejudice."[7]

Certainly South African Jews would agree with the idea that Jewish history had taught them important lessons. But they would go beyond the "lachrymose" conception of the Jewish past and would argue that Jews share humanistic values rooted in the Jewish tradition with its emphasis on social justice. Moreover, they would argue that the behavior of most Jews in South Africa was motivated by these values. These ingredients, together with disproportionate Jewish anti-apartheid activism and the record of opposition to the National Party, inform the Jews' positive self-understanding of Jewish behavior in apartheid South Africa. Herein lies the creation of a master narrative or myth.[8]

Implicit in this myth is the notion that the Jews operated on a higher moral plane than most whites. Chief Rabbi Cyril Harris intimated as much in his submission, on behalf of the entire community, to the Faith Hearings of the Truth and Reconciliation Commission.[9] Despite acknowledging a collective failure on the part of South African Jewry to protest sufficiently against apartheid, the Rabbi went out of his way to remind the Commissioners that the "Jewish community has produced proportionately more heroes in the struggle against apartheid than any other so–called white group."[10] The rabbi's "official" testimony, coupled with Mandela's generous assessment of Jewish political behavior, can be seen to validate the positive self-representation of the majority of identifying Jews in South Africa in the apartheid years.

Interrogating the Myth

Is this South African Jewish self-understanding justified? Will it survive the scrutiny of a new generation of South Africans, Jewish and non-Jewish? As is the case with all master narratives, contestation is inevitable: its contours will be informed and demarcated by new circumstances as the past is interrogated and cherished representations are challenged. The reality of Jewish political behavior under apartheid will be subject to no less revision than is undertaken in all historical analyses. Indeed, the process of scrutinizing past Jewish behavior has already begun. In addition to her critique of rabbinic behavior mentioned at the outset, Braude has drawn attention to the fact that it was a Jew, Percy Yutar, who led the prosecution that sentenced Mandela to life imprisonment. Her article on the subject, which appeared in the *Mail & Guardian*,[11] had been refused publication in a special issue of *Jewish Affairs* entitled "Jews and Apartheid"[12] as it was felt that the article could be libelous.

By focusing on Yutar, Braude exposed an important lacuna in the master narrative. Importantly, she reminds readers that Jewish leaders showered encomiums on Yutar following his appointment as Attorney General of the Orange Free State in the wake of his successful prosecution of Mandela. They considered his an "illustrious career" and praised him for bringing credit to the community that they believed he "graced." As Braude points out, it is "hard now to imagine the apologist mindset that promoted the Jewishness of the state prosecutor over that of two of the [Jewish] Rivonia trialists."[13] In due course, others will no doubt follow Braude and reveal additional lacunae.

The range of responses to Braude's article demonstrates the vehemence and vigor with which dearly-held myths are both defended and challenged. For example, Rabbi Norman Bernhard, a prominent Johannesburg Jewish religious leader, defended his role in the apartheid years, highlighting his active opposition to the regime.[14] Responding to Bernhard, Benjamin

Pogrund, a leading liberal Jewish journalist, pointed out that the Rabbi had "congratulated Percy Yutar from the pulpit on being appointed to a high legal office" and that he (Pogrund) had at the time accused Bernard of "collaboration."[15] Comments from other correspondents demonstrate that past reality is more complex than implied by the comforting phrase "community with a conscience."

In the first instance, generalizing about "the community" suggests, erroneously, that it is a monolithic entity. As is the case for all ethnic minorities, substantial cleavages exist: insularity co-exists with radical activism, strict Orthodoxy with secularism, apathy with conscience. Another question that arises is whether the behavior of individual Jews, acting as individuals, constitutes Jewish political behavior. After all, many of the individuals noted for their activism were, in the sense employed by Isaac Deutscher, non-Jewish Jews.[16] Examining individual behavior only is thus inadequate. An assessment of communal behavior needs to go beyond the behavior of individuals. It must also examine the official stance and actions of the organized community's representative institutions, of its leadership, and of the broader community.

The South African Jewish Board of Deputies (the Board), as the official voice of the community, has historically understood its mandate as representing the Jewish community to the authorities solely on matters Jewish. It insisted that because Jews, as whites, had full political rights, they were able to exercise their individual political predilections.[17] Yet in 1948, fearful of the Afrikaner-dominated National Party and its anti-Jewish record, the Board undermined its own principles by encouraging Jews to vote for the centrist United Party. Following the unfolding of apartheid and the intensification of repression, the Board began a period of intense internal debate.[18] It had to balance concern about perceived Jewish vulnerability against what it recognized as pressing moral imperatives. In the mid-1970s it called for the "elimination of unjust discrimination," but it was not until a decade later that the Board explicitly condemned apartheid.

While the Board consistently grappled with the moral dilemmas generated by apartheid, the actions of Jewish Communists and others deemed subversive by the state provided an ongoing focus—for some, an embarrassment—for its deliberations. In the main, however, ambivalent and subtle innuendo characterized official statements, especially in the 1950s and

1960s. This equivocation was rationalized, by and large, by deflecting moral issues onto the rabbinate.[19]

Did the rabbinate take up the Board's challenge? Here the record, to be charitable, is patchy.[20] Certain rabbis did engage the moral conundrums. Some were pressured by their lay committees to moderate their condemnation. In one case the residence permit of an outspoken rabbi was withdrawn by the government. Although several rabbis, even Chief Rabbis, participated with leaders of other faiths in protests against specific inhuman acts, in the main sermons steered clear of the political issues of the day. Unlike some other religious denominations, a collective Jewish religious condemnation of apartheid was absent, or muted at best. Given the dearth of outspoken rabbis relative to the number serving congregations, it seems clear that an opportunity to give Torah-based moral leadership and guidance by those purportedly best qualified to do so was lost, or at least squandered.[21]

What emerges from the foregoing is a communal leadership content to have Jewish individuals "legally" oppose the regime, while the representative body accommodated itself to the apartheid order. Jewish organizations even went so far as to invite apartheid leaders, including cabinet ministers, to formal communal functions. This is not to say that the leaders condoned or welcomed the apartheid order, or never questioned the system. However, by and large, they turned inward and focused on self-preservation, echoing the long-established tradition of *dina d'malchuta dina* ("the law of the land is law [for the Jews]"). They were unable or unwilling to recognize the inherent contradictions in their own behavior or to separate their functions: to oppose apartheid as a community, while continuing to represent Jewish interests within the ostensibly democratic segment of the polity.

The Board's equivocation and muted voice was well recognized by those individuals who founded Jews for Justice (JFJ) and Jews for Social Justice (JSJ) in the mid-1980s in Cape Town and Johannesburg, repectively. Had the Board been unequivocal in its condemnation of apartheid, there would have been no public space for these two organizations to protest explicitly, as Jews, against ". . . any form of discrimination against any people."[22] Both organizations sought to enlighten Jews about South African realities, to build bridges to black community organizations, and to participate actively in changing South African society. While their criticism of the Board had much in common with that of the radical left, the activist founders, largely of a younger generation, and their supporters were not "non-Jewish Jews." Among them were many Jewish day school and youth movement graduates who continued to participate in mainstream Jewish life. But they rejected a bystander role and argued forcefully for direct and explicitly Jewish involvement in the unfolding political process.

What of the broader Jewish population? Like all other whites, Jews were the beneficiaries of a colonial order built on racial exploitation and inequality. As a tiny immigrant community at the turn of the century, survival was their primary concern. The newcomers soon adapted to the prevailing norms and structures, with the majority seemingly oblivious to the plight of black South Africans, notwithstanding their own experience of discrimination and oppression. Fashioning a cohesive and supportive communal structure took precedence over social action.

Segregationist policies in the interwar years hardly attracted Jewish attention or concern and the transformation and formalization of segregation into "separate development" or apartheid in the 1950s was, for the most part, ignored. Even the full force of state repression, including draconian race-based legislation, failed to galvanize the community, as a community, to action. With the exception of a few individuals, in the immediate postwar period Jews did not support the Communist Party or the Liberal Party, available options for those appalled by the unfolding legislation. As Shimoni has shown, Jews gravitated towards "the conservative centre of the political spectrum, namely the United Party . . ."[23]

Jewish quiescence in the 1950s and 1960s can be explained, at least in part, by a sense of vulnerability occasioned by the manifestations of serious antisemitism in the South African polity during the 1930s and early 1940s,[24] and by the knowledge of the tragic fate of their coreligionists in Europe.[25] Their fears were exacerbated when the National Party, with its blatantly anti-Jewish record, came to power in 1948. Once that party ceased to focus on what it had termed the "Jewish problem," and instead sought to co-opt Jews, as whites, into the apartheid project, the temptation to acquiesce was powerful. The National Party government's recognition of Israel and Prime Minister D.F. Malan's visit to the Jewish state in 1953 further seduced this intensely Zionist community to virtual silence.

By the 1970s, and in the wake of a crumbling United Party, the majority of Jews had found a political home in the more liberal breakaway Progressive Party. In this choice their political behavior was little different from that of non-Jewish urban English-speaking middle-class voters. While most Jews continued to support opposition parties, there is evidence to suggest that an increasing proportion supported the National Party through the later 1970s.[26] The move to the right continued through the 1980s as the National Party shifted to the center of the political spectrum. In essence, Jewish opposition to the status quo was at best exercised through the ballot box, or, in some cases, through emigration. After the Sharpeville massacre of 1960 and again after the Soweto uprising of 1976, substantial numbers of Jews left the country.[27] It would serve the "community with a conscience" myth to be able to say that these emigrants left in disgust at South Africa's racist policies. But they may have been motivated as much by fear of the collapse of the apartheid order as by revulsion at state repression or by particular sympathy for the oppressed. However, there can be no doubt that South African Jews—notwithstanding considerable apprehension, shared by many—by and large welcomed the momentous changes inaugurated by President De Klerk on February 2, 1990, which in effect ended the apartheid era.

Reflecting on the Myth

Juxtaposing the idealized notion of a "community with a conscience" against the much more variegated and complex reality of Jewish political behavior in South Africa, exposes the partial and selective nature of myth-making. However resistant to change entrenched and widely-shared self-conceptions may be, new conditions will always provide the impetus for challenges to interpretations of the past. Such contestation will be ongoing because myths are situationally defined: they are born in particular places and circumstances, and serve specific functions in particular periods. Over time, and even if the specific function is no longer served, collective self-understanding, forged in a particular historical context, becomes collective memory, "truth," or "our tradition." The present and past—that is, current self-understanding and memory—not only allow for selective reinterpretation but are also implicated each in the other. It is in this sense that Croce's well-known contention that "all history is contemporary history" resonates with particular force. Given the inevitability that in the ongoing production of Jewish memory changing circumstances will open the way towards recasting the past, it is to be hoped that Michael Ignati-eff's summation of Isaiah Berlin's approach to historical judgement will be followed: "The function of historical understanding [is] to identify the precise range within which historical actors enjoyed room for manoeuvre, to understand how and why they used their freedom, and to evaluate their actions by the standard of what real alternatives were possible to them at the time."[28]

In the apartheid era—and particularly in the wake of the Holocaust with its indictment of bystander behavior—a progressive or liberal self-image served to assuage the troubled South African Jewish conscience. No Jew could avoid comparisons being made between the treatment of blacks under apartheid and the treatment of Jews under Nazism. In a new South Africa, closely reflecting upon and analyzing its past, it is of inestimable benefit to be able to recite a proud record of opposition to the previous regime. Thus the imprimatur of someone of Mandela's stature becomes an invaluable asset in the repertoire of communal representations. Indeed, this was evident in the foregrounding of Mandela's comments on Jews (re-ferred to above) in a recent photographic exhibition "Looking Back: Jews and the Struggle for Human Rights and Democracy in South Africa."[29] Interestingly, and not insignificantly, the exhibition included a celebration of the "hard left," among them the very people whose behavior only three decades earlier had embarrassed the Jewish establishment. That a Jewish doyen of the Left, Albie Sachs, could share in the conceptualization and preparation of this exhibition shows how new circumstances and goals— in this case reconciliation and "nation-building"—can serve to smooth over fundamental tensions and divisions of yesteryear.

At this time in South Africa—a moment of "nation-building," of elab-orate attempts at reconciliation, and of the celebration of cultural diver-sity—the edifice, the "community with a conscience" myth, so carefully constructed over half a century, is only beginning to crumble. New gener-ations, untainted by association with the apartheid regime and scornful of their predecessors, will no doubt create their own version of past reality. The richness and variety of collective memories and historical records, coupled with engaged contestation by concerned South Africans, holds the promise of dynamic ongoing creativity and reflection. In the mean-time, Jews have a role to play as full and free citizens in the country of their birth. They have much-needed expertise in many fields—certainly recognized by the ANC-led government—as well as a heightened sensitivity to the minority psyche and a proven talent for survival.

1. "Jewries at the Frontier," Isaac and Jessie Kaplan Centre for Jewish Studies and Research, University of Cape Town, August 11–13, 1996.

2. The proportion of Jews decreased to approximately 2 per cent of the white population in 1991. The Jews numbered 108,497 or 4.1 per cent of whites in 1951, and 117,963 (2.6 per cent) in 1980. See A.A. Dubb, *The Jewish Population of South Africa: The 1991 Sociodemographic Survey* (Cape Town: Jewish Publications South Africa, 1994), p.7.

3. In its current incarnation, the Democratic Party, led by a Jew, Tony Leon.

4. See Gideon Shimoni, *Jews and Zionism: The South African Experience 1910–1967* (Cape Town: Oxford University Press, 1980), pp. 227, 231.

5. Shimoni, *Jews and Zionism*, chap. 9. See also Gideon Shimoni, "South African Jews and the Apartheid Crisis," Philadelphia: *American Jewish Year Book*, 1988.

6. Nelson Mandela, *Long Walk to Freedom: The Autobiography of Nelson Mandela* (Randburg: Macdonal Purnell, 1994), p.66.

7. Ibid.

8. Another powerful aspect of South African Jewish self understanding, not addressed here, is the notion of the community's deep commitment to Zionism. This "myth" too would be worthy of scrutiny.

9. In addition to gross violations of Human Rights Hearings, there were special sessions that included Faith Hearings in which religious leaders made submissions. Chief Rabbi Cyril Harris appeared on behalf of the Jewish community.

10. *The South African Jewish Times*, Hanukkah, 5758/1997, p.36.

11. March 27–April 3, 1997.

12. Vol. 52, No. 1, Autumn 1997. *Jewish Affairs* is a journal published under the auspices of the Jewish Board of Deputies.

13. *Mail and Guardian*, March 27–April 3, 1997.

14. *Mail and Guardian*, April 11–17, 1997.

15. *Mail and Guardian*, April 18–24, 1997.

16. Isaac Deutscher, *The Non-Jewish Jew and Other Essays* (London: Merlin Press), 1968.

17. That stance goes back to the inception of the Board early in the century. See Milton Shain, *Jewry and Cape Society: The Origins and Activities of the Jewish Board of Deputies for the Cape Colony* (Cape Town Historical Publication Society, 1983); also Gustav Saron, "The Long Road to Unity," in Gustav Saron and Louis Hotz, eds., *The Jews in South Africa: A History* (Cape Town: Oxford University Press, 1955).

18. See Shimoni, *Jews and Zionism*, chap. 9, pp. 274–75; 276–77.

19. See Shimoni, *Jews and Zionism*, p. 277.

20. See Solly Kessler, "The South African Rabbinate in the Apartheid Era," *Jewish Affairs* 50,1 (Autumn 1995): 31–35 and Gideon Shimoni, "South African Jews and the Apartheid Crisis," pp. 34–37.

21. See Claudia B. Braude, "Rabbinic Writing Under Apartheid," in Sander L. Gilman and Milton Shain, eds., *Jewries at the Frontier: Accommodation, Identity, Conflict* (Urbana and Chicago: University of Illinois Press, 1999).

22. *Newsletter of Jews For Social Justice*, November 1985.

23. Shimoni, *Jews and Zionism*, p.304.

24. See Milton Shain, *The Roots of Antisemitism in South Africa* (Charlottesville: University Press of Virginia, 1994), chap. 7.

25. Milton Shain, "South Africa," in David Wyman, ed., *The World Reacts to the Holocaust* (Baltimore: Johns Hopkins University Press, 1996).

26. See Henry Lever, "The Jewish Voter in South Africa," *Ethnic and Racial Studies* 2,2 (1979): 428–40.

27. See Sergio DellaPergola and Allie A. Dubb, "South African Jewry: A Sociodemographic Profile," in *American Jewish Year Book 1988* (Philadelphia), vol. 88.

28. Michael Ignatieff, *Isaiah Berlin: A Life* (New York: Metropolitan Books, 1998), p.206.

29. Presented in 1998, under the auspices of the Isaac and Jessie Kaplan Centre for Jewish Studies and Research, University of Cape Town.

The Myth of Masculinity Reflected in Israeli Cinema

Introduction

In its early years, the Israeli cinema was a propaganda tool in the service of Zionist ideology, and as such it expressed, directly and explicitly, the Zionist myths that prevailed in various forms in many popular texts of the time (theatrical productions, children's stories, journalistic reportage, commemorative writings). Early Israeli films therefore provide us with a convenient way of examining the translation of Zionist ideology into a cinematic propagandistic language, comparable with similar efforts in other media and genres. In subsequent years, Israeli cinema shed its propaganda role, undermined Zionist ideology, and dismantled its myths. Israeli cinema is therefore an appropriate medium for an examination of Zionist ideology, its myths, and its deconstruction in Israeli culture.

Early Zionists, who fashioned Hebrew Israeli identity by rejecting the diaspora, needed the diaspora Jew's identity to define their own, by contrast. This dichotomy of diaspora Jew and Palestinian Hebrew was shaped in many texts of the pre-state and early independence period, including Israeli cinematic texts. In the cinema, the diaspora Jew became a background element against which Hebrew identity and culture were built within an ambivalence of attraction and repulsion. In this sense, this diaspora Jew belonged to a larger group of "others" who defined and even strengthened the national identity.

Israeli society was not homogeneous at that time. Societies are rarely homogeneous. Israel's was composed of immigrants and non-immigrants, members of different ethnicities, nationalities, and races. The films of that era[1] invoked a myth that attempted to purge these differences of their dynamism, to organize them within an order that consolidated all outsiders, and to create a hierarchy that would support the homogeneous facade of the new Hebrew identity.

At the top of this hierarchy and as the final goal of the plot that transformed the Jew into the Israeli, stood the Hebrew Israeli male. He controlled space with his action and gaze; he dominated all of its dimensions—length, width, and height. The topography beneath his feet and before his eyes represented his connection with the homeland and his ability to control it. This power was shaped and glorified by the camera and cinematic language. The camera fixed itself to and identified with his point of view, and the finest cinematic techniques of the time amplified his image and portrayed his domination of space. This hero determined the shape of history, the structure of the plot, and the nature of the Zionist order to be masculine. The places of the three "others"—Arabs, women, and diaspora Jews—were determined relative to the male and his position in the film. The "others" functioned as metaphorical symbols that reinforced and defined male Hebrew identity by shedding light on his identity from different angles. At the beginning of the films, the diaspora Jew displayed feminine, savage, or passive traits associated with a barren desert, and with the women and Arabs who appeared in the films. As the plot developed, he experienced a process of initiation in which he died symbolically and was reborn with Hebrew masculine traits.

The films of the 1940s and the 1950s dealt, for the most part, with Holocaust survivors. The heroes were children and the initiation process transferred them from childhood to adulthood, from Jewishness to Hebrewness, and from a relationship with a real father in the diaspora to the acceptance of an adopted Israeli father. Women survivors symbolized this process metaphorically. At first, they were permissive, seductive, or lascivious, but still represented the desert and the diaspora and shared the Arab's place. Later they became collective mothers (kindergarten teachers, child caregivers) who represented fertility and reinforced the transformation of the male hero.

In all the early films, the moment the hero changed his identity he shed the characteristics that identified him with the repulsive, threatening "others." He revealed his virility by working the land (an act portrayed as erotic),[2] by going to war, and by maintaining "normal" relations with women. At this stage, his environment and its components ceased to be repulsive or threatening, and started to be controlled by and united with the more attractive Zionist identity. Thus, the desert became a flourishing settlement and the woman, who was characterized at the beginning of the film by negative metaphors (as a barren or licentious figure who belonged to the desert) now emerged as a pure mother. The Arab did not find his place in this transformation, but he served it indirectly by disappearing from the landscape, supporting the Zionist enterprise, or allowing the recent immigrant to discover his new Hebrew attributes—in war. The myths about the desert made to blossom and the Jew who became an Israeli converged into parallel myths in the plot of the newly-arrived immigrant, the Jew-turned-Israeli.

This image, however, was merely an artificial structure intended to camouflage contradictions in Zionist ideology and merge them into a homogeneous account in which the perfect male figure attained all ideals. Everything that threatened him—including the diaspora Jew, the woman, the Arab, and the desert—was expunged. This artificial structure was a device that concealed the dependence of Israeli-Hebrew identity on other identities that reinforced it by negation and contrast. A subversive reading of the films reveals the uncertainty of this structure and illuminates the changes that swept Israeli culture in subsequent years—changes that brought the embedded elements in the cinematic texts to the surface and shifted marginal features of the early culture to the centers.

In the 1960s, the various genres of Israeli cinema attempted to expose what the earlier cinema had repressed and to restore the situation preceding the coalescence of the male-Zionist myth, in a quest for a different gender and national identity—one that neither delegitimized other groups nor disregarded the multiple identities of which the Hebrew-Israeli nation itself is composed.

However, by examining the subtext of these films, we find that the mere reversal of the hierarchy of images and values did not suffice to criticize the male Zionist myth of the early cinema. Pnina Werbner[3] discusses the danger of simplification that threatens the alternative discourse by treating the hegemonic identity as monolithic without variation or diversification. Nira Yuval-Davis[4] develops these themes in her critique of multiculturalist attitudes that assume the existence of fixed boundaries between minorities and disregard power struggles that occur within them.[5] Both scholars identify the problem that occurs when the identity of a rival, be it a hegemonic rival or an oppressed minority, is regarded as essentialist, permanent, and unchanging.

In our discussion of various currents in the deconstructive branch of Israeli cinema, we must distinguish between films that reduced various pairs of identities, Israeli/diaspora, feminine/masculine, Jewish/ Arab, to a single opposition, and films that attempted to dismantle the opposition, examine the diverse and changing relations among its components and, as a result, allowed all types of discourse, including the Zionist, to be heard.

Admittedly, the first type of film reversed the old myth, placed in the center the elements that the old myth had rejected (strangers and others), and marginalized its centerpiece, the Israeli male. However, it left intact the divisions and images that had essentialized diaspora Jews, women, Arabs, and children at one pole of the dichotomy, the one opposite from the adult heroes, the Hebrew Israelis. Thus, instead of taking a dynamic step toward diversification and heterogeneity, it allowed essentialist, homogeneous identities to survive.

The second type of film revealed two processes that Yuval-Davis discusses: "rooting" and "shifting." On the one hand, it acknowledged the complexity of the hegemonic Israeli culture in which it was rooted; on the other hand, it distanced itself from this culture in order to examine the other cultures it had rejected. By changing its position vis-à-vis both cultures, it could contemplate each from within and without. In this sense, it did not "eradicate" the old Israeli discourse but reduced it to its component parts and opened it up to other identities and cultures that were recognized as part of Israeli identity itself.

By contemplating the new deconstructive cinema from a historical perspective, we see that the more consolidated this model became, the more vigorously it freed itself of the old discourse and adopted more diverse ways of dismantling the identities and values that the discourse had built. This recalls Itamar Even-Zohar's theories about the consolidation of models in a culture[6] and describes the way in which the Zionist-male myth of the early cinema was relegated to the margins and replaced by cinema that was critical of it. Early on, this cinema preserved the old myth even as it criticized it, but it later examined it as part of a dialogue with other types of discourse.

Shattering—and Safeguarding—the Old Myth

The film *Three Days and a Child* (Uri Zohar, 1966), based on A.B. Yehoshua's short story, challenged the dominating macho image of the early films. As this persona was challenged, so was the myth of pioneering Zionism for which the hero nostalgically yearns. The film questions his values by revealing the violence embodied in them—a violence that erupts with the disintegration of values in the new bourgeois urban reality. However, a subversive reading of the film shows that it safeguarded the myth it criticized by retaining images of women that remained constant from the earlier period.

Three Days and a Child is anchored in nostalgia for the "Zionist era," which was dominated by the illusion of a homogeneous masculinity manifested at work, at war, and in the family. Early Zionist films attempted to create this homogeneity and only by interpreting them subversively can one determine at whose expense this manhood was built and who was excluded from it or affirmed it by becoming "other" to it. In *Three Days and a Child*, the film itself conducted this inquiry by dismantling the old myth and examining the migration of identities and attitudes underlying it.

The past of the plot is represented by the kibbutz. The hero perceives the kibbutz period as a time of harmony and integrity, as opposed to the dystopian nature of the urban present. The film represents these two periods in the hero's life, which correspond to two eras in Zionist history—the socialist pioneering period on the kibbutz and the era of bourgeois urbanization—by means of two feminine stereotypes. Both dominated the pioneer and Holocaust-survivor films: the woman as a symbol of fertility and the woman as the barren desert. In *My Father's House* (Herbert Klein, 1947–49) for example, Miriam is a prostitute for the Nazis, who have murdered her children. Once in Israel, she refuses to be the caregiver of the kibbutz children and a mother to David, the protagonist of the film, to whom she is strongly attached.

At this phase of her life, the camera contemplates her against the background of the Judean Desert, identifying her with the aridity of a desert. After her transformation, that is, after she accepts the role of David's caregiver and is willing to forget her past, the camera "rewards" her by portraying her against the background of dancing kibbutz members. She has shifted from one extreme, outside the Zionist pioneering reality (desert, barrenness, prostitution) to the other extreme, part of Zionist reality, represented by motherhood and fertility. In Zohar's *Three Days and a Child*, this duality suggests the dismantling of Israeli-Zionist reality from within into very different settings: city and kibbutz, the bourgeois present and the pioneering past. This fragmentation is represented by the fragmentation of the woman's body.[7]

This film, like many subsequent films, attempted to shatter the masculinity of the Zionist national cinema by retreating into its "pre-Oedipal phase,"[8] in which the symbolic order and its language had not yet been imposed on the child, in which the mother and the surrounding world could be merged into a total unity, and in which relationships were not set out in terms of defined heterosexual opposites. However, the reconstruction of this phase was impossible, and the attempt released a host of destructive urges. Moreover, the male identity of the earlier films remained intact, predicated and dependent upon the feminine image that played its customary roles. The woman was portrayed either as a threatening symbol of desert and barrenness or a representative of fertility and growth.

Eli, the hero of *Three Days and a Child*, lives a loveless urban life with his girlfriend, Yael. One day, his former lover, Noa, calls and asks him to take care of her young son for three days. During those three days, Eli is beset by memories and nostalgia for his erstwhile love and its setting, the kibbutz. In the course of the film, these memories cross two zones of time and space: the enchanted, idyllic past on the kibbutz and the repulsive present in the city.

Throughout the film, Eli repeatedly takes off his glasses, cleans them, and puts them on again, reminding us of the diaspora Jew in the early films who could not use his eyes to control his surroundings. In *Avodah* (Helmer Larsky, 1935), for example, the hero does not look around before he comes to Palestine; the camera observes nothing but the puddles through which he treads. Only after he reaches the country is he capable of contemplating its landscapes, which are now filmed from his point of view.

In *Three Days and a Child*, doubts about Eli's manhood are expressed in various ways. At certain junctures in the film, Eli (like all the men in the film) is observed lying in bed heavily and helplessly. He spends nearly the entire film at home where he feeds and cares for his former lover's son. The setting is domestic and feminine, the hero's posture is passive and feminine, and his preoccupations are feminine as well. Even though he is played by Oded Kotler, who was identified with markedly masculine roles on the stage, the film threatens this masculinity. Eli's loss of manhood is further emphasized by the women who threaten him: his neighbor's wife, who demandingly courts him; his present girlfriend, Yael, who, at the beginning of the film pricks him with a thorn; and his female students, who surround him noisily and threateningly at the swimming pool.

The film fractures the heterosexual orientation considered desirable by the previous cinema—not only by creating an effeminate male figure, but also by rupturing the binary relationship model. In fact, all of Eli's relationships in his city life are focused on the "wrong" subject. He shifts his erotic feelings for his former lover to her son, whom he caresses and kisses. When he sleeps with Yael and when he attempts to sleep with his neighbor, he needs to be watched by a third party. The peering gazes of Yael's friend Zvi or of the boy stimulate his desire, which is directed not only at the two women but at the onlookers as well.

In fact, Eli's relations concern threesomes rather than couples: he, Noa, and her husband; he, Yael, and Zvi, who is also courting her. In the final analysis, the film devotes its lengthiest attention to his relationship with Zvi. Together they care for the child; together they search for a snake Zvi has brought to the apartment and which has escaped from its box. As they search for it during the night, they form a friendship whose warmth is absent from Eli's relations with his women. The snake, which was supposed to have bitten Noa's son (Eli had opened its box the previous evening), eventually bites Zvi. This may represent a different masculinity, a violent eroticism suggested by an obvious phallic symbol and directed at a man.

Thus the film leads its hero back to the stage before the symbolic heterosexual order prevailed—the imaginary phase, in which nothing was governed by either paternal or Zionist law and order. However, within the attempt to reach this phase, violent urges erupt—urges previously organized and regulated in the persona of the warrior-hero, who channels his aggression toward the enemy. In the new urban bourgeois order, they burst out without inhibition.

Eli's kibbutz memories are diametrically opposed to his life in the city. Instead of Yael, whom he first sees in a field of thorns and scorpions, Noa, the kibbutz girl, walks barefoot in the cultivated fields of the kibbutz. She is filmed in the white, filtered light of recollection, and the sounds of bells and a guitar envelop her in a dreamlike aura. Eli himself was a different person while on the kibbutz. In the flashback there while on furlough from the army, he walks in the fields, in uniform and without glasses, as a tractor passes him. These expansive fields, observed in a series of long shots, are reminiscent of the fields in which the hero of *Avodah* strides, and recall the work-and-fight combination that fashioned the masculine image of the hero in the early films.

Although the kibbutz portrayed in Eli's memories through gentle filters is a bright and quiet place, its nature as a place of darkness and disquiet becomes increasingly apparent until he is finally reminded of his only sexual encounter with Noa, behind the creaking door of an unlit shack. This moment reveals the similarity of the woman of the present to the woman of the past and exposes the falsehood of the so-called purity of platonic love. In place of the unsullied woman she has been until now, Noa becomes a physical, sexual woman. Instead of representing life, she represents death, with her silent, corpse-like body. Thus the film ostensibly confronts the feminine stereotype by shattering it and revealing the falsehood of the fragmentation of the feminine image into two clashing entities. Actually, however, it does not fracture the stereotype; it replaces it with another one.

On the one hand, the film points to the savage, destructive violence that lies beyond the pioneering Zionist myth, a violence that now dominates the new urban life. On the other hand, it fails to confront this myth and the ideology underlying urban life because it continues to use the woman as a symbol of the schism between them. She remains where she was in the early films: confined either to deserts of desolation or fields of fertility. These old images reconstruct the old myth, which is still invoked to depict both the kibbutz and the city.

The film *Atalia* (Akiva Tevet, 1984), based on Yitzhak Ben-Ner's short story, appeared seventeen years after *Three Days and a Child*. Like the earlier film, however, it retains the old images unchanged. At first glance, it attempts to undermine the myth that transforms the Jew into the Israeli and the flaccid immigrant into a working, fighting hero who controls his surroundings. It elevates the persona this structure has rejected—the woman. It allows her to express the values of creativity and criticize those of the collective—that is, socialist ideology, which has become an instrument of repression of individuals; and Israeli masculinity, with its assimilation of militaristic values. However, because it fails to modify the male-female images and actually reconstructs them, this film still reflects the original myth. Instead of heterogeneity, dynamism, and amenability to change, its images and plots propose uniformity, stasis, and constriction, thus restoring the early myth's homogeneity.

At the beginning of the film the hero, Mati, is not a complete man. Like other heroes at the beginning of the early films, he embodies characteristics both childish and feminine: he is utterly incapable of interacting with women; his friend Ofer attempts to "get him laid"; he plays the role of a woman in a play put on before he joins the army; he needs his mother's permission to enlist in a combat unit. In the course of his military training, he fails to perform like a man and spends most of the time being carried prostrate on a stretcher. After he is discharged because of a heart defect, he reverts to boyhood: he mingles among the children in the kibbutz yard; his mother makes his bed and serves his needs; and he turns down a masculine job in the tractor garage. His manhood resurfaces not in war, but when he has an affair with Atalia.[9]

Early in the film, his situation is similar to that of the survivor-hero in the early films, and he is therefore identified with other outsiders. Like Atalia, he is rejected by the kibbutz members, who condemn him as insane and subject him to scorn and ridicule. These characteristics create a unity between him and Atalia's father, one of the first members of the kibbutz, who has become a senile old man derided by the other members. They consider him crazy as they do Mati and Atalia. The film also portrays the old man as a new immigrant of sorts who has not acclimatized himself to the country. He speaks German and fractured Hebrew—hardly a credible situation for a man who built the kibbutz and who would have lived in Israel for half a century. However, this very implausibility reinforces the necessity for integrating the new-immigrant persona with the other alien characters in the film. The camera's parallel shots and the presence of another outsider, an Arab, reinforce the relationships between father, daughter, and Mati.

In the midst of their affair, Mati and Atalia meet at the haystack, where Mati recalls how the kibbutz counselor had once told them about Arabs who had set fire to the kibbutz. At this moment the camera focuses on Atalia's father banishing the Arabs working in the kibbutz fields and insisting that "Hebrew labor" be reinstated. At the end of the film, Atalia sets the haystack alight in revenge for Mati's having joined the army during the war, and in so doing assumes the role that the earlier myth had reserved for the Arabs. Such repetition of motifs, reinforced by the editing of the shots, shows how the outsiders, including the woman, identify with one another, an identification strongly proposed in the early films. In the case of Atalia, the recent immigrant is merely a new addition to other outsider figures in kibbutz society.

As in the old films, the plot transforms the hero from an effeminate boy into a man. Here, however, he is allowed to display his masculinity in love and family relations instead of war and labor. In this way the film criticizes the old myth, but it does so hesitantly and ambivalently. Mati does discover the possibility of a different life when he falls in love with Atalia, but he ultimately manifests his manhood according to the old cinematic conventions. At the end of the film, precisely as the war rages, he returns to farming. As he tills and irrigates the fields, slow and long shots show how he dominates the land like the Zionist heroes who preceded him. Although he is not called up for military service, he perpetuates the mythic virility of the farmer-warrior by returning to the soil in the midst of the war.

Atalia, the ostensible heroine of the film and the bearer of its conceptual values, does not participate in the transformative process the man experiences. She merely serves as a marker and a metaphor, a background object against which he is examined. She does not function as a mother for she fails to tend to her daughter's needs. Her daughter reprimands her: "How is it possible that a daughter has to tell her mother what's right and what isn't?" Atalia positions herself at the prostitute extreme of the mother-prostitute polarity as the kibbutz members regards her as a whore. She reverts to motherhood only in an act that verges on incest: she falls in love with Mati, who is twenty years her junior and for whom she cared in his childhood.

Throughout the film, Atalia is incarcerated in closed rooms. This is most obvious during the war, when Mati returns to work in the open fields and she moves between the kibbutz kitchen and her room, where she lies in a fetal position as the sounds of war reverberate on the radio. When she burns the haystack, the images of mother, prostitute, and housebound woman (as opposed to the farming man) merge to form the feminine stereotype of the early cinema. It is precisely after Mati discovers the possibility of cultivating the fields and making them fertile that Atalia causes the film to revert thematically to desert and destruction. She is consequently identified with the Arabs, like the heroine of the early films.

Atalia allows Mati to rebel against society and reach adulthood through a means different from that ordained for him within the framework of customary metaphorical stereotypes: mother and prostitute, the housebound woman and the farmer, fertility and desolation. But in the mythical design that unites recent immigrants, women, strangers, and Arabs, the world Atalia offers him is replete with the conventional images of the world he has tried to reject.

Toppling the Old Structure and Discovering an Alternative

Although the films *Three Days and a Child* and *Atalia* apparently set out to rupture the old Zionist pioneering myth, they left the myth intact by preserving its main supporting images. As the new model solidified, a growing number of films adopted various devices to shatter the usual patterns and fixed identities, and to create an open discourse in which everything was subject to re-examination. The more dominant the new model became, the less remained of the original Zionist myths, which were replaced by other types of discourse that provided a range of identities, attitudes, and truths. Several films predated this new cinematic discourse, including those of Dan Volman: *My Michael* (1974), based on Amos Oz's novel, and *Hide and Seek* (1980/81).

My Michael does not ignore the male and female images of the early cinema. On the contrary, it multiples them several times over. It is this very effect, combined with new characteristics, that explodes the myth from within. *My Michael*, like *Three Days and a Child*, fractures the supremely self-confident male figure of the early films and brings his contradictions to the surface. By doing so, it creates a basis, as does *Three Days and a Child*, for subsequent films such as *Stretcher March* and *One of Ours*, which features a flawed male figure. However, in contrast to these films and even somewhat in contrast to *Three Days and a Child*, *My Michael* still presents pronounced masculine characteristics that recall those of the pioneer hero, mingled with the diaspora-Jewish and feminine labels that challenge them. By attempting to construct its heroes out of various clashing attributes, *My Michael* strives to undermine the old patterns and images.

Unlike Eli in *Three Days and a Child*, Michael goes to work in the morning and comes home in the evening. He holds a distinctively male job: as a geologist, he penetrates the soil and plumbs its depths. What the pioneer does with the plow, he accomplishes with his research tools. His life, and that of Hannah, his wife, is determined by his interests and goals. However, feminine and masculine identities converge in his character. Michael, like Eli in *Three Days and a Child*, cleans the house, provides child care, serves his wife milk and, at least at the beginning of the film, fails to satisfy her in bed. Although he is an active figure, most of his activities as shown on the screen are feminine, and some of them are observed through Hannah's dominant, condescending gaze. From this standpoint, Michael is the mirror-image of the hero of the early films who had yet to assume a masculine Hebrew identity. Michael has even lost the masculine ability to dominate space. While he penetrates the soil, it is Hannah, as we shall see, who controls the surface.

Michael's "Jewish" characteristics accompany his "feminine" ones. In fact, he is a typical student in Jerusalem of the 1950s and in this sense no different from Eli, the hero of *Three Days and a Child*. Unlike Eli, however, Michael is consciously in touch with his Jewish family tradition: by en-rolling in the university, he dreams of affording his father the privilege of calling him "doctor." In addition, he follows the example of his grandfather, Zalman, who was a teacher in Poland, and after whom he names his son. Moreover, Hannah's mother offers him her husband's suit to wear at his wedding, and by accepting her offer he stands in the man's shoes, as it were.

In general, Michael embodies a male figure other than that fashioned by fighting-and-working Zionism—a figure more reminiscent of the Jewish scholar, the *talmid hakham*,[10] than of the commando warrior-laborer. Indeed, when he returns from the war, he admits that not only did he not kill any Arabs but that the Israeli army almost killed him.

At first glance, *My Michael* appears to rebel against the old norms by reversing roles: relegating the male to the fringes of the plot and depriving him of his masculine characteristics while allowing the woman to drive events in time and space. However, these role-reversals do not occur in the film: both Michael and Hannah embody a broad, heterogeneous range of images and roles. At the most salient level, Hannah is constructed in accordance with the earlier cinematic stereotype. Like Atalia, she is a bad, neglectful mother who appears at the negative extreme of the mother-prostitute duality: instead of taking care of her family, she wallows in fantasies of rape and orgies with a pair of male Arab twins. Thus her erotic daydreams represent a threat to two basic areas of the Zionist order: the masculine, manifested in the heterosexual family, and national security.[11] The domains of gender and nationhood are interrelated in all the previous films, and here they appear as the double threat.

In her fantasies, Hannah not only prefers the twins to her husband, but also chooses three-part sex with them. In this sense, like Eli in *Three Days and a Child*, she dismantles the bipolar equation in favor of an impossible pre-Oedipal unity. The untamed expanses of which she dreams are parallel to the vastness of the desert that women occupy in the early films. Her very choice of the enemy as the object of her fantasies places her, like those women, on the Arab side. Her threat to the nation is particularly ominous as the Arab twins increasingly fill her dreams within the setting of the Sinai Campaign of 1956. In her last fantasized orgy with them, they crawl about in commando fatigues for the evident purpose of committing a terrorist attack against a Jewish settlement.

Hannah is also a maternal image. Although she is an inadequate mother to her son, she works as a kindergarten teacher—a later version of the collective mother in the Zionist-pioneer films. When she discovers that she is pregnant, she insists on her right to give birth, despite her husband's objections. And while in her fantasies she liberates the Arab twins during the war, in reality she sits at home awaiting Michael's return, and anxiously monitors his growing relationship with a woman friend.

Indeed, like the Arab twins, Hannah plays the role of a fetish in Israeli society. The twins' two aspects—romantic, alluring "noble savages" vs. carnal and violent threats—correspond to her own twin facets of mother and prostitute, the passive woman who sits at home and the woman who betrays her home and family. However, the film blurs these stereotypes by adding others, chiefly masculine, with additional labels and metaphors. Hannah fantasizes about being raped by the Arab twins, thereby becoming a "penetrated object," and at the same time she controls them by forcing them to struggle over her ("I was a princess and they were my subjects"). By actually controlling Arab men with her gaze as she wanders through the market, she assumes the role Hebrew men played in the early cinema.

She represents the male national values again when she urges Michael not to give in but to fight the British scholar who has challenged the accuracy of his Ph.D. dissertation. In the shot that follows this demand, Michael and his neighbor discuss evicting the British from the country. Thus, the film associates Hannah's demand of Michael with the pronouncedly masculine values of the struggle that eventually caused the British to leave.

This duality of male and female images accompanies Hannah throughout the film. She both represents the soil, and she is housebound. Generally such figures who cross boundaries and move between closed and open places, thus controlling the space, are men. Now Hannah resides in both domains, the male and the female. Like the heroines of the early Zionist films, she is identified with the soil and blends into it (by means of a dissolve sequence) when she tells her husband about the Arab twins. Yet she controls space and therefore plays the masculine role as well.

Throughout the film, she crosses from her home and the constricting alleys of her town into the open spaces of the imagination. She therefore crosses the boundaries between inside and outside and totally controls the cinematic space. This control is also reflected in the cinematic language. The entire film is integrated into her point of view from which the world that surrounds her is observed. It is a world painted in pastel shades and illuminated in veiled light, delicate combinations of light and shadow that isolate her on the side of the frame and present her against a background of walls and a foreground of metal grilles. This is a language that evokes feelings and psychological states that cannot be expressed in the overt language of the film, that of the plot.[12]

Hannah's control of space is especially evident at the beginning and end of the film. It begins with landscape shots that dissolve into each other, observed from Hannah's point of view with her voice the voice-over. At the end of the film, the same landscape scenes recur and the opening voice-over is heard again: "My power to love is about to die. I don't want to die." At this stage in the film she becomes insane and utterly passive. However, the shots of the landscape reveal that she still controls it, contemplating it in view of her own interior dualism. The male phallic landscape of towers and turrets alternates with a female landscape of open spaces and plains. The film's alternating light and shadow intensifies this dualism.

Alongside her female characteristics, Hannah displays male characteristics by controlling space, the gaze, the voice-over and (through her memories), time. However, she also rebels against this male culture when she replaces its masculine gaze with a personal feminine look, one that brims with emotion and memory.[13]

Basing her work on Lacan, who describes the gaze as an expression of symbolic order in the field of vision, Kaja Silverman[14] distinguishes between the productive look and the gaze. She depicts the gaze, identified with the camera, as one that essentializes, preserves, perpetuates, and "kills" the object. The productive look, by contrast, undermines it through memory, desire, and fantasy, permitting the recollection of others' memories and, in so doing, returning the marginal and rejected to the field of vision.

The undermining of Zionist manhood in a film like *My Michael* may be defined as the imposition of look over gaze. While Hannah's gaze is masculine, returned to the men who contemplate her, it alternates with a look replete with memories, emotion, and identification with the "other." While controlling the environment and the people around her, Hannah projects her emotions upon them, seeing herself in others and others in herself. The landscape she sees contains memory of the pre-statehood past and the Arabs who inhabited it, the "others" excluded by the Israeli gaze. In subsequent films (such as *Avia's Summer* and *New Land*), the feminine view attempts to revise the conventional definition of reality. In *My Michael* Hannah does not attempt to change anything, but by projecting herself onto the reality that has excluded her and painting it in her own colors, she makes parts of it her own.

The film also breaks down the unity and homogeneity of the "others" in the previous films. While Hannah strives to restore the Arab "other" to Israeli memory, Michael strives to integrate the Jewish past into the present. The two pasts, those of two different "others" in Israeli culture, are mutually exclusive. Hannah is threatened by the Jewish past, just as the twins represent a threat to Michael (even though he is unaware of their existence). Michael's attachment to the past is embodied in the figure of the insane Mrs. Glick, who in moments of lunacy reverts to Yiddish and the religious environment in which Hannah's apartment is located.

Perhaps Hannah's escape into the open spaces and the twins is, inter alia, an escape from this Jewish world, from the narrow alleys of the city that envelop her like ghetto walls, and from the Orthodox Jews who inhabit them.[15] In all the early films that dealt with Holocaust survivors, the child survivors liken their new environments, kibbutz or boarding school, to the ghetto and the concentration camp and attempt to escape from them into open space. There they become acquainted with the country and undergo an initiation process that transforms them from Jews into Israeli Hebrews. Hannah makes similar attempts to escape, but the open spaces to which she runs are alien spaces, controlled by Arabs.

In the film *Hide and Seek* (1980–81), produced about six years after *My Michael*, Dan Volman juxtaposes images and outlines of identity that prevent the viewer from placing the characters into defined groups. In addition, he further develops the special language of *My Michael* into an ambivalent, non-absolute language in which the male/female, diaspora Jew/Israeli dualities are blurred.

Hide and Seek concerns games played by a group of children in the period of struggle that preceded the War of Independence. The children's games represent a parodic imitation of the adults' war, and their devastating results portray Zionist discourse as a myth of heroism and war that obliterates anything and anyone outside it. The film criticizes the myth by grouping together all those excluded from Zionist identity—women, diaspora Jews, the insane, the Arab, and the effeminate male—and then dismantling the group the myth constructed. By placing its hero among different cultures and identities, the film distances itself from its own culture, and examines it in other cultural contexts.[16] However, instead of replacing Israeli identity by the other identities, it creates a dialogue among them.[17]

The film comprises two plots. One tells of a spy who provides the British with information with which they discover arms caches in the neighborhood. The second plot focuses on the children's games and their surveillance of the teacher Balaban, whom they consider a spy, and on their final discovery that the spy is not Balaban but a waiter in one of the cafés in town. They also realize that Balaban's relationship with young Arab men is not for the transmission of information but for homosexual affairs.

In superimposing a spy story upon a personal relationship, the children reconstruct their own experience and that of Uri, the film's hero. His parents have sacrificed their private life on the national altar by moving to Europe and spending their time bringing Holocaust-survivor children to Israel instead of caring for their own son.

The thrust of this plot is the opposite of the plots of the survivor films of the 1940s and 1950s, in which the children are orphans, alone and im-

mersed in their private world. Only through initiation do they fit into Israeli society and acquire adoptive Hebrew-Israeli parents, individually and
collectively. The Hebrew collective redeems them from their diaspora Jewish past and from their personal isolation. *Hide and Seek* leads its hero, Uri,
in the opposite direction. Although his parents are away from home
throughout the film (except for a brief visit by his mother), only towards
the end, after the truth about Balaban has come to light and after the Palmach commandos have beaten Balaban up and killed his Arab friend, does
Uri become aware of his loneliness, his "orphanhood," and his affiliation
with the alien diaspora Jewish world. In one of the final scenes, he visits
his mother at the youth village where she works. She invites him to remain there and join the class of orphaned Holocaust survivors. By focusing on his darkened face, the camera shows that he understands the symbolic implication of the invitation: like the orphaned children, he is alone,
rejected, parentless, and distrustful of the Hebrew collective.

As this revelation occurs, the type of gaze changes. When Uri monitors
Balaban's movements in the company of his friends, his gaze is the collective national gaze observing what appears to be espionage. Balaban moves
around in the Arab town, nervously looks right and left, slips a note to his
Arab friend, and so on. The collective gaze mimics the collective gaze of
the Palmach commandos who will eventually murder the Arab lover.
However, when Uri is separated from his friends, he views matters differently and observes the true story, that is, his teacher's relations with his
Arab friend. Thus Uri's initiation is expressed in the exchange of a gaze for
a look, which also allows him to substitute a personal plot for the national
one. At the end of the film this look leads him to the truth of his being an
orphan among orphans, a survivor among survivors.

In *My Michael*, Hannah imposes her subjective look on reality, thus
forcing the onlooker to view this reality differently. The Israeli cinema has
taken the first step toward changing its own gaze. *Hide and Seek* makes an
initial attempt to change the gaze—to see how the children, imitating the
adults' gaze, learn to view things differently, to recognize themselves in the
images of the "other" and thereby to transform what is theirs into the
other's and vice versa.[18]

In fact, however, *Hide and Seek* does not settle for replacing the national
plot with the personal account it has stifled. The film invokes a different
language that interposes itself between national and personal, Hebrew and

diaspora Jew, and male and female. Balaban attempts to teach Uri that there is no single truth and no homogeneous collective; instead there are individuals, each of whom has his or her own truth that varies with changing situations. This is the film's own point of view.

Hide and Seek defies clear and unequivocal judgment. Its underpinnings of masquerade, parody, and mimicry create the impression that the national identity itself is only an imitation with unfounded pretensions. The children play make-believe spy games, draw mustaches on themselves, and shed make-believe blood. By doing so they depict war, masculinity, and death in battle—landmarks in the national ethos—as child's play. Concurrently, however, the British arrests and manhunts, underscored by the melancholy strains of a cello, communicate the Zeitgeist and the struggle against the British, which is shown here not only as a parody of Zionism but as a genuine and painful struggle.

Having shattered the idea of Israeli manhood, the film focuses instead not on its female opposite nor on the diaspora Jew, but rather on something that lies in between: the teacher, Balaban, who plays blatantly masculine alongside feminine roles throughout the film and is revealed as a homosexual. At first, Uri rejects Balaban as a teacher but changes his mind after seeing him tenderly holding his dog, which has been killed. It is this display of feminine and slightly maternal tenderness that paradoxically allows Balaban to play a masculine role in Uri's life as a brother and father. Balaban is also an authoritative and beloved teacher, but in his hurtful behavior toward a neighbor, Hayaleh, he appears to be somewhat uncouth. However, he rebukes those who abuse and ridicule her and, in this context, tells the story of a crazy, mistreated Holocaust survivor. By identifying with the woman and the survivor, Balaban further distances himself from his previous macho image.

Hide and Seek, like the early movies, ostensibly draws the equation that identifies the outsiders with each other. In fact, however, the film does no such thing. Since Balaban is repeatedly defined in terms of his changing relations with his surroundings, neither he nor his homosexuality are portrayed as fixed and essentializing. The film fragments the homosexual's identity into several identities, both male and female, and shatters the unity of the "others." Homosexuals, women, Holocaust survivors, and Arabs are not arrayed as victims facing a well-defined front of oppressors; instead, the oppressors and the oppressed intermingle.

In fact, no one in *Hide and Seek* honors his or her defined role. At first, when Uri sees Balaban seated on his father's chair in the kitchen, he asks the teacher to vacate it even though the father is not at home. Elsewhere in the film, it seems that Uri has taken over his father's place. He enters his father's room, looks into the mirror, touches his father's suit, and puts on his hat. At the same time, Balaban also serves as a father. The place of the absentee mother is taken over by Uri's grandfather, who occupies the kitchen, does the cooking, and defines himself as a housewife.

The film's ambiguity and its shattering of fixed, essentialist definitions is reinforced in its cinematic language, which achieves either a dim light or unembellished, ordinary daylight shifting between light and shadow and portrayed in delicate, warm colors. The film's language expresses its mission: an attempt to lead its characters toward ambivalence, doubt, and ideological uncertainty.

The plot also tries to achieve this kind of vagueness. It is composed of episodes separated by fadeouts, some of which are presented merely to evoke the period: eating fruit from a dish, furniture in an apartment, manhunts and roadblocks in pre-independence Jerusalem. These details are valuable in themselves: they stop time, force the viewer to dwell on them, and avoid oppositions from which clearly defined meaning can be derived. This blurring corresponds to the general ambivalence of the film and the dialogue it creates between complex and diverse identities and cultures.

Conclusion

The early national Zionist cinema set up the Israeli Zionist male as a super-persona and the center of gravity in the Zionist myth. However, this cinema was not able to hide the differences in class, sex, and race this persona was supposed to obliterate. Since the 1960s these differences have been revealed to a growing extent in films that expose the diaspora-Jewish past, Israel's Arab past, and the female identity repressed by the unifying myth of the Hebrew male.

From this standpoint, the new films fall into two categories. The first, composed mainly of films made in the 1960s and 1970s, rejects the male Zionist myth while preserving it to a certain extent by leaving intact the binary oppositions the myth has created. The second is composed of films that transform this myth into one voice in a broad dialogue, creating an opportunity for the emergence of a new type of open, tolerant Zionist discourse attentive to the voice of the "other," whoever he or she may be.

1. The films include *Avodah* (1935), directed by Helmar Larsky; *My Father's House* (1946), directed by Herbert Klein and scripted by Meyer Levin; *The Great Promise* (1948), directed by Joseph Leits; *End of Evil* (1946–1949), directed by Helmar Larsky and Joseph Krumgold; *It Is No Dream* (1948–1949), directed by Joseph Krumgold; *The House on the Hill* (1949) and *A Tale of One Village* (directed by George Lloyd George); *Adamah and Tomorrow is a Wonderful Day* (1946), directed by Helmar Larsky; and *Faithful City* (1952), directed by Joseph Leits. These films are analyzed in Nurith Gertz, "The 'Others' in Israeli Films of the 1940s and 1950s: Holocaust Survivors, Arabs, Women," in Nurith Gertz, Orly Lubin, Judd Ne'eman, eds., *Fictive Looks at Israeli Cinema* (Tel Aviv: Open University, 1998), pp.381–403.

2. In this matter, see Ella Shohat, *Israeli Cinema* (Austin: University of Texas Press, 1989). Also, Yosef Raz, *The Military Body: Male Masochism and Homo-Erotic Relations in Israeli Cinema* (Master's Thesis, 1998).

3. Pnina Werbner, "Introduction: The Dialectics of Cultural Hybridity," in Pnina Werbner and Tariq Modood, eds., *Debating Cultural Hybridity* (London and New Jersey: Zed Books, 1997), pp.1–36.

4. Nira Yuval-Davis, "Ethnicity Relations and Multiculturalism," in *Debating Cultural Hybridity*, pp. 193–209.

5. Feminism, according to Yuval-Davis, accepts as a basic premise that all oppressed women have a permanent identity and do not consider that the feminine identity is a collection of diverse identities built through a "performative" process, to use Butler's term (1990), of constant evolution.

6. Itamar Even Zohar, *Polysystem Studies/Poetics Today* vol.11, no. 1 (Spring), 1990.

7. See analysis of this in Michal Friedman, "Between Silence and Abjection: The Cinematic Medium and the Israeli War Widow," in *Fictive Looks at Israeli Cinema*, pp. 33–44.

8. Michal Friedman analyzes this phenomenon and, following Kristeva, describes the cinema of the 1970s and the 1980s as a voyeur cinema situated in the pre-genital stage, in which a child is still engrossed in the abject, including his emissions, and is preoccupied with exploring possibilities of controlling himself and others.

9. This brief summary is based on Nurith Gertz, *Motion Fiction* (Tel Aviv: Open University of Israel, 1994). See also Friedman, op.cit.; Yael Schub, "The Female Persona and the Dynamic of Fracturing the Narrative in Modernistic Israeli Cinema" in *Fictive Looks at Israeli Cinema*, pp. 215–23.

10. As described by Daniel Boyarin in *Unheroic Conduct: The Rise of Heterosexuality and the Invention of the Jewish Man* (Berkeley and Los Angeles: University of California Press, 1997).

11. According to Lushitzky, Hannah expresses the fantasies and fears of her culture, in which woman is identified with the Orient and defeated by the id, chaos, and insanity. On the basis of this interpretation, one may regard her fantasies as combinations of both feminine and Oriental threats, both symbolizing the repressed desires of Israeli male culture. Yosefa Lushitzky, "From Orientalist Discourse to Woman's Melodrama: Oz and Volman's *My Michael*," in *Edebiyat* 5 (1994), pp. 99–123. See also Shohat, *Israeli Cinema*.

12. Gertz, *Motion Fiction*.

13. In an analysis of the possibilities of cinematic subversion, Orly Rubin points out that the Israeli cinema could not cope with the marginal professional status of women. Therefore, its subversion took the form of restoring the mechanism of the gaze and positioning the sexual female body in the center. The examination of Israeli films produced in the 1980s, as of *My Michael*, shows how this cinema used the "look" to reposition the formerly marginalized persona in the center. Orly Lubin, "Women

in Israeli Cinema," in Yael Atzmon, ed., *A Glimpse at the Lives of Women in Jewish Societies* (Jerusalem: Zalman Shazar Centre, 1995), pp. 349–75. See also Friedman, "Between Silence and Abjection."

14. Kaja Silverman, *The Threshold of the Visible World* (London and New York: Routledge, 1996).

15. Lushitzky, "From Orientalist Discourse to Woman's Melodrama."

16. Werbner, "Essentializing Essentialism, Essentializing Silences: Ambivalence and Multiplicity in the Constructions of Racism and Ethnicity," in *Debating Cultural Hybridity*, pp. 226–57.

17. As stated, Yuval-Davis characterizes these two directions as "rooting" and "shifting."

18. Silverman, *The Threshold of the Visible World.*

"So Sarah Laughed to Herself"[1]

Sarah "our Mother," wife of Abraham, the "Father of the Hebrew nation," is mentioned in the sources: in the Bible, the Talmud, the midrashim, and the legends—but always at the side of her husband and subservient to him. Like other female biblical figures, she "appears on stage only when she is of an age to marry and her term of stay is generally determined only for as long as her status as a mother affects that of her son, [for] biblical mothers simply disappear from the narrative the moment their sons become independent."[2]

Sarah's "life history" in the Bible and the Midrash[3] attests to a problematic relationship between the first Hebrew couple. Abraham discovers his wife's beauty for the first time only when he goes to Egypt and the Egyptian king covets her. He does not confront the king, or another would-be suitor, Avimelech, King of the Philistines; neither does he protect his wife from their advances. Instead, God enlists His angels to strike down these kings. Sarah and Abraham's relationship is also a sterile one, for it appears that she cannot bear a child. She gives her handmaiden Hagar to Abraham for her to bear him a son. Only when Sarah reaches the age of eighty-nine and Abraham ninety-nine do the angels inform them that a son will be born to them. These are the tidings that cause Sarah to laugh, and thus to name her son Isaac [Hebrew: Yitzḥak, "he will laugh"].

Sarah was 127 years old when she died. When she heard that Abraham had bound Isaac upon the altar and almost slaughtered him, she swooned and died.[4] This act of binding Isaac bestowed independence upon Isaac and annulled any need for his mother's continued existence.

The sole event in which Sarah is seen acting on her own volition, in both the Bible and in other, later sources, shows her committing an act of cruelty. She casts out Hagar (mother of the Arab nation) and her son Ishmael into the desert. *Pirkei Rabbi Eliezer* (an eighth-century book of legends) blames Sarah for the expulsion and absolves Abraham of any guilt "And of all the hardship *that had come to Abraham* [italics mine], this thing was very hard and bad." (chap. 30). Although several sources excuse Sarah because Ishmael plotted against Isaac, the impression remains, particularly from Genesis 21, that this was an ugly act by a jealous woman, sending a mother and her child out into the arid desert where, had they not been helped by an angel, they would have surely died.

This essay focuses on two Israeli plays from the 1990s that examine the myth of Sarah and rewrite it from a feminist perspective. First, however, we shall take a look at the place of women in Israeli theater; a look that will explain the acuteness of this deconstruction of the male myth as executed by Shulamith Lapid on a major Israeli stage in *Womb for Rent* (1990); and by a fringe theater group in a Jerusalem theater in *Sarah* (1993).

Women in Israeli Theater

The Hebrew theater has been perceived since its inception in the 1920s as a highbrow cultural activity whose contents are given great importance and often arouse public controversy. Its audiences, generally well-educated, often deliberately choose original plays in order to examine for themselves, in a public place, and within their own social context, the problems and conflicts that disturb them, including those questions of cultural identity that so bother an immigrant society. This combination of elements explains the importance of the public discussion of various issues in the Israeli theater, and it also reveals the absence of certain subjects and "voices" from the plays. For example, according to Yona Hadari-Ramage, women, oriental Jews, and Palestinians are rarely found among the participants in Israeli social discussion.

> In the arena of public thought, Israeli discourse is generally one of
> men among themselves. A discourse of warriors, of fathers and sons,
> of buddies and even of rivals, and so on. In the main the discourse
> is still that of the pioneering Ashkenazi Jew [of European origin],
> the white, blond, pure-in-deed male [. . .] his acts and words . . .
> they have suppressed all the others, the religious, Asian and African
> immigrants, and women.[5]

Most of the Israeli theater repertoire has been a dialogue of male playwrights, with female characters depicted in the main from a male point of view. From the early period of settlement, before the establishment of the State, men were presented as the ones who made the desert bloom and who provided a defense against marauding Arabs. Women were restricted to mother-wife-sister-daughter roles: they were lovers, cooks, laundresses—and only rarely "allowed" to help on the land, perceived at that time to be holy work.

Two plays are characteristic of the early period: *He Walked in the Fields*, by Moshe Shamir (staged in 1948 by the Cameri Theater) and *In the Plains of the Negev*, by Yigal Mossinsohn (staged in 1949 by Habima Theater). In both these, and in other plays of the time, the central recurring motif of sending a son to the battlefield is perceived as a "binding of Isaac" (Genesis 22). Just as the original biblical story does not relate to Sarah and transforms this divine test of faith into one in which only the man is tested, so too in these plays the men are the "binders" or the "bound," while the women remain passively behind, anxious, weeping, and suffering.

In plays from the period following the establishment of the State, women in many cases present the changing values in Israeli society and are blamed for the disintegrating pioneering ideal and for the hedonism and selfishness that have negatively influenced the world of the male, who had formerly devoted all his energy to the Zionist enterprise. It is particularly interesting to note that from the beginning of the 1970s, female characters in the plays of Hanoch Levin, the most successful of Israeli playwrights, constitute a sort of caricature of the Jewish mother, depicted as a domineering, graspingly materialistic monster.

The Hebrew theater has produced few women playwrights and the number of their plays that have reached the stage is low, even in the 1980s and 1990s, despite an increase in the overall number of playwrights. Male domination of Israeli theater extends beyond its playwrights. Administrative positions (artistic and otherwise) in the large theaters were always reserved for men and few women have administered or are currently administering small theaters. While at first glance it would appear that Israeli theater has reserved an important place for its actresses, their status as stage figures is determined by texts written and directed by men. Under such conditions, it is not surprising that women's theater in Israel has been consigned to the fringes and that the repertoire of its plays dealing with women's issues is surprisingly small. It contains theatrical texts presenting the "authentic" views of women on events involving men, such as

women's conversation about war, or social plays dealing with family violence or battered women. The number of plays aimed at "re-writing" the
place of women in Jewish and Israeli myths is particularly small.

The few plays that succeed in constituting a feminist theater are therefore important. Of equal importance is the interpretation these plays give
to Hebrew-Jewish myths from a women's point of view, including the two
contemporary feminist versions of Sarah's life history.

Womb for Rent (1990)

Shulamit Lapid's *Womb for Rent* (Cameri Theater, directed by Ilan Ronen),
a bourgeois-feminist re-reading of the myth,[6] is unusual in being a feminist text staged by one of the mainstream theaters. The circumstances of its
staging in a public theater also imply a covert feminist criticism of the
myth of Sarah.

In an article entitled "Embarrassing details about our Mother and Father," Amir Peleg summarizes Lapid's interpretation of the Sarah myth in
her play:

> The first Hebrews, the Fathers of the Nation, Abraham our father
> [Avram in the play] and Sarah our mother, are the mythological he-
> roes of *Womb for Rent,* which uncovers their degeneracy, from a dis-
> tance of almost four thousand years. It is only natural that the fa-
> thers of the Cameri Theater were chosen to present them on the
> stage. Shulamit Lapid, the playwright, transferred their story to
> Palestine of the early 1930s, a place in which Sarah (Hannah Mar-
> ron) and Avram (Yossi Yadin) are still new immigrants, wandering
> from one architectural dig to another. Lapid herself dug into and
> researched the biblical sources and discovered the following embar-
> rassing details about our "father" and "mother": they were, it would
> appear, uncle and niece—"a cursed family, with everyone marrying
> one another." The barren Sarah, in the play as in the Bible, exploits
> her beauty to get officers and governors into her bed, in order to
> obtain benefits for herself and her husband. Her brother Lot . . . is
> the first to express the idea of putting his adopted daughter, Hagar
> (a minor), into Abraham's bed, and thus to arrange the matter of in-
> heritance. Our father Abraham—who according to the sources led

a life of celibacy with his wife, which according to Lapid was because of his secret affair with his young and handsome lieutenant,
Eliezer—is much taken with the idea, and even after this union results in the birth of Ishmael, he will not forgo the favors of Lot's
daughter. Little wonder, therefore, that Sarah cries out in protest
and throws out the daughter and her baby, including the nurse. That
way, at least, she and her Abraham will be able to grow old quietly.
Then, however, the angels Gabriel, Michael, and Rafael arrive and
reveal to the pair that even at the age of seventy the pistol can still
fire and hit the bullseye. And thus, in the end, Isaac is born.[7]

The interesting component in the tale of the play is what is missing from
it—the Binding of Isaac does not suit a narrative that deals principally
with dwindling femininity, and therefore its plot ignores the biblical story.

The theater generally attempts to relate to reality, to describe it, to criticize it, and to translate it into an "autonomous" fictional world, with the
help of artistic codes clearly separated from the real world. However, some
theatrical components complicate, deliberately or inadvertently, this creation of a credible fictional world. Two of these components, comedy and
celebrity status, are linked to the actress Hannah Marron, who plays the
role of Sarah in *Womb for Rent*. Comedy, like other popular genres, often
involves the audience directly. "The resolution of a comedy," notes
Northrop Frye, "comes from the audience's side of the stage."[8] Such direct
confrontation by comic actors undermines, sometimes deliberately, the
credibility of the stage reality, when they "raise" the spectators onto the
stage or "lower" the actors into the audience. Celebrities, too, unravel the
fabric of fiction—mainly through their own presence, of which both they
themselves and the spectators, who identify them as celebrities, are aware.
This can be confirmed by the reactions of the spectators. Whenever a famous actor makes his first entrance on stage in a French Boulevard theater, this entrance is accompanied by applause even if it takes place in the
middle of the second act. The combination of celebrity and the comic, or
the casting of stars noted for their comic ability, can therefore effectively
serve ideological arguments as an amusing and instructive means of "alienation." A play written for an actress with both comic talent and celebrity
status can thus be particularly useful for ideological purposes.

Hannah Marron has a rare comic talent. She addresses the audience directly, thereby ironically creating and enjoying her own success. While she has indeed played many roles, including tragic ones, it would nevertheless appear (also confirmed in confessional magazines) that she herself particularly enjoys the comic roles; and she brings a comic quality even to her serious roles, releasing tension within the audience and returning it for a moment to extra-theatrical reality.

In Israel, Marron is a celebrity—that is, someone whom we know from outside the theater too; someone who has particular qualities that continue (albeit not indefinitely) to keep himself or herself within the public eye. The celebrity status sustained, therefore, by public acknowledgment is not always based on familiarity with his or her theatrical roles. Michael L. Quinn claims that "the celebrity figure is an alternative reference, competing with and structuring the role of the stage figure as it promotes its own illusion. The sequence can be graphed this way: actor—celebrity figure—stage figure—audience.[9]

To these components we should also add famous roles associated with the celebrity in the past and impressions of the celebrity's acting already stored in the spectators' memories. The enjoyment is doubled for spectators watching a celebrity act. They enjoy both the play itself and the pleasure of the acting, which is linked in their minds to the "real" biographical details of the actor and their recollections of his or her previous roles. If the actor has also appeared in a television series, their enjoyment may be even greater; for a series, which involves frequent encounters between actor and spectator, engraves the actor even more deeply upon their memory, and may endow him or her, according to Martin Esslin, with a special status somewhere between fiction and reality—that of an almost mythological figure.[10]

For the audience then, Marron brings with her her previous roles, mainly the comic ones; the image she developed in the Israeli television sitcom *Close Relations*; the special quality of her voice; and the so-called "cynicism" that several critics marked in her manner of expression; all of these combine in the audience's perception of Marron as Sarah in *Womb for Rent*. The appropriate graph for this play (and others) is circular: Hannah Marron—Hannah Marron as celebrity: her personal biography her professional biography—the image of Sarah (a role written specially for her)—Sarah in *Womb for Rent* as perceived by the audience as a celebrity version of Hannah Marron.

From the spectators' perspective, "Hannah Marron" is a text supported by biographical elements incorporating past appearances in the theater and other media. Within this text certain characteristics dominate, such as her sexual attraction, sharp tongue and sense of timing, her laughter; even the name—*Hannaleh*—frequently used by journalists, and implying familiarity—indicates a special closeness, an intimacy that her stage personality solicits. Her biography has been summarized in the press, starting from the very outset of her career as an actress in Israel and continuing to to her seventieth birthday. Many articles recount her life history, from child wonder in the German theater to the present, interweaving her relationship with her mother, her parents' divorce, her three marriages, her special relationship with her first husband, the actor Yossi Yadin, who was also her permanent stage partner.

At the same time, they frequently emphasize the barrier she erects, and wishes to maintain, between her private life and her professional one. She herself characterizes her life as "schizophrenic": "So there's the stage Hannah Marron and then there's Hannah Marron-Rechter, who is a person with different problems entirely."[11] Little wonder that the spectators (who are also the readers of the above-mentioned texts) relate to her "biography" when they encounter her on stage. As a text she is also characterized by her intertextuality with other similar/different texts, as are other actresses. She herself, as mentioned, supports "secondary texts" such as newspaper interviews, pre-performance articles, critics' reviews. All these nourish her existence as a celebrity both within and outside the theater.

Several of these interviews are also instructive regarding her fear of losing her actress-celebrity status (for example, her story about the taxi driver who called to check whether she was "Hannah Rovina," "Ilana Rovina" or "Hannah Aharoni"—actress, singer, and film star, respectively[12]); or her reservations about being eternally typecast by her television sitcom role, as well as fears that her success as a comic actress might affect her status as a serious dramatic actress. The unique nature of Marron's celebrity status in *Womb for Rent* lies in the dramatic text having been written for an actress who is herself already a text, and making use in it of this celebrity element, deliberately directed at her comic talent.

From the playwright's perspective, *Womb for Rent* is "a play about the mother and father of our nation—Sarah and Abraham. Hannaleh is Sarah our mother and Yossi Yadin is Abraham our father."[13] It is reported elsewhere that the Cameri theater approached Shulamith Lapid with a request to write a special play for Marron, who is considered in the public consciousness as one of the "founders" of the Cameri Theater. The press also notes that Lapid hoped that an additional founding father of the Cameri, Yossi Yadin (son of a well-known Israeli archeologist), would take part in the play, "and thus on the associative path, the family of Abraham and Sarah became the archeologist's family," linked in her mind with "digging," "also in its sense of soul-searching, like an archeologist of the soul."[14] Lapid also revealed an additional layer of the text and performance: "Fantasy constitutes redemption for my characters, which depend upon the imagination as something consolatory, compensatory and enriching, just like finding a refuge in the theater, cinema, or literature, that amuses and entertains the imagination."[15] Her remarks here apply more to the world of the performing actors than to the dramatis personae, for a barrier has been lowered between actors and their roles that may not have been there at the beginning.

The appearance of a celebrity in the theater may undermine authority, which is placed in conflict with the celebrity status. The celebrity may cause a breakdown of order by not fitting into the ensemble of characters and by shattering the illusion of coherence of the fictional world, meant to be established in a theatrical text by the presence of the character who is herself a familiar text to the audience. Marron recognizes her own celebrity status: "I've been in the theater for many years and 'legends' have already sprung up about me."[16] If we add to this her comic ability, which in itself can contribute to "disrupting" the rules of the fictional world, we can understand the deep connection between Lapid and Marron in a text that contains, as noted by several critics, feminist intentionality: a connection within the Israeli theater system in which men have a "natural" senior status. Such intentionality is perhaps to be found in the weak roles given to men in the play, as noted by the men themselves. Yossi Yadin almost grumbles in an interview: "It's been said that Shulamith Lapid wrote a feminist-chauvinist play in dealing mostly with the character of Sarah." He continues: "The figure of Sarah was tailor-made for Hannah Marron. And she [Lapid] still claims that she tailor-made Abraham for me—she seems to have erred by a few centimetres here and there."[17] It may well be that this is what Lapid aimed for, in wanting to strengthen the female image and the "female voice" at the expense of the male figures, whose common

denominator is their wretchedness, and who are made only to play supporting roles to Sarah (Hannah) and not to be the center of attention.

The process of spectating, in which the audience is invited in *Womb for
Rent* to participate, is complex and constructed upon a row of di-
chotomies, each of which presents the conflict between man and woman:

1. For the cultural background we have the Abraham–Sarah dichotomy. Parents of the nation, their biblical myth presents the man
as superior and the women in his shadow. Lapid is interested in replacing the masculine approach to the myth with the feminine one;
from this point of view the play is not "a deconstruction of the
myth," as claimed by one critic,[18] but rather its feminist reading.

2. The "husband" and "wife" dichotomy: It is the "husband," of the
biographies about her that Marron presents to the public through
the press. This husband makes demands upon her, among other
things because of her roles as wife and mother, and restricts her
theater appearances. "I try to perform only once a year. . . . I have,
God bless them, three very nice children. It's important that I'm at
home occasionally and get involved in the problems of football.
And I have a husband, and he too wants to see his wife at home
from time to time—definitely not an exaggerated request. You
should know that my profession is not a particularly good one for
women.[19]

3. The dichotomy of Avram–Sarah in the play: he is a well-known
archeologist and she is his aging wife whose beauty has faded.

4. And, principally, the dichotomy of Marron as Sarah and Yadin as
Avram. In a reversed patriarchal order to that of the previous di-
chotomous pairs, Marron, as one critic described her acting: "makes
full use of her dramatic power and comic talent," while Yadin, like
the rest of the male figures, "is made of cardboard!"[20]

The feminist discourse in the play challenges the conventional female status vis-à-vis men as well as the presentation of women as sexual objects
who exist for men's pleasure. Already in the first scene of the play, Marron
has her bottom pinched, and her Sarah is being used sexually by men for

their own self-serving purposes. Marron is particularly suited to this role as an actress whose sexual image is part of her celebrity text. Like Sarah in the play, she too "confesses": "When I was young, I was very successful, I always had suitors. I think I still do today. What do I care if they gossip about me? It's flattering."[21] Indeed, one critic found that Marron "really does look ageless, sexy and amusing."[22] However, "aging is a particular problem for a beautiful woman,"[23] stated Marron in an interview, which in the play becomes a monologue in which Hannah-Sarah describes her fading beauty when faced with Hagar, a young woman and her adopted daughter, who is reawakening her husband's sexuality. For, indeed, if the success of an actress in the Israeli theater depends upon beauty and "sexiness," she will surely be replaced by a younger woman who will serve those same male needs.

Many details in the play support Marron the actress and celebrity playing Sarah: her age and her image as a desirable woman. The playwright directs Hannah-Sarah to laugh (her well-known rolling laugh) at the "masculine" biblical myth, which enables such "miracles" as a ninety-year-old woman giving birth to her hundred-year-old husband's child. At the end of the play Sarah sums up its feminist message as one of male exploitation and the contrasting effect of time on the two sexes: "Yes, Avram investigated the past, so now he has a future. I was interested in the present, so now I have a past."[24]

In sum, *Womb for Rent* is a play written by a female playwright for a woman functioning in a masculine system. The play incorporates the "biography" and theatrical career of Hannah Marron in a feminist effort to invert the biblical myth of Sarah. The masculine narrative is contested by Marron's celebrity and comic talent in order to present a modern version of the feminine voice of the past.

Sarah, 1993

The affiliation of women's theater with the fringes of the system is particularly apparent in its specific forms. Mainstream repertory theater tends toward coherent, well-made narratives, often produced on technologically advanced stages with sophisticated scenery, varied lighting, and a wide selection of costume and props. Women's theater, on the other hand, has developed from its objection to the central, patriarchal mainstream, and has consequently chosen alternative characteristics. Both fringe and women's theater tend towards the fragmentary and minimalist, characteristics that emphasize their message and contradict those views and beliefs that are routinely accepted.

In works by the all-women Theater Company of Jerusalem (TCJ), the experimental form serves the company's demand for "a new Judaism"—a Judaism in which there is a well-deserved place for women. Following the path of the American writer Cynthia Ozick, it sets out to redress the injustice inherent in the sub-human status demonstrated toward women by the Torah:

> If we look only into Torah, we see that the ubiquity of women's condition applies here as well. . . . Women's quality of lesserness, of otherness, is laid down at the very beginning, as paradigm and as rule: at the start of the creation of the world woman is given an inferior place.[25]

The masculine model of theater is presented in one of the TCJ's productions, *The Last Play* (1992), as a model to be rejected. The TCJ's philosophy reflects that of the French poet, playwright and essayist, Hélène Cixous. Although they are not familiar with her writing, it is helpful in understanding their theatrical activity. In a short essay "Aller à la mer,"[26] Cixous refers to the problematic link between women and theater: the theater serves the "male fantasy" in which well-known female figures (such as Electra, Ophelia, or Cordelia) are always the victims, are always exploited and disappointed, and serve as a mirror for the heroic male. Such a theater suppresses femininity which refuses to remain silent: "and if, like Cordelia, she finds the strength to assert a femininity which refuses to be the mirror of her father's ravings, she will die."[27]

The Last Play, a collaborative work by Joyce (Rinat) Miller and Aliza Elion-Israeli, offers a rewriting of feminine characters—"writing as reenactment" from the masculine model, according to Cixous:

> So he gave me the stage as if it belonged to him [. . .] he wants a monodrama? Monodrama? He probably thinks that I'll begin with a major classic role. Medea (acting): "We women are a cursed race." That's what Euripides put in her mouth before he let her kill her

two children. Why do I need to be a party to this perversion written by men? Why do I constantly continue doing exactly what
Michel wants, even now, on the stage that is all mine, when there is
nobody here to bother me with their Doll's House fantasies. Michel
wanted me to play Medea like a witch and Ophelia like a betrayed
and innocent virgin [. . . .] What's he afraid of? I've actually played
both of them as clever women with great sensitivity, standing on
the brink of an abyss.[28]

The TCJ has several features in common with other women's theater: its
organization, themes, and theatrical forms and strategies. From the organi-
zational point of view, it has no hierarchy: its female participants share
their ideas, the writing, acting, and directing. They are assisted by guest di-
rectors and additional actors, male and female. They work as an ensemble,
with most of the writing done by Elion-Israeli. Preparation is accompanied by research by all the participants and does not cease with the first
performance. Decisions frequently involve the audience, and it is not unusual for the company to continue shaping the play even after its preparations are complete (as in *Sarah Take 1*, which was changed and updated to
Sarah Take 2). This continuous process leads to extensive examination,
throughout the life of the play, of questions relating to feminist issues. The
playwright and actresses use various techniques of persuasion, such as different theatrical styles: comedy, musical or cabaret. Among the accepted
distinctions between the different directions of women's theater—"bourgeois" feminism, radical and "socialist/materialist"—the TCJ tends towards
the radical, which proposes a feminist counter-culture. This direction is
characterized by Elaine Aston as "investigating the possibilities of a gender
based ritualized style of theater which seeks the emotional, mythical and
historical keys to woman-centred culture."[29]

The TCJ has been active since 1982, mainly with plays derived from
Jewish sources. Each of its participants brings to the company her own
Jewish identity. Lev, Wieder and Elion-Israeli refer to Jewish tradition in
both their work and lives. Lev and Wieder are sisters who grew up in Aus-
tralia in a religious family of Holocaust survivors, while Elion-Israeli was
born in South Africa and raised in a secular Israeli home. They keep many
of the mitzvot, "but the concept 'religious' means little to me," states
Elion-Israeli.[30]

In contemporary feminist theater, in which women seek to present an "active subject," they tend towards an "interrogative style" of text and performance practice.[31] According to Elion-Israeli: "Our process evolved from within the tradition . . . study as a way of life [. . .] the creative system is therefore a process of study. We thus approach the material as it has been taught in the *ḥavrutot* [groups of students] throughout the years in the *yeshivot.*"

Burdening the women with "dumbness" is also described by Hélène Cixous. In one reference to her own Jewishness (which she terms *juifemme–Jewoman*), she explains the subordination of the *juifemme* as an arbitrary act by a male whose claims to the superiority of a father as God she refutes:

> What is a father? The one taken for father. The one recognised as the true one. "Truth," the essence of fatherhood, its force as law. The "chosen" father.[32]

Cixous believes that the main political and ethical functions of the theater are to correct injustice and to rehabilitate disabilities, as well as to create an unbiased openness to the "other."[33] There is a clear trend in the TCJ's repertoire towards those "other(s)" in Israeli society: women, oriental Jews, and Arabs.

An important part of Cixous's theoretical and practical work relates to deconstruction: "Derridean deconstruction will have been the greatest ethical critical warning gesture of our time: careful! Let us not be the dupe of logocentric authority."[34] Deconstruction serves her as a strategy for demolishing those myths that support the patriarchal system and for abrogating their "natural" status. She conceives the Oresteia as a narrative in which patriarchism overcomes and defeats matriarchism and firmly installs father and son, Agamemnon and Orestes, at the center of things. The daughter, Electra, also serves the aims of phallocentrism, for her voice is the clearest in its demand to avenge her father's death by killing her mother.[35] Like Cixous, the TCJ studies, dissects, and rewrites the myths from a feminist point of view. According to Elion-Israeli:

> One can approach the sources from contradictory directions. As in the case of Sarah. One can claim: How does one turn the mother

of the nation into a barren woman? And not just barren, but without a womb? What sort of culture are we? In which a woman who is supposed to be the "fertile mother", has her tale told by a male culture that removes her womb so that she will not be able to give birth naturally but only by means of a miracle from God—who is a man. The image of Sarah in particular is important because historically she is situated on the border between matriarchal and patriarchal cultures. This does indeed generate anger. But that's the way it is, that's the tradition we have for Sarah. Sarah does not speak out in any of the Bible stories. She is a silent character.

We do not set out against what is told. We understand it in our own way. For us, Sarah is the hero of the play. She speaks throughout the play and we give her many opportunities to say what we think she says; mainly to say the world of Abraham her husband is not her world. She says to her son Isaac: "The world that you and your father have created is not my world
[. . .] my world is a world of plenty [. . .] of embryos and of benediction.

French feminists, principally Cixous, present the male/female dualism as deterministic. They do not believe in a harmonious solution. The TCJ raises both questions and doubts in this regard. The "duality" of Sarah is recognizable in what Theresa De Laurtis has called a feminist narrative structure, which sharply diverges from the masculine narrative characteristic of mainstream theater. In her semiotic research into cinema, De Laurtis characterizes narrative strategies according to gender, and most of them fall into the masculine category. Between the genders, on screen (and on stage) there is a rigid division of labor: the man in many narratives is the subject who initiates the path to adventure, while the woman (the "princess") is merely the sought-after object, neither active nor activating.[36]

To contest this dominant model, Cixous proposes a theater with a powerful physical female presence at its centre. "Non-theatrical. Without a barrier between stage and auditorium." And there is "no need for plot or action."[37] Like Cixous (and Teresa de Laurtis), Gabriella Lev distinguishes between the male and female models:

The model of western theater—a linear plot constructed towards a climax followed by relaxation of tension—is a masculine model. Our plays are constructed along feminist lines: they are episodic, circular, containing various interwoven elements, all equally important. We leave things open, which also contrasts with the masculine model.[38]

The play *Sarah* is constructed like a lesson in a *ḥavruta*. The spectators' seats are arranged around the acting space. The texts relating to Sarah are projected onto the wall; the audience sits up close, experiencing and learning together with the actors. During the performance the various midrashim recounting "Sarah's life history" are examined, and emphasis is diverted from the heroic image of Abraham to the almost reticent figure of Sarah. By means of masks and a slide projector, the spectator becomes aware of her multi-faceted image. The director Serge Ouaknine "was fascinated by the dialogue between the archaic and mythological Sarah and her image as our contemporary."[39] We therefore find three Sarahs on stage—the biblical Sarah, the Sarah of the Talmud and Midrash, and the contemporary Sarah. During the course of most of the scenes, the actresses represent a transition from ancient biblical times to the period of the Talmud and Midrash and to a feminist present in Israel—seeking the common denominator, whose main issue is the status of women in Judaism.

A sense of tension emanating from insoluble contradictions accompanies a study of the play. Clear expressions of that tension can be found in its emphasis on duality in all components of both its form and its content, which explore the sharp divide between man and woman. Occasionally it seems to be offering solutions within the framework of the existing halakhah; but this is only an intermediate strategy, enabling the playmakers to progress in a radical direction. In this way it can serve as a feminist case study that questions the spirit and authority of the harsh male halakhah and attempts to reveal another halakhah and a different Judaism—a Judaism in which there is not only a place for woman, but in which the female spirit guides the way of life.

The two theatrical versions of "Sarah's life history" considered here differ greatly from one another. Common to both, nonetheless, is their understanding of the severity of Hagar's banishment, as well as their anchor-

ing the tale in present-day Israeli–Palestinian reality. Ann Hackett cuttingly
formulates the injustice done to Hagar in the biblical account (Genesis
21:9–21):

> . . . this story can be seen to make a point about the kind of power
> some human beings have over other human beings, and perhaps es-
> pecially over a human being who is in the most vulnerable position
> possible: female, slave, and foreign.[40]

In *Womb for Rent*, which was staged during the period of the Intifada (the
Palestinian rebellion in the Occupied Territories), there are a few references to the Palestinian offspring of Hagar who have been humiliated and
suppressed and who have finally rebelled.

In contrast, *Sarah* not only deals with the Israeli–Palestinian dispute but
includes a request for Hagar's forgiveness; this is nonetheless accompanied
with a justification for banishing her, together with Ishmael:

> . . . I ask forgiveness . . . (turns to audience) I ask forgiveness from
> all of you. In the books—they didn't let me speak. I stood there
> hard as iron: "Go, Hagar!" I said to her. "Now! For this dispute is
> not only between you and me. It belongs to all the generations to
> come. Go! And only an angel from heaven can help you. For know
> that this quarrel is not only about position." And I let her go and
> watched how her child was thirsting in the desert. And I was right,
> yes Isaac, I was right. But there has to be some other way that does-
> n't end in a mother sitting at a distance from her child, watching
> him starve.

Sarah, who was wronged, in turn wronged Hagar and Ishmael. Neither of
the two playwrights approves of this turn of affairs in "Sarah's life history,"
but they both deal more with the insult to one woman and less with the
tragedy of the other.

Citations with no reference to source are all taken from my interviews with Aliza Elion-Israeli and
Gavriella Lev.

1. Genesis 18:12

2. Ilana Pardes, *Countertraditions in the Bible: A Feminist Approach* (Tel Aviv: Hakibbutz Hameuchad,
1996), 61. [Hebrew]

3. In the chapter on Abraham on the book by Louis Ginzberg, *The Legends of the Jews* (Ramat Gan: Massada, 1967), vol. 2, 1–68. [Hebrew]

4. Targum Jonathan for Genesis 22:20.

5. Yona Hadari-Ramage, *Thinking It over: Conflicts in Israeli Public Thought* (Ramat Efal: Yad Tabenkin and Yediot Aharonot, 1994), p.20. [Hebrew].

6. Elaine Aston, *An Introduction to Feminism and Theater* (London and New York: Routledge, 1995), pp. 65–66.

7. Amir Peleg, "Embarrassing facts about our Father and Mother," *Ḥadashot,* March 30, 1990.

8. Northrop Frye, *Anatomy of Criticism* (Princeton, New Jersey: Princeton University Press, 1971), p. 164.

9. Michael L. Quinn, "Celebrity and the Semiotics of Acting," *New Theater Quarterly,* May 22, 1990, pp. 154–61. See also Marvin Carlson, "Invisible Presences: Performance Intertextuality," *Theater Research International,* 19,2 (Summer 1994): 111–17.

10. Martin Esslin, *The Age of Television* (San Francisco: Freeman, 1982), pp.41–45.

11. Hannah Marron (interview), "This Nation is Expecting to be Told: No!" *La-Ishah,* December 29, 1975. [Hebrew].

12. Hannah Marron (interview), "This Terrible Compulsion to be Otherwise," *Ha-Aretz,* October 22, 1976. [Hebrew].

13. Haim Nagid, "Hannah our Mother and Yossi our Father," *Ma'ariv,* January 22, 1990. [Hebrew].

14. Daniella Fisher, "Who will be the Mother?" *Al Hamishmar,* April 8, 1990 [Hebrew].

15. Ibid.

16. Yirmi Amir, "I've always had Suitors," *Yediot Aḥaronot,* April 20, 1990 [Hebrew].

17. Dan Urian, "Theater Needs to Arouse, not to Give Answers. Dan Urian Interviews Yossi Yadin," *Bamah* 13, (1991): 123–24 [Hebrew].

18. Michael Handelsaltz, "Deconstructing the Myth," *Ha'aretz,* June 18, 1990 [Hebrew].

19. Rachel Inbar, "From the Creator's House," *Bamah* 36 (1968): 56 [Hebrew].

20. Shosh Avigal, "They Missed the Biblical Story," *Ḥadashot,* May 22, 1990 [Hebrew].

21. See n.13.

22. Giora Manor, "Meteorological-Archeological and Madatory-Biblical," *Al Hamishmar,* June 18, 1990 [Hebrew].

23. See n.13.

24. Shulamith Lapid, *Womb for Rent* (Tel Aviv, 1990), p. 95.

25. Cynthia Ozick, "Notes toward Finding the Right Question," *Forum* 35 (1979): 56.

26. This title can be translated as "Going to the sea" or "Going to the mother."

27. Hélène Cixous, "Aller à la mer," *Le Monde* Avril 28, 1977, trans. Barbara Kerslake in *Modern Drama* 27, 4 (December 1984): 546–48.

28. Unpublished text.

29. Aston, op.cit., p.68.

30. See n. 2 above.

31. Lizbeth Goodman, *Contemporary Feminist Theaters: To Each Her Own* (London and New York: Routledge, 1993), p.21.

32. Hélène Cixous and Catherine Clement, *The Newly Born Woman,* trans. Betsy Wing (Minneapolis: University of Minnesota Press, 1991), p.103.

33. Cixous, p. 124–44.

34. Hélène Cixous, "Preface," *The Hélène Cixous Reader,* Susan Sellers, ed., (London and New York: Routledge, 1994), p.xviii.

35. Hélène Cixous, *The Newly Born Woman,* p.191–98.

36. "The mythical subject is constructed as human being and as male; he is the active principle of culture, the establisher of distinction, the creator of differences. Female is what is not susceptible to transformation, to life or death; she (it) is an element of plot-space, a topos, a resistance, matrix and matter." Teresa De Laurtis, *Alice Doesn't: Feminism, Semiotics, Cinema* (Bloomington: Indiana University Press, 1984), p.119.

37. Cixous, "Aller à la mer," p. 547.

38. Lee Evron, "Blessed be He for Making Me a Woman," *Jerusalem*, October 29, 1993 [Hebrew].

39. Motti Neiger, "The Chapter on Sarah's Life," *Kol Ha-ir*, October 29, 1993 [Hebrew].

40. Ann Hackett, "Rehabilitating Hagar: Fragments of an Epic Pattern," in Peggy L. Day, ed. *Gender and Difference in Ancient Israel* (Minneapolis: Fortress Press, 1989), p. 25.

Jonathan Webber

Lest We Forget!

The Holocaust in Jewish Historical Consciousness and Modern Jewish Identities

Introduction

A few years ago, when I first started doing anthropological fieldwork in Poland at the Auschwitz State Museum, I spent quite a lot of time seated at a suitable vantage-point observing the throngs of visitors as they passed through the place.[1] I noticed a high proportion of young people, parties of Polish schoolchildren, earnest groups of Germans, old-age pensioners from Denmark—in fact, a very wide range of people from all over the world, including the occasional lone intellectual clutching guide-book and notebook. The Museum authorities told me that they estimated that there were about half-a-million visitors per year.

No one had any idea, of course, how many Jews were among this figure, although registered groups of Israelis at that time numbered about one percent—that is, about five thousand people in all. I must confess I was surprised to see comparatively few Jewish visitors in evidence: I had arrived in Auschwitz armed with a Jewish preconception of the place as one forgotten by the world at large. Auschwitz, and the Holocaust in general, did not—in this stereotype—belong to British history, European history, or world history. It belonged exclusively to Jewish history, and it was our job as Jews to remind the world of the appalling crimes committed against our people.

It wasn't particularly difficult to find evidence for this Jewish belief: from time to time I would see Jewish youth groups and parties of Israeli schoolchildren making their way round the site bearing huge flags, with the single Hebrew word *Zakhor!* inscribed on them in large letters. Certainly it gave a somewhat surreal impression: wending their way through the throngs of the ninety-nine percent other visitors were these people, openly identifying themselves as Jews, declaring the single imperative

"Remember!" Behind these flags lay a deep cultural belief: memory as an essentially Jewish value, remembrance as a Jewish moral duty, *zakhor* as a holophrastic statement of Jewish identity to declare to the world at large. I was therefore not surprised, on a recent visit to the Holocaust Memorial Museum in Washington, to see badges for sale with the single word "Remember!"

The stated desire to remember is not to be taken as a measuring-rod of what Jews actually remember about the Holocaust—but rather as a statement of belief about what constitutes the nature of the central Jewish purpose or mission. But in fact, the idea that Jews form and have always formed their identity as a people of remembrancers does not derive from the empirical facts: it is a contemporary Jewish myth.

In this paper I propose to explore this theme, with particular reference to the way in which the Holocaust has become mythologized, so as better to instantiate and substantiate the content of modern diaspora Jewish identities in the West. For "myth" here, read "belief": what I mean by "myth" is the belief that something that happened in the past is true, regardless of whether it is possible to disprove it, or show it to be false. "Mythologization" thus refers to the emergence and consolidation of beliefs about the "true nature" of the historical past. Sociologically speaking, the construction of contemporary attitudes to the Holocaust offers interesting insights into the general process by which a group of people mythologizes its past, for in this case we have the opportunity to observe beliefs about the recent past actually coming into existence before our eyes. This paper attempts to chart something of this process. Unless otherwise stated, I am therefore concerned here with the more popular aspects of the subject rather than those expressed by theologians or philosophers.

Zakhor: The Strong View

The basic memory argument is easily stated. To summarize the main points very roughly: since the duty to remember the past derives from the Hebrew Bible, Jews today are being authentically Jewish if they go about remembering the past. Furthermore, since one of the main biblical instructions to remember concerns the catastrophe inflicted by the Amalekites on the Hebrews when they left Egypt (Deut. 26: 17–19; the text actually uses the word *zakhor*), the implied moral lesson is that Jews ought to remember the major catastrophes. Since the Holocaust was a major catastrophe—certainly the largest catastrophe in the two thousand years since the destruction of the Temple in Jerusalem—it is a moral Jewish duty, deriving from the Bible, to remember it. Hence the badges and flags saying "Remember!"

This, in brief, is the core popular belief. It is a mythical construction in at least two senses: (1) the facts used in support of it are selectively drawn (a procedure typical of any mythological construction, which by definition cannot be inclusive of all the facts and indeed is not intended to be); and (2) the logic used to link the various propositions together is a form of syllogism, which as everyone knows is analytically unsound but nevertheless seems compelling (again, a form of mythological reasoning that in the field of religion is often used in homilies, a technique designed to exclude rational counter-argument). There is, for example, no reason to suppose that remembering the Holocaust is in fact a moral Jewish duty analogous to remembering the damage inflicted by the Amalekites on the ancient Israelites; and if the Bible meant the Israelites to remember all future catastrophes, it could just as well have said so—but it did not.[2] (It is, after all, very explicit about many things to be done in the future.) Why then, one might ask, is the claim made that the Bible stresses the need to remember the past?

The short answer to this question is that Jewish identity, at least until the modern period, was based not on personal faith or on personal choice but explicitly on the practice of the inherited collective tradition. Being Jewish meant being a member of a social group that inherited its culture from the past. And in that culture were certain key texts, liturgies, and rituals that specifically invoked elements of that past. Traditional Jewish culture can perhaps be summarized schematically as consisting of four theological propositions, all of which were presented in the Hebrew Bible as a core narrative of four founding events that took place in the past:

(1) God created the world (a fact of permanent relevance, but presented in the text as a historical event).

(2) God made a series of promises to specific people, named in the text as Abraham, Isaac, and Jacob—promises described in the text as historical events—that their descendants would possess in perpetuity a special relationship with the divinity, notably an existential claim to the Holy Land as their home.

(3) God performed an act of liberation, allowing the people to become a people (the so-called departure from Egypt, also a historical event).

(4) God revealed himself to the whole people at Mount Sinai (yet again a historical event) and gave them details of the basic principles of correct behavior. This confirmed a covenant between God and his people, now redefined as a theological community.

Putting the matter very crudely, being Jewish meant being an inheritor of this history. It was impossible to be Jewish without also experiencing a deep sense of historical consciousness, at least as interpreted in this theological mode. Furthermore, the annual cycle of Jewish festivals hinged specifically on a domestic Passover ritual when fathers had the ritual duty to explain to their children the historical facts concerning the liberation of the people at the time of their historical departure from Egypt. The regular daily liturgy also included explicit references to this event. History, so to speak, was the key mode in which the whole system was framed and elaborated. It is little wonder, then, that when transposed into a modern or contemporary idiom, "remembering the past" has become for many Jews the banner of their identity.

As I have implied, the whole structure is not without its difficulties. Although certain scholars, notably Yosef Yerushalmi, have argued very vigorously that the Hebrew Bible is essentially a text firmly anchored in a historical way of looking at the world,[3] it may be that the case is overstated and that there is a danger of misunderstanding here. This is not the place to go into a detailed biblical exposition, but a few remarks may be in order, merely to suggest that the biblical evidence could indicate the possibility of a different view.

The four key events enumerated above do not constitute disinterested history; that is, they do not constitute a writing of history for its own sake. On the contrary, the way the biblical text frames the relevant narratives is that it was through certain sets of historical events that major collective beliefs and values came into existence. These in turn were to be articulated or enacted through the medium of specific rituals or other social practices.[4]

This is why the Pentateuch is not a seriously sustained piece of historical writing, in the sense of having something to say about each generation. There are indeed large tracts of dead stretches where "nothing happens"—for instance during thirty-eight of the forty years that the

Israelites spent in the desert. Very little historical fact is actually recorded; in practice, only a core narrative, only certain key events, need to be remembered. Yerushalmi notes that the Pentateuch is organized chronologically, in other words a sure sign of a commitment to the narrative mode rather than (for example) a mere recitation of miracles; but more to the point is that there are numerous events that are out of order, so much so indeed that rabbinic commentaries felt bound to insist on the principle of *ein mukdam u-me'uḥar ba-torah* ("there is no chronology in the Torah").[5]

Thus, despite Yerushalmi's claim, the Pentateuch cannot be said to follow a strict chronology. The Torah just seems chronological, an illusion that helps to frame the sense of historical events on which matters of greater importance depend. It is this illusion that should engage our attention here, as it gives the game away. In building a mythologized presentation of the historical past, the underlying structure of the Torah necessarily has to hover between narrative and non-narrative styles, where some events are given dates and others not. Pastness was built into the system, so to speak, in order to provide a rationale for the society's cultural values—the non-historical preoccupations in which the Torah is deeply and thoroughly soaked. It was not the historical past as such that had to be commemorated, but rather the principles that it framed. Not everything needed to be located in historical time, and not everything that happened in the past needed to be remembered.

The idea, then, that the Bible identifies Jews as a people of remembrancers is indeed partly true, but only partly. Late in the twentieth century, after a period of great catastrophe, "remembering" has become emblematic of Jewish culture, worthy of being written on a flag—but only as a new mythologization of the essence of the Jewish tradition. For once the biblical canon was closed and the Temple in Jerusalem destroyed, the preoccupations of the learned Jewish world came to rest on talmudic exegesis: history left the stage and seems to have become forgotten altogether. New events were seen merely as further examples of what was already known about the nature of the world. Nothing essentially new could happen in any case—*ein kol ḥadash taḥat ha-shamesh* (Eccles. 1: 9 "There is nothing new under the sun")—since everything of cosmological importance had already occurred.[6]

During the many centuries down to the modern period there was no such accepted concept as "Jewish history," and very few historical works were composed, let alone read and discussed. But once again it is worth noting that there was an illusion of interest in historical detail: recounting the story of the departure from Egypt was a ritual duty; but although elaborating on the basic story was considered praiseworthy, it was not part of the duty itself.[7] Filling in additional historical details was not a central part of the model of Jewish virtue—and in any case depended on traditions whose historicity could be challenged on the basis of other traditions.

Just to give one example, drawn from a recent article by Sacha Stern in the *Journal of Jewish Studies*: the Talmud seems to be extremely meticulous in recording the historical details about just who it was who said what to whom and when as far as legal and theological opinions are concerned. The Gemara in Berakhot (27b) has the following passage, fairly typical of its kind:

> R. Zera said, quoting an opinion that R. Assi had said, in turn quoting an opinion that R. Elazar had said, in turn quoting an opinion that R. Hanina had said, in turn quoting an opinion that Rav had said: at the side of this pillar R. Yishmael ben R. Yosé used to recite the prayer of Shabbat on the eve of Shabbat.

So far so good, you might think: how seriously the rabbinic chronicler attempted to record the details of history! But then the passage continues:

> When Ulla came he said: it was at the side of a palm-tree and not at the side of a pillar; and it was not R. Yishmael ben R. Yosé but R. Elazar ben R. José; and it was not the prayer of Shabbat on the eve of Shabbat but the prayer of the end of Shabbat.[8]

So much for Jewish memory. But it is this myth that in the twentieth century has come to be given a central position in the features widely regarded as constitutive of Jewish identity.

History, so it is claimed today, has finally returned to the Jewish people after a long absence; and central to this sense of history is the overwhelming need to remember the Holocaust. I should of course add that the beginnings of modern Jewish historiography, and the desire to salvage Jewish history from the documents available, go back to a time well before the Holocaust. But interest in the findings existed mainly among the scholars themselves, rather than in the general public as it does today. The Holocaust has given the process a particularly striking new popular twist, although undoubtedly the establishment of the State of Israel also contributed to that widespread interest: the very creation of a nation-state, and its sustainability in the popular mind, inevitably depend on the construction of a suitable history that both accounts for its creation and provides a rationale for its continued existence.

Modern Jewish Identities

The point has probably now been reached in this essay when generalized references to matters Jewish should give way to something a little more specific about the range of diaspora Jewish identities today, in particular regarding which kinds of Jews have developed which kinds of attitudes towards the memory of the Holocaust. There is, after all, no such thing today as one Jewish historical consciousness, any more than there is one Jewish people—a concept that today should be taken more as an imaginary construct rather than as some objectively measurable single community. There are so many divisions or subdivisions within the contemporary Jewish world as to make it rather difficult, if not also pointless, to offer generalizations.[9]

Perhaps the most significant distinction within the diaspora Jewish world concerns the cultural and cognitive gap between secular Jews and religious Jews. In some respects the gap is simplistic and terminologically misleading, for the great majority of Jews today neither wholly practice their religion nor wholly neglect it. On the other hand, it has become conventional among Jews to impose some form of order on the nature of their contemporary world by sensing an increasing polarization of attitudes towards religion. Although this polarization is rarely institutionalized in diaspora Jewish society, there are contexts in which relations of perceived dominance by one group over the other are taken very seriously.

As far as the Holocaust is concerned, it does not possess equal self-evident importance to all Jews as a historical event. Indeed much of my preceding discussion about whether or not the Jews are a people of remembrancers can be closely mapped onto the divide between secular and religious approaches to the nature of Jewish identity.[10] Identity in any case is closely linked with attitudes to the past: it is a commonplace that different social or political groupings, even notionally within a single community, will produce competing approaches to the past. Or, to put the point in stronger form, if it is true that the writing of history is usually to be understood in relation to the legitimation of power (or its reverse— that is, the attempt to delegitimate existing power structures), then an understanding of how power is distributed in the present-day Jewish world forms an indispensable background to understanding how the Holocaust catastrophe is broadly conceptualized and assimilated into popular understanding.

The rise of the new Jewish historiography, referred to above, was from the beginning linked with movements of enlightenment and reform, and more recently with an explicitly secularist, if not also Zionist, mode of engendering Jewish historical consciousness. To put it another way, history became part of a new discourse about the nature of Jewish experience that was, broadly speaking, foreign and also inaccessible to the classical Orthodox world, and, as such, part of the intellectual weaponry whereby the monopoly of power held by the traditional rabbinate in defining Jewish experience could be broken—and indeed has been broken. The secularist view, in promoting what we would today call a new but "authentic" style of Jewish self-awareness, was that the Jewish people has always been concerned with history, and particularly so in the founding texts of the Hebrew Bible. From this perspective it goes without saying that the Holocaust unquestionably must figure substantially in any contemporary rendering of modern Jewish history, particularly a secularist one.

How people actually make sense of the past is not, however, something that is easy to observe in ordinary daily life. To the extent that collective memory is at all visible ethnographically (as opposed to the assumption of its existence in the collective subconscious), it is a process that, one might say, lies at the intersection between scholarly histories and community rituals based on founding myths of some kind. In the absence of formal histories in the modern sense, the traditional religious Jewish response to catastrophe tended towards a collective, timeless view of tragedy— mythologizing it ritually or liturgically and thereby endowing it with a redemptive, life-affirming sense of closure.

Some examples may be helpful here by way of illustration. An interesting ethnographic one was a Sabbath sermon delivered in the synagogue in Cracow by the emeritus Chief Rabbi of Britain, Lord Jakobovits, the day after the official ceremonies in Auschwitz in January 1995 commemorating the fiftieth anniversary of its liberation from the Nazis. As in any such case when an Orthodox rabbi would speak in a synagogue on a contemporary subject, Jakobovits drew on what he felt to be an appropriate analogy from the classical sources.

When the Israelites left Egypt, he pointed out, the biblical text records that the first thing they did was sing a song in praise of their divine liberator. There is no reference to any grieving. Although they had just suffered four hundred years of slavery, the systematic murder by the Egyptians of all their newborn male children, and doubtless many other bitter experiences that we today would call genocide and/or the slow murder of the population through forced labor, Moses did not institute any memorial day. All this suffering in Egypt was forgotten immediately.

I think that Jakobovits is a reliable informant here, expressing the widely held view that the text did not see any good reason for the people to commemorate this particular historical catastrophe. On the contrary, it implies, they should let the memory of it subside and concentrate on deliverance and national liberation. His message was quite clear: Jews should focus on the divine promise for the future and should devote their resources to rebuilding Jewish life rather than squander their spiritual energies by contemplating the Holocaust. The Bible commands the commemoration of the catastrophe inflicted by the Amalekites, and the later rabbinic tradition imposed a series of fast-days, mainly in connection with the destruction of the Temple. Further encroachment into a religious calendar often seen as already overloaded with melancholic recollections would be regarded as improper and wrong.

But note the selectivity in Jakobovits's argument: the Passover ritual, as described both in Exodus and later on in the book of Numbers, clearly instituted the eating of bitter herbs, and this has remained part of the ritual, in specific memory of the suffering, down to the present day.[11] When I later challenged him privately on his omission, he was prepared to concede the point; nevertheless the sermon is instructive in showing how minimalist a position a religious Jewish view would like to accord to Jewish tragedy.

This is not only a matter of power relations within the rabbinate—for example, the reluctance of Orthodox rabbis to introduce a new memorial fast-day for fear of being accused of reformism.[12] The pattern of downplaying catastrophe also clearly illustrates a more pronounced characteristic—historical indifference and selective forgetfulness in general. The traditional Jewish cyclical calendar enables a particular fast-day (such as the Ninth of Av) to encompass more than one historical tragedy. To put it another way, discrete tragedies that a modern historian would see as quite different events were commonly seen from a mythological point of view as repetitions of one another, the historical details that would differentiate them having been forgotten. It was the essential meaning of such fast-days that was important, not their historical features as such. As Yerushalmi points out, the catastrophe marked by the fast-day of the twentieth of Sivan to commemorate the Chmielnicki massacres of 1648–1649 was seen at the time merely as a further iteration of events already commemorated by an existing fast-day on that day: the burning at the stake of thirty-two Jews in the city of Blois in 1171 who had refused to be baptized. The liturgical commemorative dirges were already in place; there was nothing new to add.[13]

This is by no means a unique case. A memorial prayer was instituted after the catastrophes at the end of the eleventh century, when Jewish communities in the German Rhineland, then one of the main centers of Jewish life in Europe, were all but obliterated during the First Crusade. Interestingly enough, neither the victims of the massacres nor the perpetrators are specifically named in the contemporary version of this memorial prayer (*Av ha-raḥamim*, used to this day in the Ashkenazi Sabbath liturgy), nor is there any date given. The prayer only commemorates a category—"Jewish communities that gave up their lives as martyrs" (*kehillot ha-kodesh she-maseru nafsham 'al kedushat ha-shem*)—and provides no further particulars. The memory of the historical details about any specific catastrophe was not a major long-term Jewish preoccupation, any more than it was regarding the details of the liberation from ancient Egypt.[14]

As a final example of this point of view I should like to quote the Divrei Chayim, Rav Chaim Halberstamm, the distinguished nineteenth-century founder of the Zanzer dynasty of Hasidim from the town of Nowy Sącz in Galicia. He was once asked whether it was permitted for a Jewish woman to wear the same kind of head-covering as that worn by local Polish women, or whether this contradicted the principle of *ḥukat ha-goy* (the general ban on imitating Gentile customs). His answer was an interesting one in the present context: he quoted the verse from

Deuteronomy (23: 8), *lo teta'ev mitzri, ki ger hayita be-artzo* (which roughly translates as "you should not abhor an Egyptian, because you were allowed to live in his country"). If the Bible says that attitudes towards Egyptians should be based on gratitude, regardless of all the suffering that had been endured at their hands, then, in elaborating an attitude towards the local Polish population, the Divrei Chayim's opinion was that Jews should always recognize that they were "guests" in Poland and should therefore accord the Poles every respect.[15]

On further inspection it turns out that the Divrei Chayim was in fact on rather strong ground here, for the biblical text clearly shows that the people themselves rapidly forgot their suffering. Less than a month after they had left Egypt, they were already recalling with evident nostalgia the food they had eaten there: "We remember the fish, which we used to eat in Egypt for nothing, the cucumbers, the melons, the leeks, the onions and the garlic" (Num. 11: 5). In other words, there is room in the text to support the argument that both the folk view and the elite view converge in the need to see the Egyptian past in a positive light. I think this case shows rather nicely that the process of remembering the past may therefore also include another sequence of steps: forgetting the past, and reconstructing and mythologizing it. What is meant here by reconstruction and mythologization is the procedure—sometimes quite consciously undertaken—of adapting the historical memory so as to suit cultural values, social priorities, and moral or ethical predispositions that are deemed appropriate in a given place or period.

Sources for the Secular Jewish Mythologizations of the Holocaust

The above considerations and examples may help to frame our analysis as we explore the broader issue of contemporary secular modes of Holocaust memorialization. It may well be that the evidently negative attitudes of most Orthodox rabbinic authorities to the specifics of present-day Holocaust memory largely derive from an awareness that such remembrance is too overtly secular in content—although, as I have argued, the deeper issue of just how Jews have traditionally dealt with the past and flattened or mythologized a long history of Jewish persecution and tragedy in any case suggests that there are probably more fundamental differences of approach operating here than the conventional dichotomy between religious and secular would suggest. To be sure, Orthodox rabbis have written at length on Holocaust matters, most notably on the moral, ethical, and ritual quandaries that Jews had to face under Nazi rule, whether inside the ghettos, on the deportation trains, or inside the concentration camps. But in this perspective the Holocaust appears not as a historical event or set of events to be commemorated but rather as a set of human problems to be studied and contemplated as morally instructive in their own right.[16]

Be that as it may, outside the religious Jewish world the ethnography of the historical memory is exceptionally diverse, providing very large scope indeed for secular reconstructions and mythologizations, and indeed for competing models of the Holocaust itself. There would seem to be three broad reasons for this state of affairs, and I would like to make a few remarks about each of them.

My first point here is that whereas the Holocaust is often spoken of as if it constituted one historical event ("The Holocaust"), the truth of the matter is that the term "Holocaust" is really a historiographic category that has been retrospectively applied to the entire period of the German persecution and murder of the Jews of Europe. In practice the term is primarily intended to subsume the many different ways, in many different places and contexts, by which six million lives were brought to nothing. In a more general sense, however, it also refers to the sheer brutality of the period and therefore includes the experiences of those Jews who survived the German occupation or arrest by the SS, as illustrated by the term "Holocaust survivor." In other words, it encompasses many different kinds of possible memory—not only the shooting, the gassing, the deportations, but also the survival in ghettos, the survival in attics or under floorboards, the survival on the Aryan side of town, the survival in concentration camps—as well as the wartime separations, friendships, acts of courage and even heroism, betrayals, the constant fear, the witnessing of atrocities, and so on. Given these realities, it is surely inevitable that despite the use of the blanket term "Holocaust" one cannot find significant internal consistency in the types of memory that are commonly proposed, except perhaps the general rubric of man's inhumanity to man—though even this somewhat bland motif far from covers everything that people feel needs to be said.

The second reason for the diversity of Holocaust memory concerns the considerable range of forms used in describing and representing the Holocaust, namely through such media as photography, painting, sculpture, museums, monuments, survivor testimonies, films, commemorative lectures, exhibitions, prayer meetings, study tours to Holocaust sites—or even, for that matter, the representation of the Holocaust in the writings of professional historians. The very diversity of these activities itself testifies to the functional impossibility of unified presentation to the public of what the Holocaust was, and what it might mean. But, in addition, its representation in any of the forms I have just mentioned raises a series of difficulties. If the Holocaust was historically unique, it is not a straightforward matter to describe it adequately in such a way that it can be accounted for or understood—the categories used to portray or explain it will by definition either be unintelligible or alternatively so trivial that they will not do justice to its uniqueness.

If, on the other hand, the Holocaust was not historically unique, but rather the convergence of a series of individual factors that in themselves were not exceptional, how can one provide a coherent representation of it, say in a work of art or in a liturgy, that at the same time adequately conveys a proper sense of the extraordinary combination of the relatively commonplace factors that brought it about? How does one really depict the total abnormality of the Holocaust, yet at the same time reveal the banality and normality it also consisted of? How is an artist supposed to create something to represent total destruction?

Once the questions are put in this way, it becomes clear that the sheer scope of possible description and representation is immense—as well as inadequate. In practice, however, the range of representations with which people are familiar has an enormous hold over them, in telling them what the Holocaust was like and indeed providing them with what they should in effect be thinking of when trying to conceptualize what the Holocaust was, or what it might mean. After all, the only way to get hold of the past, in any case, is through some form of representation, most commonly today visual rather than textual. But not all of it can be shown at once; on the contrary, all that can usually be managed is to show some element or aspect of it at any one time. Unfortunately, the consequence of doing so is to overload the particular aspects being portrayed or represented with more symbolic meaning (and emotion) than they historically deserve. And most people are not aware that any representation usually shows only one aspect—hence the popular acclaim of *Schindler's List* as *the* Holocaust movie, or indeed *the* representation of the Holocaust. In reality, this is nothing more than wishful thinking; the selectivity upon which it rests is an example of a mythologized understanding of the past.

To take one concrete case: How does one depict Auschwitz in a Holocaust exhibition? Very often this is done by showing a photograph of the famous entry-gate, with the inscription "Arbeit macht frei." One problem with this representation is that visitors to such an exhibition would be tempted to reduce their image of Auschwitz to just this entry-gate, thereby substituting a part for the whole and giving that part more meaning than it really deserves. A related problem is that the comparative normality of the appearance of this entry-gate may also act in such a way as to shield visitors from the horrific realities of what went on beyond. The combined effect of this process of metonymic reduction is thus ultimately to mystify. During my own fieldwork in the Auschwitz Museum I have in fact regularly encountered visitors who turn out to be confused just because of the widespread use of this image of the entry-gate. Why, they ask, does the inscription refer to work or forced labor when everyone knows that what really was important at Auschwitz were the gas-chambers?[17]

Maybe there are makeshift solutions to all these epistemological difficulties; but the truth is that however well-educated about the Holocaust the public may theoretically become, there will inevitably be a gap between the representation of the Holocaust and its realities. Or, to put it more crudely, it may be that representing the Holocaust properly cannot really be done at all. "The logic of representation," as Dan Stone has written, "includes its own impossibility, [namely] the desire to give presence to what is not present."[18] I am sure he is right; but in the meantime both artists as well as organizations struggle with the conceptual problems as they furiously produce more and more exhibitions and monuments. I think one can expect even more imaginative types of Holocaust representation in the future; in Germany in particular, the range of new memorials being constructed—for example, to mark the sense of the loss or absence of the Jews of a specific town—is becoming very extensive. No doubt the very awareness of these difficulties of representation is generating the increased diversity in markers of historical memory.[19]

My third point follows from this: historical memory does not just appear from mid-air but is usually the product, the self-conscious product, of some institutional source that has some motive in delivering a particular rendering of the historical past. Photographs are taken or selected for a reason; exhibitions are put together with a particular purpose in mind. In past centuries the institutional source for the elaboration of Jewish historical memory were the rabbis—they decided what should be commemorated and how. The steady loss of their authority and power over the past two hundred years has been accompanied by the steady rise of quite new institutional sources for the consolidation and dissemination of Jewish memory, reaching remarkable new proportions in recent decades.

All this, of course, matches the veritable explosion in the democratization of memory that has taken place in wider society, particularly among groups hitherto marginalized but now demanding recognition as part of their agendas of discovering or rediscovering their identities—for example, working-class memory or women's memory. Their expression usually has to depend on a reconstruction, based on newly discovered or indeed newly created archives. The analogy here between Jewish and other institutional forms of memory is I think instructive, because in many cases Jewish groups have in effect modeled themselves on procedures commonly adopted in the wider environment, in particular as regards the energies spent on collecting oral materials as the basis for the new type of archive for the preservation of the memory of the past. The videotaping of survivors at the initiative of a whole range of new kinds of Jewish agencies is a good case in point of this decentralization process and democratization of Holocaust memory. What it all means is that there has come into existence a new range of institutionalized Holocaust-memory practitioners, though also including a penumbra of freelancers.

For those who like typologies, one can suggest at least three types of institutionalized practices, discourses, and narratives. First, there are the museums—those at concentration camp sites such as Auschwitz, Majdanek, Buchenwald, or Dachau, but also dedicated specialized ones such as Yad Vashem in Jerusalem and the United States Holocaust Memorial Museum in Washington and a host of other such museums across the world. Then there are the organizations of Holocaust survivors. Lastly there are the scholars and other intellectuals from a wide range of disciplines, including history, literature, and psychiatry. All of these sources possess their own internal histories, and especially of course the history of their own reconstructions and mythologizations of the Holocaust. To be sure, there is contact and cross-fertilization between them; but the overwhelming feeling of people who are familiar with the competing materials, terminologies, time-frames, or with the moral, intellectual, and financial priorities generated from all these disparate sources is that the overall discourse is chaotic, unstructured, and incoherent—a true reflection not only of the democratic process but perhaps of the Holocaust itself.

Professional historians, of course, find the problem of reconciling the subjective experience of survivor testimony with ordered historical narrative a matter of particular frustration; and it is not infrequent for a survivor to stand up at the end of a scholarly lecture and criticize the eminent historian for too much emphasis on bookish knowledge and thus not really having properly captured the true Holocaust experience. But the truth is that both parties here have reconstructed and mythologized; and that their respective discourses do not always mesh.

The passion that one sometimes sees in encounters of this kind should be understood not only as the reflection of the profound moral and emotional questions that any exposure to the historical consciousness of the Holocaust is likely to engender. Out of this chaos of competing institutional histories there has also been emerging something of a consensus in the public Jewish mind of the need somehow to protect the memory of the Holocaust from trivialization and banalization. It is noteworthy that the word "sacred" is steadily becoming more widely used to refer to this memory—as if to hedge it off from desecration. It may be that the fury directed against Holocaust deniers and revisionists should perhaps best be seen as an expression of a sense that they have trespassed onto a sacred space—a place from which foreigners, that is, people who do not share your values, must keep out. I suspect that if Holocaust deniers hadn't existed, they would have been invented.

The point here is that the phenomenon of Holocaust remembrance is beginning to develop many of the signs of a new secular religion of Jewish identity. Thus, for example, the erection of magnificent and imposing Holocaust museums, particularly in the United States, represents a major new type of monumental building that Jewish communities construct today, usually at vast expense. These edifices, with the fetishization they accord to "original Holocaust artifacts," and with their new commemorative liturgies, archives, specialists, dedicated newsletters, adult education classes, and so on, are beginning nowadays to assert themselves as the only truly "authentic" voice of the modern Jewish experience. The annual cycle of Holocaust commemorations—Kristallnacht, the Warsaw Ghetto Uprising, and Yom Hashoah (Holocaust Day, as established by the Israeli government, but very widely observed outside Israel)—supplies, furthermore, sufficient scope for these new secular Jewish rituals and endows these museum temples with the function of meeting-places for the enactment of this new post-Holocaust Jewish identity.

Indeed, the Holocaust has become one of the two or three principal subjects of Jewish public discourse about Judaism—a development that Jewish intellectuals conscious of traditional Jewish values find deeply disturbing. The preoccupation with mass murder is nothing less than a shocking reversal, in fact, of the biblical emphasis on the deliverance from Egypt, which hitherto had constituted the basis for a Jewish raison d'etre.[20] The secular terms of reference—notably the post-Holocaust obsession with Jewish survival for its own sake and the alleged "lesson" of the Holocaust that Jews should depend on no one but themselves in order to ensure this survival (and note the absence of any reference to God or any spiritual mission of the Jewish people)—should not be allowed to obscure the essentially religious aspect of this mythology, when understood analytically. The Holocaust here is "an event," functioning as a founding myth that explains to contemporary Jews that they are a single people; its "lessons" explain why Jews must be Jewish and what they have to do to stay Jewish. It occupies the key place in modern Jewish history. Not only was the Holocaust by definition unique. It was the great catastrophe that was then followed by the redemptive event of the establishment of the State of Israel. The two taken together offer a transcendent perspective on the recent past, a classic mythical structure of salvific religion.[21]

It may be that the catastrophe-redemption model is less commonly articulated nowadays than it was in the first decades after the events, but no other meta-historical myth has emerged as a frame of reference in which to locate the Holocaust.[22] The point is that it is precisely through a mythological structure of some kind that there is a Jewish concern with the Holocaust at all. This is how it is remembered by Jews today, and this is probably how it will be remembered in the future. Memory, as part of the collective consciousness of a people, is not the same thing as scholarly historical understanding. History as understood by the professional is concerned with nuances, complexity, differentiation. Memory eliminates nuances, and opts for a global and schematic rendition of the past. The mythologizing that stands behind populist memory shapes a sense of coherence out of the chaos of a complex subject. The anxiety of certain Holocaust historians today that Jewish Holocaust commemoration has become loud, simplified, and vulgar (especially through the influence of the mass media) helps to draw attention precisely to this crucial mythological component—which indeed may be accounted for by the simple fact that Nazism left an imprint on the imagination independent of whatever its historical significance might otherwise have been.

It is as if memory constitutes those aspects of the past that historical reason cannot reach. Maybe, in today's world, only memory in this sense can resolve an important contradiction: in the commercially dominated sector of the culture industry, the past is everywhere (historical museums and memorials of all kinds have proliferated in popularity). At the same time, however, the past is fundamentally irrelevant (action is not determined by past behavior). Thus it is perhaps through this new secular religion of the Holocaust—whatever its profound shortcomings in relation to classical Judaism—that these contradictory treatments of the past can be transcended in the popular imagination, so that the catastrophe can be hedged off from the fear of irrelevance and given proper status in the context of contemporary Jewish needs.[23]

Mythologizations

So what, finally, can be said about the reconstructions of the Holocaust that function as the central myths or beliefs of this new religion? The first point to make here is that one of the functions of a myth is to be selective and shrink the complex details of the past down to a manageable size. Thus, as with the fundamental structure I proposed earlier in relation to the Pentateuch, there would appear to be a core historical narrative that is constructed in such a way as to embody the main values of those who today choose to identify themselves as post-Holocaust Jews. This core narrative consists basically of four features: (a) antisemitism; (b) the total powerlessness of the Jews facing a violently antisemitic dictator egged on by bloodthirsty antisemitic sadists and murderers; (c) post-Holocaust survival; and (d) the moral imperative for both Jews and the rest of the world to remember the catastrophe, that it should never happen again.

The existence of this core narrative, which seems to underlie so many of the disparate Holocaust stories and representations, also means that there is comparatively little that people really need to know about the Holocaust itself—or indeed do know about it. There is far too much for people to know anyway. What is important about this structure is that it provides Jews with a series of justifications and a charter for action for maintaining their identity as Jews: (a) that the outside world is hostile, or at least potentially hostile; (b) that Jews should, however, no longer be afraid to assert their identity, as there is now a State of Israel, which among other things has redeemed them from powerlessness and (c) substantially contributed to the belief that Jewish survival is now guaranteed; and (d) that the principal moral obligation on each Jew, in the face of the appalling catastrophe, is to find suitable ways of remembering what happened and transmitting this knowledge into the future. This act alone is enough to confirm one's identity as a Jew.

But much of all this constitutes new Jewish values. There is no reference here, let alone any systematic reference, to anything readily identifiable as classical Jewish values—apart, that is, from the claim that remembering as such is a Jewish value of great antiquity. In this sense, I think this claim fits rather well with the widespread contemporary Jewish definition, particularly in the United States, of the Jewish community as an ethnic group rather than an ancient religion. The irony, of course, is that the expression and content of this post-Holocaust ethnic Jewish identity has taken on a number of forms, as we have shown, more usually associated with popular religion.

For example, what people actually know about the Holocaust beyond the core narrative may give the illusion of historical precision but on closer inspection often turns out to be little more than a religious litany. "Six million" seems to be a concept, one that links up with the customary lighting of six candles at commemoration ceremonies; but beyond the phrase there is not even statistical substance to it—no common awareness of a breakdown by country, by age, by gender. Similarly, one finds a series of famous words, names, photographs, and stereotypes that together pass for knowledge of the Holocaust, but in essence, these details comprise only a symbolic, quasi-liturgical knowledge. It seems to be chronological but often isn't, and moreover tends to rest on a belief in the certainties of what happened rather than on a continuous quest for knowledge about the great unknown. The parallels with religion will be immediately apparent.

Then there are the taboos—for instance the question of Jewish complicity in the Holocaust, such as the betrayal of other Jews—the widespread popular confusion over details of chronology, and of course the historical inversions. Perhaps the most notable example of historical inversions is the common substitution of Poles for Germans: in the elaboration of this reconstructed popular Jewish history of the Holocaust, it is the Poles who are largely identified with the antisemitism responsible for it all. "The Poles were much worse than the Germans," as Holocaust survivors confidently tell their audiences.

The role of survivors as the main contemporary pillars, if not the priests, of the new religion is something I must touch on here, even if briefly. The antisemitism they knew from before the war in eastern Europe was certainly real enough, as was the antisemitism they often would have encountered from the forest partisans and village peasants, on whose help they had to depend in order to survive in making their escapes. But this sort of antisemitism can certainly not account for the totality of the Holocaust as such. Survivors continue to represent one of the principal sources for popular Jewish knowledge about the Holocaust, and in many respects have provided the main contours of Jewish historical consciousness on this subject. But their own knowledge is partial, in both senses of the term. Those who survived the concentration camps or the firing squads of the Einsatzgruppen would have known nothing of the Wannsee Conference in Berlin in January 1942; they could have had no grasp of the totality of the German plan, its motives, and how it fitted into German war aims— all of which they could learn only after the war was over. And yet they participated in the historical event, they saw it from close up. What they came back to tell us was what happened to them; and there were many tens of thousands of them who had once been inside Auschwitz and lived to tell the tale. This is one reason we have all heard of Auschwitz and why it came to be the main representation of the Holocaust. Yet 600,000 Jews were gassed to their deaths in Bełżec: but who ever heard of Bełżec? From Bełżec there were only three survivors—and I think by that contrast, between Auschwitz and Bełżec, hangs an important tale about what it is that entered popular knowledge of the Holocaust.

A sociology of memory, in other words, may turn out to be critical in understanding how the myth is put together, as for example in the case of Bergen-Belsen, which was liberated by the British and thereafter entered popular British representations of the Holocaust. A further set of difficulties that one must remember in treating survivor testimonies as serious analyses of the Holocaust: most of these people were quite young at the time of the war (mainly in their teens or twenties); their testimonies are today often given in languages other than their mother-tongues and are obviously prone to all sorts of embellishment—in the years that have elapsed since the end of the war these survivors have inevitably been influenced by books and films—not to mention their reliance on stories they heard from other former ex-prisoners or escapees about what really happened.[24] All these factors can be taken into account by the professional historian trying to make sense of the testimonies or integrate them into a larger narrative; but in practice (as remarked above) these concerns of scholars have not significantly affected the perceptions of the ordinary Jewish world. On the contrary, one dare not criticize Holocaust survivors; their writings have become quasi-sacred texts that should be treated with reverence, and indeed are ceremonially read from at Holocaust commemoration meetings.

Not all survivors have given testimony or joined the survivor organizations; but the latter nevertheless are strong contact groups for the exchange of experiences and information, often reinforcing the conviction among many survivors that their experience of having survived the Holocaust is the defining social and personal fact in their lives and identity—a conviction that became the paradigm for the new Jewish values. Being the child of a Holocaust survivor, or even the grandchild of one, has in recent years become a source of meaningful social status in the Jewish world and often leads to being asked to read an extract, give a lecture, lead a tour, or light a commemorative candle. After all, in this new Jewish myth, all Jews are to see themselves in some sense or another as Holocaust survivors—that is, as long as they continue to remember this about themselves.

Conclusions

In traditional diaspora Judaism before the modern period, there was no elaborate disinterested writing of history; new events, as we might today perceive them, were seen as reiterations of previous events. This is why, for example, even the Chmielnicki massacres in the middle of the seventeenth century largely disappeared from the public Jewish memory. Such catastrophes had occurred before—for example, during the massacres accompanying the destruction of the Temple—and they would occur again. This sense of déjà vu may explain not only why Orthodox Jews have largely turned their backs on Holocaust commemoration; it may perhaps also partly explain why Jews seemed so unaware during the Holocaust itself of the totally new form of systematic genocide that they were being confronted with. Familiar with what is today called antisemitism, even murderous antisemitism, they accommodated the new to the old.[25]

But now a new Jewish approach to history has arisen. This new understanding has drawn its main strength both from a sense of opposition to the old order and from conventions found in wider society. The closed set of meanings supplied by the past, as understood in the old system, was now to be replaced by studious attention to the details of history, even though (as indeed is now often complained) history could supply no meanings to those details. Despite the outpouring of Holocaust representations in an ever-increasing flood of books, exhibitions, films, and conferences, the meaning of this past remains elusive. In this breakdown of classical Judaism meaning has been replaced by history—but at the same time the cultural predisposition for using a highly selective form of memory, together with its consolidation into myths as a charter for action, remains unchanged. And the new Judaism claims its authenticity in its assertion that the need to remember as such derives specifically from the Bible, an assertion that itself represents a totally new interpretation of biblical religion and long-standing patterns of Jewish historical consciousness.

It is not clear how all this came about, especially given the silence of survivors immediately after the war and the myths that were conventional at that time that the Jews allowed themselves to go like sheep to the slaughter.[26] Maybe indeed there was at first an overwhelming sense of shame that the whole thing had happened at all. Perhaps, as I suggested earlier, Jewish needs changed in the meantime: the new Jewish mythology fits the contemporary need of the broad masses of Western Jews, whose ethnic identity as Jews has become highly attenuated, selective, and intermittent. In some respects they may have less in common with each other than with the non-Jews among whom they live, and in such a context a central founding myth that appropriately explains their identity both to themselves and wider society was in any case needed. It may also be that a post-Holocaust identity gained validation as a substitute for the secular alternatives that were in vogue up until a generation ago: socialism, which has steadily declined in popularity since 1968, and Zionism, which equally has lost much of its appeal among the secular Jewish intelligentsia over the past ten to fifteen years.

One feature of post–Holocaust Jewish identity that also enhances its value as a charter for action is the sense that Auschwitz is contested space—not only because of the existence of Holocaust deniers but also, and perhaps more insidiously, because the Poles and the Catholic Church also seem to claim it as theirs. In fact, the Jewish claim that Auschwitz has been Christianized or otherwise dejudaized is itself a mythologized reconstruction, drawing only very partially on the empirical facts; but it provides the devotees of this new religion with the sense they also have something to fight for. This is another myth, and itself a new value. It is certainly true that the Auschwitz site was never specifically dedicated to the memory of the Holocaust during the years of Polish communism, when the camp was promoted as an official state symbol of Polish suffering during the German occupation. Things have changed very substantially since Poland became a free country in 1989, but the stereotypical Jewish grievance not only lingers on but has been reinvigorated by beliefs deriving from an earlier time: the denunciation of Polish ill-will has become a commonplace of contemporary Holocaust activism. But on the other hand, Jews, as well as Poles, have still not properly come to terms with the reality that they all were put to death together at Auschwitz (albeit in very unequal proportions) and that the ashes of both Jews and Catholics were indiscriminately strewn over the fields. Both groups thus share a common history of the Auschwitz terror; and there is no objective reason for treating it as contested space.

But the erection of such a boundary, fencing off the Holocaust founding event from all would-be trespassers, leaves pre-Holocaust time as prehistory. The implications for Jewish historical consciousness are profound. The Bible had nothing to say about thirty-eight of the forty years that the Israelites were in the Sinai desert: in its construction of a specific kind of historical consciousness the period was irrelevant. A similar structuring process has been in evidence in early Zionist perspectives of Jewish history: the diaspora Jewish experience of two thousand years largely disappeared from view in order to enable Israelis to feel themselves reconnecting with the ancient Hebrew settlement of the land in biblical times.

Today's new Holocaust-derived Jewish historical consciousness has like-wise restructured its apperception of the landmarks of the past. Most significantly, Auschwitz seems to have had the effect of crossing out the ethnic memory of prewar Polish Jewish culture. Who amongst these Holocaust buffs can for example name, say, ten famous Jews who were murdered in Auschwitz? The Holocaust finally finished off any real sense that the great majority of today's Ashkenazi Jews descend from an experience of eight hundred years in Poland. It's now almost completely forgotten, having been reduced to a stereotyped ethnic Jewish memory of Polish antisemitism.[27]

And this forgetting, of course, is what the new myths are there to deal with: they substitute alternative preoccupations and then explain them. Perhaps this is how Jews as a people have survived at all: if indeed they had scrupulously preserved the memory of the countless pogroms and other humiliations of past centuries, maybe they would have lacked the cultural confidence to keep moving forward and adapting to new circumstances. Certainly there are Holocaust survivors today who run to the cellar when they hear a knock on the door, or who refuse to install showers in their apartments or to let their children sleep in bunk-beds; but, from what I know, such people are comparatively rare. People forget much more than they remember. Today's post-Holocaust slogan "Remember!" covers up this very widespread forgetting and remythologizes the nature of Jewish historical consciousness and Jewish identity. But in the final analysis it should be said that in the circumstances of today's Jewish world, the injunction to remember represents only a very vague attempt to come to terms with the ruins of the past.

1. I should like to record my grateful thanks to the Economic and Social Research Council of the United Kingdom for offering me the research grant during the years 1992–95 that enabled me to carry out the fieldwork on which much of the material presented in this essay has been based.

2. An obvious example of a major catastrophe that the Bible nowhere mentions as worthy of remembering as such is the major defeat of the Israelites at Hormah following the abortive first attempt to enter Canaan by force (Num. 14: 45; Deut. 1: 44). The rout at Hormah is explained in the text as a consequence of the people's lack of faith and the confusion brought about by the report of the twelve spies, the majority of whom emphasized the military impossibility of an attack. (The *victory* at Hormah, as reported at Num. 21:3, probably took place at a much earlier date.)

This resounding defeat for the Israelites, which in effect condemned them to spending thirty-eight years in the desert before a fresh attack could be undertaken, is thus linked to a major episode in the spiritual history of the people. Even though the text implies (Deut. 25:18; Ex. 17: 8–16) that the cowardly attack of the Amalekites on the Israelite rear at Refidim also had something to do with the lack of Israelite confidence in God, it is clearly different from the defeat at Hormah in terms of its power to generate the need for memory.

It could be, perhaps, that Refidim was simply the first defeat after the departure from Egypt and therefore became the prototype event of the category of defeats, to which other, later defeats would be mythologically merged (as indeed happened later with the mythological merging of Jewish tragedies in the Middle Ages, as discussed below). Another interpretation could be that Refidim was to be specially remembered because of the cowardly nature of the attack—and thereby a prototype in a different sense, namely as a founding event (a relatively small massacre, perhaps) characterizing the barbarism of neighboring societies, as opposed to the intrinsic goodness of one's own. It otherwise is hard to explain the longevity of such massacres or pogroms in the folk memory; but founding events of this type are, after all, well known from many societies across the world.

3. Yosef Hayim Yerushalmi, *Zakhor: Jewish History and Jewish Memory* (Seattle and London: University of Washington Press, 1982).

4. For example, the introduction of the Sabbath is described in the text as a historical event connected with the interruption of the manna food-supply (Ex. 17). "Long ago," the story seems to be saying, "when our people had to live in a desert for a generation after leaving Egypt, we had to rely on 'food from heaven' [Ex. 17:4], which we had to go out and collect; for some miraculous reason this food did not arrive on the Sabbath but came down in a double portion on Fridays. It thus became the custom not to go out looking for food on the Sabbath, but to stay at home instead; it was pointless going out, because there would be nothing there to collect. This situation was then codified into a set of detailed laws concerning the observance of the Sabbath, which was explained as possessing many spiritual meanings—including references to the creation of the world and the liberation of the people from Egypt." It is worth noting that from the way the story is told in Exodus 17, the people are not deemed to have been previously aware of the concept of Sabbath observance as such—that is first mentioned only three chapters later, within the context of the Ten Commandments.

5. See for example the Gemara at Pesachim 6b, which discusses the point in the context of the biblical narrative in Num. chap. 9, chronologically identified in the text itself as one month earlier than the narrative in Num. chap. 1—for which the commentaries suggest a variety of implicit reasons and messages. It is not only events, of course, that may be out of chronological sequence: for example, the reference to the "testimony" at Ex. 16: 34 presupposes the presence of these two tablets of stone (Ex. 31: 18), which in turn presupposes the relevant elements of the construction of the sanctuary, mentioned at Ex. 25: 21–2.

6. In accordance with this principle, specific historical miracles (which might otherwise seem to be in contradiction with it, or at least exceptions to the rule) are explained in the Mishnah as having been accounted for at the time of creation and therefore part of the intrinsic nature of the world rather than interruptions of it (Avot 5: 9).

7. The contrast is terminologically quite clear in the liturgy of the Passover Haggadah: "even if we were all wise . . . and all knowledgeable in the Torah, we would still be obliged [*mitzvah 'aleinu*] to tell the story of the departure from Egypt, and [but?] he who elaborates on the story . . . is worthy of praise [*harei zeh meshubbah*]." The obligation to tell the story aloud is a ritual one, provided by the liturgy, and has nothing whatever to do with the state of one's own personal knowledge.

8. Quoted by Sacha Stern, "Attribution and Authorship in the Babylonian Talmud" in *Journal of Jewish Studies*, 45:1 (1994): 28–51.

9. On this subject see, for example, Jonathan Webber ed., *Jewish Identities in the New Europe* (London and Washington: Littman Library of Jewish Civilization, 1994).

10. If there is such a straightforward binary division, "religious" versus "secular" does not quite

capture it, as other parameters—sometimes following this boundary, sometimes cutting right across it—are also involved. For example, "religious" might also be taken to include such features as committed, affiliated, traditional, communitarian—as opposed to assimilated, unaffiliated, modern, individualistic. New terms and new distinctions are also constantly being proposed, such as Michael Goldberg's "covenantal Judaism" versus "consumer" or "civil" Judaism, which in some contexts supports the religious–secular divide but in others supersedes it *(Why Should Jews Survive? Looking Past the Holocaust toward a Jewish Future* [New York: Oxford University Press, 1995], pp. 43 ff., 136–41).

There are difficulties with all these terms, which are little more than vague approximations, leaving behind a good deal of unrepresented overlap of features across this notional divide. They therefore cannot be taken literally but rather as heuristic devices to be read in the context of an author's particular exposition about the nature of Jewish society today. My own use of the terms "religious" and "secular" here is thus not intended to be comprehensive. To give one specific example of the point, such a distinction leaves open the place of religiously minded Reform Jews. The outlook of these Jews, and indeed the various positions that have been suggested regarding a non-Orthodox Jewish theology of the Holocaust, is a large subject on its own and one that is unfortunately beyond the scope of this article.

11. This is to simplify quite a complex picture. Eating bitter herbs as part of the Passover ritual is mentioned only twice in the whole Hebrew Bible (at Ex. 12:8 and Num. 9:11), despite many other references to the Passover both in the Pentateuch and elsewhere in the later books of the Bible (for example, Deuteronomy 16, Joshua 5, II Kings 23, Ezekiel 45, Ezra 6, and II Chronicles 30 and 35). One is tempted to suggest that it lost its symbolic force—came to be forgotten?—once the generation of survivors who had personally witnessed the horrors of the slavery and persecution in Egypt had died out, and that it was reinstated by the tannaitic rabbis—on the basis not only of the two biblical source-texts mentioned but also of their own experience of persecution under Roman rule in Palestine. Note that these two lone biblical references give no reason for the practice.

However, the idea that this gastronomic ritual intrinsically symbolizes the bitterness of the Egyptian experience is not only given explicit mention in the rabbinic liturgy for Passover; the text of this liturgy actually goes out of its way to emphasize its importance, identifying bitter herbs as one of the three symbols (alongside unleavened bread and a representation of the biblical Passover sacrifice) that require specific ceremonial explanation. In addition, the physical act of eating the bitter herbs is even accorded a formal ceremonial benediction—a liturgical status unequivocally emphasizing its ritual importance, in this sense comparable only to the ceremonial eating of unleavened bread. In short, the relatively wide range of biblical ideas concerning the meaning and significance attached to the Passover festival has been restructured in the rabbinic Jewish tradition—specifically to make room for a restated emphasis on the commemoration of suffering.

12. On the history of the introduction in Israel of *'Yom ha-shoah ve-hagevura'* (Day of Remembrance of the Holocaust and Heroism [sic]), and the debates over the religious and other issues involved, see James Young, *The Texture of Memory: Holocaust Memorials and Meaning* (New Haven and London: Yale University Press, 1993), chap. 10.

13. See Yerushalmi, *Zakhor*, pp. 48–52. The twentieth of Sivan was the date in 1648 when the first of the Chmielnicki massacres occurred, in the city of Nemirov. The massacres have been all but forgotten today: that particular fast-day is no longer observed.

14. The original custom in late medieval Germany was in fact to read out a full list of the names of individuals; these were compiled into Memorbücher, for which the classic source is Siegmund Salfeld ed., *Das Martyrologium des Nürnberger Memorbuches* (Berlin: Leonhard Simion, 1898). One of the two Sabbaths when the names were read out was the Sabbath before the festival of Pentecost (the anniversary of the massacre). Following further massacres the lists were added to, but by the end of the

fourteenth century they had grown so long that room was found only for place-names where Jewish communities had been destroyed.

For some reason (lack of serious interest, perhaps?), these lists were never printed in book form, with the result that once it became common for Ashkenazi congregations to rely on printed liturgies (during the nineteenth century), the whole custom fell into disuse. The *Av ha-raḥamim* prayer that survives today is merely the remainder, therefore, of a much more substantial ritual of remembrance; the German custom of reciting it specifically on the Sabbath before Pentecost (a custom that is followed in the accepted Anglo-Jewish rite of the United Synagogue) is doubtless a relic of forgotten historical knowledge: certainly the standard liturgies in common use offer no explanation.

15. See Yitzchak Bromberg, *The Sanzer Rav and His Dynasty*, trans. Shlomo Fox-Ashrei (Brooklyn: Mesorah Publications, 1986), p.163. It would appear that the question related not to the traditional headscarves worn by Polish peasants but to some more stylish form of head-dress that was evidently coming into fashion just then.

16. For a more detailed discussion of this subject see my article "Jewish Martyrdom in the Holocaust: A Representative Category?" in Yasmin Doosry, ed., *Representations of Auschwitz: 50 Years of Photographs, Paintings, and Graphics* (Oświęcim: Auschwitz-Birkenau State Museum, 1995), pp. 71–85; republished in *Polin: Studies in Polish Jewry*, 13 (2000), in press. In recent years there has also developed a new genre of Holocaust memoirs specifically written by religious Jews (of which perhaps the best-known pioneering work is Yaffa Eliach, *Hasidic Tales of the Holocaust* (New York: Oxford University Press, 1982); but see also the "Holocaust Diaries" series put out by C.I.S. publishers of New York).

17. The main four gas-chambers of Auschwitz were in fact located at Auschwitz-Birkenau, about two miles from the main camp. Both camps also functioned as concentration camps for forced labor, the main camp almost exclusively so. The "Arbeit macht frei" inscription was over the entry-gate to the main camp, but there was no such inscription at the entry to Birkenau, whose entry guardhouse, with its railway line passing through an archway, is often confused in the popular imagination with the entry-gate of the main camp. They seem to be merged into a single image. To the extent that Auschwitz itself represents the Holocaust, the very idea that there were two "Auschwitzes" (in fact there were no less than forty Auschwitz sub-camps in all) does not correspond to popular conceptualizations of the Holocaust, and therefore the merged image comes to supersede the empirical facts.

18. Dan Stone, "Chaos and Continuity: Representations of Auschwitz," in Doosry, *Representations of Auschwitz*, pp. 25–33; at p. 31.

19. See Young, *The Texture of Memory*, chaps. 1–4. For a new generation of artists in Germany today, he writes, the question is how to avoid classic monumental forms in the light of their systematic exploitation by the Nazis. Hence the rise of "vanishing monuments" and other forms of countermonument—"brazenly self-conscious memorial spaces . . . whose primary function is to jar viewers from complacency, to challenge and denaturalize the viewers' assumptions" (pp. 27–28).

Young's emphasis, throughout this book, on the interplay between artist and audience (and sponsor) in effect expounds the scope for multiple encodings of the past as each community constructs its own Holocaust memory; in this way, the philosophical and historiographic problematic concerning the intrinsic unrepresentability of the Holocaust can be circumvented—after all, the Holocaust is being memorialized, and that is the critical issue that needs description and explanation, regardless of the numerous inherent methodological difficulties faced by professional historians (on which, for a convenient recent survey, see Saul Friedlander ed., *Probing the Limits of Representation: Nazism and the "Final Solution"* (Cambridge: Harvard University Press, 1992).

On the other hand—in a manner similar to the difficulties in interpreting biblical texts as discussed above—it is necessary to be aware of their underlying problematic, in this case in order to be able to see analytically how memorialization rests on an intermediary mythologization that makes the public memorials possible. One feature of this mythologization is the almost total lack of common Jewish awareness (outside Germany) of the scholarly debates about representations, in particular of the recent paradigm shift from the incomprehensibility of the Holocaust to its disturbing normality in the modern age: such debates belong to the literary elite, far removed from folk preoccupations.

20. See Goldberg, *Why Should Jews Survive?* p. 14 and passim; or, for a much earlier work, Jacob Neusner, *Stranger at Home: "The Holocaust," Zionism, and American Judaism* (Chicago and London: University of Chicago Press, 1981).

21. For a detailed exposition, see Neusner, *Stranger at Home*, Part Two.

22. See Yerushalmi, *Zakhor*, p. 98. He suggests that its basic image is being shaped today more by novelists than by historians.

23. The historian I have been citing here is Saul Friedlander, in particular in the context of his exchange of views with Martin Broszat. See *Memory, History, and the Extermination of the Jews of Europe* (Bloomington and Indianapolis: Indiana University Press, 1993), pp. 58–61, 95–97. Friedlander does not express satisfaction over such a division of labor between memory and historiography; on the contrary. But it should be noted that he was also concerned about such a division of labor within the German context, not merely the Jewish one.

24. Given this range of difficulties, some researchers have preferred to base their work on interviews with survivors rather than analyze their memoirs—that is, to become an active participant in the construction of a common understanding ("intersubjectively communicable discourse," as it is called), especially important at the level of ordinary language use, rather than remain passive reader (see for example Barbara Engelking, *Zagłada i pamięć: Doświadczenie Holocaustu i jego konsekwencje opisane na podstawie relacji autobiograficznych* (Warsaw: IFiS PAN, 1994), chap.4 and pp. 311–15.

The issue of historical accuracy is a particularly vexed question. Holocaust testimonies, often privately published, are seldom cross-referenced to specialist scholarly studies. Some may have great appeal as literary works of art (notably those, of course, by such well-known authors as Primo Levi, Elie Wiesel, or by non-Jewish authors such as Tadeusz Borowski or Charlotte Delbo); but the genre can also be disappointingly inauthentic or otherwise unreliable on points of historically attested detail. The purpose of testimony today, as Annette Wieviorka puts it, "is no longer to bear witness to inadequately known events, but rather to keep them before our eyes. Testimony is to be a means of transmission to future generations" ["On Testimony," in Geoffrey H. Hartman, ed., *Holocaust Remembrance: The Shapes of Memory* (Oxford: Blackwell, 1994), pp. 23–32; at p. 24].

But survivors are not necessarily experienced authors; on the contrary, as Wievorka notes (ibid., p. 29), the differential social composition of Auschwitz survivors, compared with survivors of other concentration camps, meant that the former were on the whole less educated. It meant that after the war, they would sometimes team up with a professional author in order to publish their memoirs—of which perhaps the best-known example is the memoir of Rudolf Vrba, who told his story to Alan Bestic (*I Cannot Forgive* [London: Sidgwick and Jackson and Anthony Gibbs and Phillips, 1963]).

Although in the early decades following the war such writers exercised great care in matters of detail, this has become less fashionable (and less possible) for works of this kind being written nowadays, fifty years on. Rebecca Fromer, for example, who wrote up the story of Daniel Bennahmias, one of the last surviving former members of the Sonderkommando at Auschwitz, evidently felt it quite acceptable to fill out the account with episodes she had heard of elsewhere but which the survivor had not in fact reported to her: "To my surprise," she writes in one passage, "Danny knew nothing of this incident until I informed him of it" (Rebecca Camhi Fromer, *The Holocaust Odyssey of Daniel Bennahmias, Sonderkommando* [Tuscaloosa and London: University of Alabama Press, 1993], p. 101).

It may well be in the future that Holocaust deniers will have a field-day in deconstructing this kind of literature, which does indeed seem prone to incorporate certain kinds of images (both literary and visual), regardless of their strict historical appropriateness. For example, the dustjacket of Fromer's book reproduces a photograph of the barbed-wire perimeter fences at the main camp at Auschwitz, with prisoner blocks on one side and SS barracks on the other; although captioned simply "Auschwitz" (p. 126), it has nothing whatever to do with Daniel Bennahmias's experience as a member of the Sonderkommando in Birkenau. He never set foot in the Auschwitz main camp; and the barracks shown in the photograph, typical of any ordinary Nazi concentration camp, are very far from the exceptional horror of the work of the Sonderkommando in the gas chambers. But the photo is a well-known representation of Auschwitz: popular mythologization, in other words, has entered here as a substitute for the historical realities.

One final example worthy of mention is the remark that when Danny arrived at Auschwitz (Birkenau) he saw the famous "Arbeit macht frei" inscription (ibid., p. 31). But this would have been impossible since the entry-gate where this slogan was hung was more than two miles away (see above). Many other Auschwitz survivors have made a similar error. See for example Alfred Kantor, *The Book of Alfred Kantor* (New York: McGraw-Hill, 1971), drawing on p. 34, which shows the Birkenau entry-gate with this inscription.

25. One of the key aspects of the definition of a pogrom was that it would blow over; patience (and/or confidence in God) was needed before the mob would calm down, and peace would be restored (perhaps helped along by a bribe to an important official). It may be important to bear this in mind when considering Jewish "passivity" during the Holocaust.

26. The idea that Jews were taken like sheep to the slaughter is originally a biblical image (Ps. 44:23): "For your sake, indeed, we are killed all day long; we are treated as sheep to the slaughter." (See also Jer. 12: 3 and Is. 53: 7). As a literary image, it is a bitter lament for the catastrophes experienced by a people who nevertheless would reassert their confidence and faith in their divine protector. "Why do you hide your face, forgetting our affliction and our oppression?" the psalm continues. "Rise up and help us; redeem us for the sake of your mercy" (Ps. 44: 24–26).

The image of sheep to the slaughter, which reappears in the ordinary weekday liturgy, as well as in the liturgical dirges for the fast-day of the Ninth of Av, seems however to have been reworked after the Holocaust into a sloganized formula constituting a secularist accusation against pious Jews, who by and large did not physically resist the SS, in contrast to the heroism of a handful of ghetto fighters and partisans (mostly belonging to the Zionist youth movements). In a manner somewhat reminiscent, perhaps, of the contemporary reworking of the biblical *zakhor* command, the "sheep to the slaughter" image came to be historicized—as if it were a bona fide representation of a historical reality.

27. There is virtually no sign yet of Jewish reconciliation with Poles, despite what Goldberg calls the toxic racism of condemning a whole people on the charge of genocide *(Why Should Jews Survive?* p. 145, although no specific nation is mentioned in this passage). Interestingly enough, Goldberg notes that the Bible in effect advocated reconciliation with "those Nazis of ancient times, the Egyptians," citing the identical verse in Deuteronomy (23: 8) referred to by the Divrei Chayim when discussing attitudes to Poles (see above).

Redemption from the Orient

One by-product of the short-lived western Haskalah was the deeply rooted conviction that Western Jewry could only find redemption by an increased adoption of modern, Western values and tastes. In the course of half a century much of the mythological apparatus of the Jewish communities of western Europe had been undone. The traditional Jewish models that were still alive and well in eastern Europe were disparaged and ignored in the West. This flight from tradition was accompanied by a keen desire to identify new mythologies and new models for Jewish life. The painful process of Jewish secularization and the westernization of religious phenomena took place concuurently with the discovery of Andalusian and other Judeo-Islamic models and achievements. German Jews started to embrace a portion of the past that had previously been marginal to their view of the world, and this eventually enabled them to redefine their new Western identity in a Jewish mode. These precedents were invoked in the new Jewish scholarship, in new educational institutions, in literary models and even in the form of nineteenth-century synagogue architecture, which, in many cases, was predicated upon Islamic models.[1]

The dialectic of rebellion against the past on the one hand and rejuvenation by means of a remotely sensed oriental version of the past on the other was thereafter to recur not irregularly in Jewish consciousness and literature. The great periods of Jewish-Muslim symbiosis were perceived as emanating from a Muslim civilization whose innate and essential characteristics included a highly developed aesthetic sense, cultural pluralism, and a philosophic mind-set. Like other historical myths, this one generated a selective vision of the past—one that was determined and colored by the social requirements of the day—in this case, the social need of Jews to achieve similar circumstances in nineteenth-century Germany.[2]

Somewhat later, the natural relationship of the Muslims of Palestine to the land and to their own past was similarly seen as offering a model for déraciné Jews "deformed" by the abnormalities of diaspora existence. These perceptions, whether in support of emancipation and assimilation or in support of Zionism, suggested that redemption for the Jews would come from the East. This discourse existed on a number of levels and was applied to various eastern models, both Jewish and non-Jewish. In this paper I shall attempt to place western perceptions of the Yemenite Jews within this general context.

Notwithstanding that not much is known of the early history of the Yemenite Jews,[3] an essential feature of the discourse is that they are an ancient "biblical" community. Even some contemporary scholars continue to insist that they are descended from some ancient Israelite implantation in South Arabia.[4] For most modern observers, their very appearance has automatically evoked the Bible. Yomtob Sémach, who visited the Yemen in 1910 on behalf of the Alliance Israélite Universelle, wrote: "The sidelocks around their faces, their pointed noses and dark flowing garments recall certain biblical figures . . ."[5] This perspective on the Yemenites soon gained the widest possible currency. Shortly before the First World War, Judah Magnes (1877–1948), the American rabbi and Zionist functionary, encapsulated this view, calling them "a lost tribe and the oldest community of the Dispersion who were returning with a sure and simple faith and bringing an original Judaism such as was taught and lived in the early days of the Jewish exile."[6]

Several decades later the discourse was essentially the same. A WIZO pamphlet proclaimed:

> For centuries the forgotten Jewish community of Yemen—perhaps the purest of all Jewish communities anywhere, in the most direct line of descent from the ancient people of Israel—prayed for the Messiah to lead them back to the land of their birth . . . their hands and feet retained the delicacy and grace of the ancient kings of Israel, proclaiming an aristocracy of soul and body that no amount of persecution could destroy. . . . A fabulous tribe, the most poetic of the tribes of Israel. Their features bear the ancient Hebrew grace, and their hearts are filled with innocent faith and a fervent love for the Holy Land."[7]

An Israeli correspondent covering the airlift of the Yemenite Jews to Israel in 1948 would remark that the refugees belonged to "the Bible Age" and were taking part in "a Biblical epic."[8]

The discourse insists that the Yemenite Jews retain the closest possible resemblance to the Jews of the Bible. Direct descendants of the first Exile, if not earlier, they are viewed as having lived in the same locus until finally they were redeemed. They were supposed to have preserved their distinctive Jewish characteristics, which have been unsullied by religious, cultural, or genetic interference. As Weingarten has put it,

> This originality has been claimed for such disparate characteristics as their pronunciation of Hebrew, the textual details of their sacred books, their religious customs, and indeed for their genetic identity. Whereas Jews throughout the world have changed, the Yemenites have remained the same, runs the popular myth.[9]

The idea that the Yemenites' authenticity could, in some sense, redeem the rest of Jewry, was expressed by many, particularly in the first days of the State of Israel. "To witness the arrival of the refugee convoys, to talk with the Jews and hear of their experiences, was like being taken back through time and witnessing a Biblical epic. . . .They sent me back to the Bible, whether I wanted it or not," wrote one Jewish journalist. A Jewish aid worker commented: "Aren't they all wonderful? These people have faith . . . that is faith, like the Bible come true. We with our modern world! I tell you, they give me faith too."[10] On one occasion, the renowned scholar S.D. Goitein observed: "Once when I conducted our late lamented teacher Professor Louis Ginzberg to a Yemenite synagogue, he said after the service, 'Now I know what Judaism is.'"[11] Elsewhere Goitein observed:

> It has been deeply and rightly felt by many that the Yemenites were the most Jewish of all Jews; that they had preserved in their remote isolation, in a country which was itself a monotheistic theocracy, much of the character of a genuinely Jewish society. Therefore, their ingathering to the land of their fathers was not only a redemption of the body; it was a return of the spirit."[12]

In the nineteenth century, even the Jewish world knew relatively little of the Yemenite Jews. In 1831 Rabbi Yisrael of Shklov[13] sent an emissary *(shaliaḥ)* to the Yemen on behalf of his *kolel* in Safed in northern Palestine to raise money for the *ḥalukkah*—the fund that helped to support the communitites of pious Jews in the holy cities of Palestine. The *shaliaḥ* was sent off in the serious expectation that beyond the deserts of Arabia, a mighty kingdom peopled by the lost tribes of Israel would be found. This notion had been strengthened by emissaries who had visited Yemen some years before and who had claimed to have met members of the tribe of Dan in the deserts there.[14] Among other things, Rabbi Israel hoped to recreate in Palestine the ancient institution of ordination for the Sanhedrin—a necessary precondition, as he pointed out, for the Redemption and the coming of the Messiah.[15] He believed that it was only among the lost ten tribes that this ancient practice was still followed: once the tribes in South Arabia were found, instructions could be given that would enable ordination to be reintroduced in the Land of Israel, and redemption would surely follow.

The emissary, R. Barukh ben R. Shmuel of Pinsk, arrived in the Yemen in 1833 and set off to explore the little-known desert areas of the northeastern part of the country. There he met up with a mysterious individual who claimed to be of the "Sons of Moses" and from the very "kingdom of the Jews" he was seeking. Because of the impending High Holidays, the emissary returned to Sanaa, where he was murdered. This story, along with others about tribes of Israel living in the desert regions and fighting alongside the Arab tribes, was published with no hint of skepticism in Jacob Saphir's influential and widely read book *Even Sapir.*[16] Reports from Joseph Halévy, who visited the Yemen in 1870,[17] and Yomtob Sémach, who followed him some forty years later, of warlike, armed Jews living on the fringes of the Arabian desert cannot but have reinforced the notion that the lost tribes of Israel and the Jews of the Yemen were one and the same.[18]

At the same time, the arrival of Yemenite Jews in the 1880s dressed in exotic garb and speaking their own form of Hebrew aroused considerable interest and stimulated further speculation about the lost tribes. In 1897 Avraham Luncz,[19] the blind Palestianian-Jewish writer, became so tired of the subject of the ten tribes that he complained indignantly in a letter to the influential Hebrew journal *Hashiloah* that foreign Jews visiting Palestine were much more eager to seek news of the lost tribes of Israel than they were to have up-to-date information about the history and geography of Palestine and the general state of the country and its inhabitants.[20]

These ideas were to continue to have some currency for the next few decades. In 1928 Wolfgang von Weisl, an Austrian journalist, visited the Yemen. His account of his travels was carried by a number of newspapers throughout the world, including the *Evening Standard* in London, which reported that there were several thousand Jews in the Yemen subject to the Imam. But in addition,

> To the north-east across the great Arabian desert live other Jews, possibly descendants of the "Ten Lost Tribes of Israel" who have maintained their freedom through their fighting abilities and who look down upon their brethren in the Yemen ... Then there are the independent Jews, the enemies of the Imam, the Jews of the North: they live in seventy cities and they fight against the Yemen....[21]

During the late nineteenth and early twentieth centuries, the motif of the lost tribes of Israel and echoes of travellers' reports from the Yemen are to be found in the works of a number of Jewish writers.[22] Naphtali Herz Imber (1856–1909), the central European Hebrew poet who wrote *Hatikvah*, the Israeli national anthem, wrote a Hebrew poem called "The Sons of Moses," which describes his desire to visit those parts of Arabia where the lost tribes lived and to learn from them how to wage war. The Land of Israel would have to be taken by force of arms, and the Jews of Arabia would provide the skills necessary for this enterprise.

In the early days of modern Jewish settlement in Palestine, one current of belief emphasized what was seen as the racial kinship of Jew and Arab. A number of writers took this further and wrote about Hebrew-speaking Jewish Bedouin groups that had been sighted in the hinterland of Palestine. Hemdah ben Yehuda (1873–1951), for instance, wrote in one of her stories of a tribe descended from the original Hebrews. In her description, which appears to owe something to the travellers' reports cited above, these nomads are of singular intelligence, tall, noble of bearing, and handsome. They were the very antithesis of the way in which western European Jews at the time viewed themselves. In addition, they legitimated the Zionist idea of settling Palestine: "These wild brethren of ours who have preserved our land for two thousand years ... their feet have not trodden alien soil, and our language lives on in their mouth from those times until this very day . . . faithful children!"[23]

A central view of Jewish life at the turn of the century was the idea that Judaism was in crisis, that the Jewish spirit had been warped as a result of the unnatural experience of *galut* and that something radical would have to be done to "reform" the Jewish people. The Zionist movement developed a credo that maintained that the Jewish people would be rebuilt by the very action of rebuilding the Land of Israel. As Zionist pioneers attempted to create "the new Hebrew man," various models were enlisted, including one based on the local Arabs, who had such a natural rapport with the soil of Palestine. For a while the pioneers adopted some aspects of Arab dress and used Arabic expressions among themselves. Indeed, for several decades the heroes in Hebrew Palestinian novels used Arabic slang, while the villains used Yiddish. During the same period one can see that the Yemenites, too, were viewed as a redemptive model for the European Jews. In much the same way as Rabbi Yisrael of Shklov hoped to find among the Yemenites the secrets of ordination to facilitate the final redemption of the Jewish people, so in the twentieth century European Jews hoped to find a cure for their metaphysical and existential ills through an infusion of the Yemenites' simple faith and their perceived proximity to the wellsprings of Jewish existence and to the biblical past.[24]

In nineteenth-century Hebrew literature, the Yemenite Jews were portrayed as simple but well-meaning people with a profound love for the Land of Israel. Often the Yemenite immigrants were servants working for Ashkenazi Jews.[25] One such, a certain Saadya, is a central character in a Hebrew play called *Ha-Baḥlan*, written by Y. Barzilai during the period of the First Aliyah. Saadya, a figure of fun with an odd sense of humor, a peculiar voice, and exaggerated gestures, is mistreated by his Ashkenazi master. However, it is Saadya who is responsible for curing his master's sickness.

Intriguing perceptions of the Yemenite Jews were also formed by a number of Zionist institutions in Palestine in the early years of this century. Both the Jewish National Museum, which was part of the Bezalel Institute of Art and the nascent National Library, aspired to display the shared peoplehood of the Jews. But as Michael Berkowitz has put it, "The Sephardim and other Jews from the Arab world or Ottoman Empire were made into a romantic sideshow." In the pictures of Bezalel, Yemenites were presented as industrious and useful orientals working in their traditional jewelry craft and welcomed with open arms by their European brethren, to whom they could contribute their charming traditional skills.[26] Typical of the paintings displayed were those of the Paris and Vienna-trained artist Abel Pann,[27] a teacher at Bezalel, whose romantic images of the Yemenites would set the tone throughout the Mandate years. In 1947, *A Palestine Picture Book* (with photographs by Jan Rosner) devoted some sixteen pictures to the Yemenites: seven stress their religious way of life, two show them engaged in their traditional crafts, and the rest emphasize their quaint ways—grinding grain by hand or smoking water pipes while wearing their colorful traditional costumes.[28]

These attitudes toward the Yemenite Jews (in the early days of the state, one Israeli writer called them "Israel's most appealing community")[29] were to have a marked effect on their lives. The Yemenite laborers could redeem the land with their cheap labor, while the spirit of Jewry could be redeemed by their spiritual authenticity.[30] These possibilities presented themselves to the yishuv before the First World War. It has been suggested that the real impetus for the encouragement of immigration from the Yemen came from the Jewish planter class and that, specifically, "Aharon Eisenberg, the general director of *Agudat neta'im* (The Planters' Society), the largest capitalist enterprise during the Second Aliyah, was the first to suggest the catalysis of Jewish immigration from Yemen through propaganda initiated from Eretz Yisrael."[31] The underlying reasons are clear: the Yemenites would do the dirty work in the colonies,[32] as they had done the dirty work in the Yemen: they would be the "natural workers," a "lumpenproletariat" who would provide the cheap labor previously provided by the Palestinian Arabs. They would be the shock troops in the struggle to establish "Hebrew labor" in Palestine while pursuing "a quiet, contented, and humane existence."[33]

This initial experiment was not a success and it was not long before Yemenite workers were discouraged from entering Palestine. Some in the Zionist Movement feared that the Yemenite workers in Palestine were being exploited; some feared conflict between the Yemenites and the European workers; others feared that their presence would water down the socialist ideology of the Zionist movement; others yet that the Yemenite workers would completely undermine the position of the Ashkenazi workers.

Both at this time and much later the Yemenites were viewed as primitives, and stories circulated about their extreme simplicity. This account is typical:

Flown from the Dark Ages to modern times in the space of a few hours, they had thought they were experiencing the fulfillment of the biblical prophecy of redemption "on eagles' wings." When they awoke one morning and found the ground covered with a strange white substance, the Bible again came to mind. 'Manna!' they exclaimed ecstatically. 'Manna!'[34]

Others maintained that they had never seen a car, or a plane, that the idea of a house of more than one story was foreign to them, that they were innocent of the principle of steps. Goitein was not free of such attitudes. He wrote:

I have met Yemenites with an *almost* [my emphasis] European mind, and other groups, fortunately a small minority, who are inarticulate primitives. The Yemenites are famous for their cleanliness, and I believe this applies to the majority; but I have met groups, especially from lower Yemen, with whom I was unable to make close contact because of their uncleanliness.[35]

The Yemenites in Palestine were generally regarded as having fine qualities. Their messianism and simple faith was approved of, their naive love of the Land of Israel was admired. They were liked as long as they showed no signs of changing. They were tolerated as long as they stayed in their proper place, at the bottom of the socio-economic scale.[36] The more they asserted themselves, politically or in whatever other way, as they often did, the less they were tolerated.[37]

The "biblical appearance" of the Yemenites, which had caused such a stir in Palestine when they first started arriving in substantial numbers in the 1880s, was not often allowed to survive the refugee camps in Aden, where the Yemenites were marshalled in the late 1940s before being flown on to Israel. The Yemenites were authentic Jews, no doubt, but their very authenticity now made them appear absurd. The dominant ideology now required them to change into modern Israelis as quickly as possible. As one observer noted:

> They had to hand over their old clothes, which during the long and strenuous journey had been reduced to rags anyhow. These old clothes were burnt. Then the people were sent to a shower bath. . . . The heads of the men were shaved. Before leaving the shower bath, all were treated with D.D.T., and only then were they given new clothes. . . . We did not permit the performance of the ritual circumcision, because the aseptic facilities were not considered satisfactory."[38]

Any resentment the refugees showed at the destruction of their clothes was ignored. The men were often forcibly shorn of their prized sidelocks. Their absence made them feel uncomfortable. In addition in their second-hand western clothes, "they had the ridiculous air of people returning from a fancy-dress party in daylight." To preserve their modesty, the women tried to lengthen the short western dresses by attaching towels to the hems.[39]

The idea that Yemenite Jews could be transformed from what they were into something better is immanent in the literature of all the Jewish organizations who had dealings with them throughout the twentieth century. The Alliance representative in Jerusalem noted in 1928, that "their character is transformed by contact with the normal inhabitants of Palestine. Their Orthodoxy becomes moderated, their timidity disappears, they acquire more dignity. By their marriage with Sephardi women their physique becomes regenerated and their children are no longer yellow and emaciated."[40] In 1950 Ben-Gurion wrote a letter to Yigael Yadin in which he explained that the Yemenite Jewish "tribe" would have to be completely transformed.

> It is two thousand years behind us, perhaps even more. It lacks the most basic and primary concepts of civilization (as distinct from culture). Its attitude towards women and children is primitive. Its physical condition poor . . . it does not have the minimal notions of hygiene. For thousands of years it lived in one of the most benighted

and impoverished lands . . . all its human values need to be changed from the ground up.[41]

One of the most celebrated events in the history of the State of Israel is the massive airlift that between June 1949 and September 1950 brought 42,000 Yemenite Jews from Aden to Tel Aviv.[42] Once news of the airlift became known, newspaper reports and the like customarily referred to it as "Operation Magic Carpet." On November 8, 1949 the *Palestine Post* opined that no tale out of the Arabian nights was "so romantic and picturesque, so adventurous and exciting" as this Operation Magic Carpet——which soon became the accepted name for the operation in public discourse in Israel and elsewhere. In Israel it soon became axiomatic that the Yemenites believed the Skymasters of the airlift to be the eagles of the prophecy[43] and David Ben-Gurion to be the Messiah, not in any metaphorical sense but quite literally. Neither was true. Most if not all had seen planes flying over the Yemen and knew more or less what they were. About what was happening in Palestine they had a much surer grasp. The Jews from the towns of the Yemen had been closely in touch with events in Palestine for the previous three decades. Many families had relatives in Palestine by the late 1940s. Everyone knew someone who had left. Jews from remote villages were no doubt less informed, but their journey to Aden took many weeks and during this period, if not before, they would have had sufficient time to inform themselves as to what was actually happening in the Land of Israel.

It is perhaps not without significance that the name "Operation Magic Carpet" has become unpopular among the Yemenite Jews in Israel. In recent years they have insisted that the operation should be called "On Wings of Eagles," which refers to Exodus 19.4: "You have seen what I did to the Egyptians, and how I bore you on wings of eagles and brought you to myself" (although this latter term was neither used by the people organizing and administering the airlift, nor by the Yemenites themselves). Perhaps Israeli Yemenites are sensitive to the name "Magic Carpet" with its invocation of *A Thousand and One Nights* and perceive that its use contributes to the "orientalist" field of discourse within which the Yemenites have been viewed for many decades.

1. See H.Hammer-Schenk, *Synagogen in Deutschland. Geschichte einer Baugattuing im 19. und 20. Jahrhundert (1780–1933)*, 2 vols. (Hamburg, 1981); H.Künzl, *Islamische Stilemente im Synagogenbau des. 19. und frühen 20. Jahrhunderts* (Frankfurt, Bern, Nancy, New York, 1984).

2. See I.Schorsch, "The Myth of Sephardic Supremacy," in *Leo Baeck Institute Year Book*, XXXIV (1989): 47ff.

3. Overwhelming evidence points to the likelihood that the Yemenite Jews are descended in great part from Himyarite converts to Judaism. See T. Parfitt, *The Road to Redemption* (Leiden, New York, Köln, 1996), pp.7–14.

4. Cf. for example R. Ahroni, *Yemenite Jewry*, p.42: "The conclusion is drawn that Yemen's Jewish settlements were populated not by Judaized Himyarites but by Jews from the tribes of Israel who had migrated to Yemen." Frequently the issue is ignored altogether. See for example Z.Gluska, *On Behalf of the Jews of the Yemen* [Hebrew] (Jerusalem, 1974), p. 350; R.Ahroni, *The Jews of Aden* [Hebrew] (Tel Aviv, 1991), pp.vi, 16ff. See also the slightly different English version: *The Jews of the British Crown Colony of Aden: History, Culture and Ethnic Relations* (Leiden, New York, Köln).

5. Y. Sémach, *Une Mission de l'Alliance au Yémen* (Paris n.d.), p. 36.

6. N. Bentwich, *For Zion's Sake: A Biography of Judah L. Magnes* (London, 1954), p. 66.

7. Wizo in Israel. *Special Supplement: Exodus from Yemen* (Tel Aviv, 1949).

8. S. Barer, *The Magic Carpet* (London, 1952), pp. 11–12.

9. M.A. Weingarten, "The Genetic Identity of the Yemenite Jews," paper given at the Second International Congress of Yemenite Jewish Studies held under the auspices of the Institute of Semitic Studies and the Committee for Jewish Studies, Princeton University, 1992.

10. S. Barer, p. 12.

11. S.D. Goitein, "The Yemenite Jews in the Israel Amalgam," in *Israel: Its Role in Civilization* (New York, 1956), p. 183.

12. S. D. Goitein, "The Yemenite Jews in the Israel Amalgam," p. 178.

13. R. Yisrael ben Shmuel of Shklov was a disciple of the Gaon of Vilna. In 1809 with his family he joined the third group of the Gaon's disciples to emigrate to Palestine. In time he became the head of the Safed *Kolel* of the Perushim. He died in Jerusalem in 1839. See A. Yaari, *Letters from the Land of Israel* [Hebrew] (Jerusalem, 1953), pp. 324–25; A. Luncz, *Yerushalayim*, v, 1901, p. 289.

14. A. Yaari, pp. 347–48.

15. A. Yaari, p. 353.

16. Yaakov Saphir (1822–1885), Hebrew author and traveller, was born in Lithuania and taken to Palestine when he was ten. He later travelled widely in the East. Of the Yemen he noted: "In short, the sufferings of the Jews of the Yemen baffle all description. Even in the Holy Land things did not look rosy before 1830, as I know from my own experience. But in comparison with the Yemen. . . Palestine could then be regarded as a land of freedom." See Y. Saphir, *Even Sapir* (Jerusalem, 1866), p.52; see Y. Ratzaby, *Yemen Paths*, [Hebrew] (Tel Aviv, 1988), pp. 47–66; Y. Ratzaby, "*Shelihim* to the Yemen in the years 1883, 1889" in *Shalem* 1 (1974): 427–53. For a discussion of the internal implications of these tales, see B.–Z. Eraqi Klorman, *The Jews of the Yemen in the Nineteenth Century: A Portrait of a Messianic Community* (Leiden, 1993), p. 100ff.

17. Joseph Halévy (1827–1917), French Semitic scholar and traveller.

18. See H. Habshush, *Travels in Yemen*, ed. S. D. Goitein (Jerusalem, 1951), p. 63; Sémach, op.cit., p. 21.

19. A. M. Luncz (1854–1918) emigrated from Kovno to Palestine in 1869 and became a key figure in "enlightened" circles in Jerusalem, where he was active as writer, editor, and publisher.

20. Luncz makes this point in a letter to *Hashiloah* in reply to a criticism by Ahad Ha-'Am of one

of his books. See *Hashiloah* vii (1892): 282. See also S. Werses, "Stories about the Ten Tribes and the Sambatyon and Their Absorption into Modern Hebrew literature" [Hebrew] in *From Mendele to Hazaz* [Hebrew] (Jerusalem, 1987), p. 307. I am indebted to Dr. Herman Zeffert for bringing the letter of Luncz to my attention.

21. *Evening Standard*, December 8, 1928; see also *Ha'aretz*, October 5, 1928.

22. Perhaps the best known of these is Mendele Mokher Sefarim's *The Journey of Benjamin III*, which satirized the popular obsession with the subject.

23. H. Ben Yehuda, "Havvat Bnei Reikab" in *Sippurei Nashim* (Israel, 1984), p. 69.

24. See Y. Berlowitz, "The Image of the Yemenite in the Literature of the First Aliyah," [Hebrew] in *Pei'amim*, 1981, p. 95.

25. In the works of Y. Barzilai, there are a number of such characters: Salem in *Lehem u-mayim*, Ahi'am in *Ha-kevas ha-yehudi*, Sultana in *Sultana*. See the painstaking dissertation by H. Zeffert, *The Literature and Language of the First Aliyah Hebrew Writers*, Manchester Ph.D, 1994.

26. M. Berkowitz, *Jewish Culture and West European Jewry before the First World War* (Cambridge, 1993), pp. 162–63.

27. Abel Pann (Pfefferman) (1883–1963) b. Russia, settled in Palestine in 1913, where he was one of the first teachers at Bezalel.

28. J. Rosner, *A Palestine Picture Book* (New York, 1947), cited in H.S. Lewis, *After the Eagles Landed: The Yemenites of Israel* (Boulder, San Francisco and London, 1989), p. 67 n. 73.

29. J. Comay, *Introducing Israel* (London, 1963), p. 44.

30. G. Shafir, *Land, Labor and the Origins of the Israeli-Palestinian Conflict, 1882–1914* (Cambridge, 1989), p. 92ff. See also N. Druyan, *Without a Magic Carpet: Yemenite Immigrants in Palestine 1881–1914* [Hebrew] (Jerusalem, 1981), pp. 117ff; Y. Gorni, "The Paradox of National Unity within the Workers' Party Throughout the Second Aliyah" [Hebrew], *Meassef* 9 (1974): 55–56; *Carpet: Yemenite Immigrants in Palestine 1881–1914* [Hebrew] (Jerusalem, 1981), pp. 117ff.

31. G. Shafir, p. 96.

32. Professor H. Doniach of the University of London told me that when he was at Mikveh Yisrael Agricultural College near Tel Aviv in the 1920s, he was shocked to find that Yemenites were employed to clean the toilets. Yemenites were to be engaged in this kind of menial activity for many decades to come. M.A. Weingarten, an Israeli scholar of English extraction, has observed: "I remember my first visit to Israel in 1965, when I took back with me to England a photograph I had taken of an elderly Yemenite with long side curls cleaning the streets of an Israeli town. A truly Jewish state with Jewish labor and no shame, I felt. I had no idea quite how pathetic that scene was, how it was a reenactment of the public degradation of the Jew cleaning the streets of San'a" [*Changing Health and Changing Culture*, p. 36]. Quite remarkably, a Yemenite Jew was put in charge of the sanitation of the Geulah refugee Camp for Yemenite Jews in Aden in 1949.

33. See J. Feldman, *The Yemenite Jews*, p. 26ff.

34. See, for example, M. Brilliant, *Portrait of Israel*, New York, 1970, p. 105.

35. S. D. Goitein, "The Yemenite Jews in the Israel Amalgam," p. 180.

36. Jean Jacques Berreby, 'De l'intégration des juifs yéménites en Israel' *L'Année Sociologique*, 3rd Series, 93, 1956.

37. There was a certain degree of antisocial behavior on the part of young Yemenites in Palestine, which was somewhat unusual within the yishuv, where for ideological reasons the standards of civic behavior were remarkably high. In more positive ways the Yemenites proved to be an assertive community. In the refugee camps in Aden, they stood up for themselves with considerable pugnacity, often to the fury of the Ashkenazi officials. In Palestine and later Israel, it did not take them very long before they formed themselves into a number of effective associations and political groupings. Before

and during the War of Independence, a disproportionate number of Yemenites joined the Revisionist political movement and its youth affiliate Betar; many joined the underground Etzel group led by Menahem Begin. In 1949 and 1950 the Yemenites were the only ethnic group in Israel to elect members of their group on an ethnic slate. In 1953 Raphael Patai noted: "They are the best organised of the Oriental Jewish communities in Israel." R. Patai, *Israel Between East and West: A Study in Human Relations* (Philadelphia, 1953); H.S. Lewis, *After the Eagle Landed*, p. 53. On the genesis of the Yemenites' political identity in Palestine/Israel see S. Rubenstein, "Gibeonites?" in *Sei Yona: Yemenite Jews in Israel* [Hebrew], ed. S. Seri (Tel Aviv, 1983), pp. 211–230; H. Herzog, "Ethnicity as a Negotiated Issue in the Israeli Political Order: The 'Ethnic Lists' to the Delegates' Assembly and the Knesset (1920–1977)" in *Studies in Israeli Ethnicity: The Image and the Reality*, ed. A. Weingrod (New York, 1985).

38. Dr. O. Blum, *Health Conditions amongst the Yemenites in Hashed Camp* (Aden, n.d.[1950]).

39. S. Barer, *The Magic Carpet*, p. 52.

40. M. Loupo to Board of Deputies, Jerusalem, December 28, 1928. BoD Acc 3168/318–22.

41. D. Ben-Gurion to Y. Yadin, Ben-Gurion Estate, November 27, 1950, quoted in T. Segev, *The First Israelis*, pp. 186–87. Convinced of the worthlessness of the culture that had nourished them in the Yemen, Ben-Gurion would later say in the Knesset that the Government's aim was that the Yemeni immigrant should forget where he had come from "as I have forgotton that I am Polish."

42. In addition, 1,770 Adeni Jews were flown to Israel between March and May 1949, 200 Jews were flown from Djibouti, and 200 from Asmara. Including the 5,553 Yemenite Jews who were flown to Israel between December 1948 and March 1949, the total was 49,637.

43. The myth has even entered the academic literature. Cf. R. Ahroni, *Yemenite Jewry*, p. 1: "The Yemenites, most of whom had never seen an airplane before, associated this 'miraculous' operation with the biblical verse 'I bore you on eagles' wings.'"

From Ancient to
Modern Jewish Mythologies

Modern historians and students of social sciences or the arts tend to use the term "myth" as a given, which is accepted by all. The long and complicated history of the term makes it possible for each scholar to choose the special meaning of the term as it was defined in Ancient Greece, in medieval philosophy, or in pre-modern Europe. Most scholars and disciplines that have taken myth as their main research topic agree that we have to define myth as "sacred narrative," that is, the stories told by a certain society that construct its view of the world, analyze the supreme powers, and conduct its lives and social structures.[1]

Were we to adopt the first component of this definition—the "sacred"—the myth would have only little relevance to modern life and culture. Sacred narratives cannot be produced in a secular world. However, social, political, historical, and national narratives now replace the sacred ones.

There is another aspect of myth, which for anthropologists and folklorists is included inter alia in the definition of myth—its traditionality. Myth is a narrative created not by individuals, but by society, and transmitted from generation to generation by various means, oral and written.[2]

All the myths discussed in this volume have roots in deeper structures of Jewish culture. The myths of the foundation of British Jewry as the outcome of pogroms and wanderings are not different from foundation myths of other Jewish communities and learning centers.[3] The myth of the Arab in Hebrew fiction and Zionist ideology has had deep roots in the Jewish myth of "the other" since biblical times.[4] The myth of dying for the sake of "the nation," one of the basic Israeli myths, has deep roots in the ancient martyrological theme in Judaism.[5] To these belong also a large part of Holocaust narratives (Death in the concentration camps is labelled in modern Israeli culture as death for *kiddush ha-shem,* "sanctification of the Name"—that is, martyrdom). The myths of the supremacy of the spirit, the book over matter, the body, has deeper roots in ancient Jewish cultural concepts and myths.[6]

One approach to modern Jewish myths is the synchronic—modern myth as an outcome and component of modern life and culture. This is the direction preferred by most scholars, as we can see from the studies presented in this volume.[7] Another approach is the diachronic, which attempts to consider modern myth from the point of view of traditional cultural models and sources. This is the direction preferred by folklorists, who try to understand myths as traditional cultural models transmitted from generation to generation and to study them as ancient cultural motifs that act upon the collective memory of society. The impact of myth on life cannot be explained, in my view, without these ancient, unconscious elements that myth brings with it from the past. I shall try now to demonstrate this diachronic-traditional approach to the study of myth by means of one example: the ancient Jewish myth of the Golem. Wondrous are the ways of ancient symbols and myths: one finds them in ancient cultures, as central and powerful religious symbols, in modern culture, as elements of everyday language, literature, and music; and in popular culture, in movies, science fiction, and even in the comics. How did these symbols bridge gaps of thousands of years? What was the power, the vitality, that made it possible for them to survive for centuries, while other symbols and myths disappeared in the darkness that separates us from ancient cultures? Do these particular symbols carry the same messages and fulfill the same functions as they did for our forefathers?

These questions are not new for those who deal with the development of culture, and each has been raised again and again, especially with regard to our subject, the Golem. The motif or myth of the human creation of another man-like creature (homunculus or anthropoid) was already known in ancient cultures: in Greek mythology, in the mythology of the ancient Middle East, and especially in Jewish postbiblical literature. The motif has appeared and reappeared in both Jewish and non-Jewish cultures since the beginning of the twentieth century. It presents an exemplary test-case for the exploration of continuity between the beginnings of Jewish culture—the pre-monotheistic myths and beliefs—and philosophy and science in modern times. Studies of the myth of the Golem have concentrated on the observation of cultural continuity: Gershom Scholem, Byron Sherwin, Arnold Goldsmith, and Moshe Idel have each indicated different versions of the legend in sources from various ages, in both Jewish and world literature, and have pointed to the transmission of the theme from period to period, the influences of one upon the other, and the specific meaning of this myth in the context of each period.[8]

However, it seems to me that the studies have mostly been text-oriented and not culture-oriented. At their core stands the discovery and interpretation of new texts and documents that could provide evidence of assumed cultural continuity. Now that most of the textual evidence is known to us, the time has come for a culture-oriented investigation of this most interesting theme.

The main question, in my view, is why this myth was created in the first place, and why it came to life in certain periods and did not appear in others. What is the cultural meaning of the Golem myth in its various appearances? What kind of emotions and tensions have been expressed through it? What messages did it carry for the society that created and retold it in such rich and varied forms?

The traditions concerning the Golem appear in three principal categories: in elite, learned culture; in popular culture; and in folk culture.[9] In the first category, authors, philosophers, lawyers, and mystics have concentrated on a certain aspect of the myth of the Golem and used it for the formulation of definite questions arising from the core of their studies of the Kabbalah, Halakhah, philosophy, or ethics. Some of the eminent thinkers who have dealt with it include authors such as Meirink, Leivick, Borges, Isaac Bashevis-Singer, and Wiesel;[10] mystics such as Abraham Abulafia and R. Eleazar of Worms; halakhists such as R. Zvi Ashkenazi and R. Hanoch Gershom Leiner; and modern philosophers such as Norbert Wiener and André Neher.[11]

We also find evidence of rich and various representations of the legend in popular culture. The cinema, already in its initial stages in the 1920s, has created a number of interesting movies on the theme, while science fiction stories, comic strips, television, and computer games are some of its other manifestations in modern culture.[12] The ubiquitous appearance of the theme is proof that this ancient myth has had a great renaissance in our century and that the modern mind considers it to be a part of its own period, and not just a fossil of ancient times.

Because all the early evidence of the legend is to be found in the elite, learned literature: legal (Talmud and midrashim, Responsa literature), mys-

tical treatises, philosophical discussions, novels, plays and poetry, its appearance in folkloric culture has been largely ignored. This is because this
mode of communication has been the most widespread while, at the same
time, the most unknown. A typical example of the myth's early appearance
in the folk tradition is the story told by a certain seventeenth-century
Kabbalist from Poland:

> And I have heard in a certain and explicit way, from several re-
> spectable persons of one man [living] close to our time, in the holy
> community of Helm, whose name is R. Eliyahu, the Master of the
> Name [Ba'al-Shem], who made a creature out of matter and of
> form and it performed hard work for him for a long period, and
> the name of *'emet* was hanging upon his neck, until he for a certain
> reason [according to another version: "the Rabbi saw that the crea-
> ture of his hands grew stronger and stronger. . . . R. Eliyahu the
> master of the Name, was afraid that he would be harmful and de-
> structive, he quickly overcame him and finally removed the name
> from his neck and it turned to dust."[13]

This text is of much interest for many reasons, but first of all, let us consider the question of its source: The narrator testifies that the story was cir-
culating among many of his age. This, and the fact that some versions of
the legend about R. Eliyahu Ba'al-Shem survived also in the writings of
that period, are definite proof that the story was a folk legend in the sixteenth and seventeenth centuries. Let us try to understand what happened
in this case. This legend was based on the ancient Jewish tradition about
the creation of a human-like form, on local, medieval European stories
about magicians who created homunculi,[14] and on the figure of the leg-
endary Master of the Name of Helm and his expertise in practical Kabbalah. It crystallized within the course of one or two generations after the
death of R. Eliyahu and was spread among the Jewish communities of
Poland. The few versions that have survived in writing are only indications
of a rich and colorful oral tradition. In fact, we have to be aware that the
written texts about the Golem that have survived are only the proverbial
tip of the iceberg—we are able to assess the dimensions and strength of
the myth only from these visible peaks.

And if this description is accurate regarding the period we are discussing, it must be so for other periods as well, both earlier and later—including the rabbinic period: the seminal evidence in the Babylonian Talmud about Rava, who created a Golem,[15] is undoubtedly only a suggestion of the extensive oral tradition about the creation of artificial men that prevailed at the time. The same may be said for the important account of R. Eleazar of Worms and Ashkenazi Pietism (in the thirteenth century), or the later traditions of R. Löw, the Maharal of Prague and the Golem, which were transmitted orally by the Jews of Prague in the eighteenth and nineteenth centuries.[16] Since these accounts were not committed to writing, we know very little about them.

The oral folk traditions of the myth also indicate a different point of view. Novels, operas, philosophical treatises, and mystical trends are expressions of individual minds; they demonstrate the attitudes of the few and learned towards the myth. The folk versions, however, reflect the ways in which the myth has been accepted by the people, as part of their culture. It expresses their tensions, fears, and aspirations in a way that is much more authentic than the studied and ideological writings of the learned, even if these "folk" expressions are communicated only indirectly, by means of a society's cultural symbols.

From this we can draw another conclusion: the folkloric aspect of the myth of the Golem serves not only as a proof that it has been accepted by society as a part of its collective memory, but that it reflects, in every period it has appeared, the inner tensions, the most hidden fears, and the unarticulated hopes of the generations. Thus, the myth reflects not only the interpretation and interests of Jewish religious leaders or mystical thinkers, who have been the focus of most students of the Golem myth, but the most sensitive areas in the consciousness of Jewish society.

The classical account of the Golem in the Babylonian Talmud is a good example. Inserted there as part of the discussion on magic and idolatry, it precedes and follows stories and reports about the prohibition against acts of magic of all kinds and the danger such acts pose to the people involved. We know from other sources of that period that topics related to the performance of different kinds of magic, folk medicine, astrology, and divination were among those most discussed.[17] In the rabbinic period, the formative age of Jewish religion and practice, questions of differences between the Jewish faith and the faiths of the gentiles were crucial components in those extensive debates and should be considered in the context of these formative years.

An account of the creation of the Golem is introduced as part of these discussions. And so, when the Golem that was created by Rava comes before R. Zera and is revealed as a man-made creation, R. Zera returns him immediately to dust. The Rabbi clearly considers such a creation as forbidden, as the Talmud forbids all the other acts of magic and divination described before and after this story.

It seems to me that we have to consider the talmudic text not only as a story about creating an anthropoid, but as an ongoing argument about the legitimacy of this creation. The "folk," the larger layers of Jewish society of that period, considered it an example of the wondrous powers of the rabbi-magician. We can assume that in the original folk-traditions, the story was an expression of the formidable powers ascribed to such rabbis, while the religious leaders of the age, those who strove to achieve pure monotheism, considered such performances, or stories describing them, very negatively, since such events strengthened the beliefs of the folk in the liminal stages of religion and society and were considered dangerous to the integrity of Judaism.[18] This difference of approach is expressed clearly in the talmudic text.

Let us take, as a second chronological example, the text presented above about the Golem of R. Eliyahu of Helm. The differences between it and the talmudic text are clear: there is no hint of any dispute between the rabbis and the folk concerning the legitimacy of either magic or the creation of an anthropoid. Indeed, the accomplishment of the Master of the Name is not only considered as normative, but is the reason he became known throughout Poland. No prohibition of magic, as in the talmudic text, is suggested; on the contrary, the Master of the Name, using the *Sefer Yetzirah* and the *shem ha-meforash* (the hidden Name of God), is described as having reached the highest level of religious achievement.

During the sixteenth and seventeenth centuries, there was what one scholar labelled an "explosion" of hagiographical literature in Jewish culture.[19] The reasons for this important cultural development are not of concern here; however, the story about the Master of the Name of Helm is a typical saint's legend and only one of a large cycle of legends about his wondrous deeds that were widely disseminated in the Jewish community. The purpose of the Golem creation story was to promote the saint's name and enhance his status among Jewish communities of Poland, confirming his exceptional supernatural powers. It also undoubtedly represented these communities' need to believe their spiritual leaders could save them, through the use of sacred means and names, from individual (sicknesses of the body and mind) and communal hardships (the aggression of the Christians).[20]

A third example is from modern times. In the popular culture of the twentieth century, the Golem, in its different forms, is created by a mad scientist, or by order of a military administration, to fight enemies, to conquer the world, or to pursue a "pure" scientific investigation. In the modern myth, the Golem runs out of control, kills his creator, destroys neighborhoods and villages, and becomes a threat to the whole world.[21]

It is difficult to find a more accurate expression of the fears and tensions of the modern world vis-à-vis the real or imagined dangers of science than these stories. Biotechnologies, cybernetics, genetic engineering, nuclear physics, have all opened potentially fantastic opportunities to modern mankind, but at the same time, they have introduced new dangers to human life. The improper use of scientific powers, the possibility that mad or ambitious persons will possess or control such powers, are a real threat to the existence of the world. The fact that the Golem motif has become a part of modern popular culture testifies that these fears are, consciously and unconsciously, part of all layers of modern society.

In the last example we have seen how the myth of the Golem presents the discourse—ideological and psychological—of a specific period. This validates my basic argument, that we cannot concentrate solely on the study of texts and their relationships—the text-oriented interpretation—as has been the approach of most previous studies. Expressions of the Golem myth did not appear by chance in a particular time and cultural context. Our tendency to consider all cultural phenomena as if they were created by "texts," and not by people, cannot be valid. Thus to try to understand the legend of the Golem in the talmudic age, as separate from the dispute between the rabbis and the "folk" concerning the question of magic and idolatry, means to miss the whole cultural meaning of the legend. It is the same thing as consideration of the legend in the middle ages without also placing it in the context of the hagiographical literature of the German Pietists and the development of charismatic religious leaders in central Europe at the beginning of modern Jewish history.

One question that has not been asked in depth in the various studies about the Golem is why, according to the texts that survive from the different ages, did people create anthropoids? Students of Jewish mysticism cite mystical purposes, while modernists give scientific reasons. This element of the myth in particular requires a comparative investigation. Is there a structural or conceptual resemblance in the motives of the various creators of a Golem? Already in the myth's first appearance in Jewish culture, in the Babylonian Talmud text, it is clear that Rava and his colleagues created the Golem as an intellectual exercise—to test their mastery of *Sefer Yetzirah*. The later mystics, who were engaged in similar practices, considered such a creation as a means to know God by imitating his most complicated creation. All were motivated by personal interest: to develop mystical practice; to prove one's closeness to God. Very different in practice are the stories of those who created homunculi for obvious personal benefit: for example, the rabbis who created a calf every Friday in order to eat it during the Sabbath, or Eliyahu of Helm, the Master of the Name, who created a Golem as a personal servant. But there is a common thread to both types of creation: an intellectual motive may also be for personal benefit.

Even the modern versions of the myth—in science fiction, comics, movies, and the like—are based on similar desires. Here, the mad scientist is creating a robot that has a life of its own, but like his predecessors in earlier centuries, he seeks to perform or test his scientific superiority, or to use the robot as a servant. As Mary Shelley's Frankenstein, the robot's creator, explains his motives: "A new species would bless me as its creator and source." Alternatively, a wicked superpower orders its scientists to create artificial men for the purpose of oppression, world conquest, and so on.

In most of the variants mentioned here, the anthropoid becomes uncontrollable. The Golem in the Talmud escapes the hands of the group who created it, and R. Zera has to eliminate it immediately. The Golem of Eliyahu, the Master of the Name, grows to monstrous dimensions and becomes a threat to society. The most powerful danger is posed by the modern robots, who are a threat to the entire human race. Only by using very complicated procedures can the scientists succeed in neutralizing their power.

The most important expression of the Golem legend throughout its history is the 1909 publication of *The Wonders of the Maharal*, by Judl Rosenberg. As I have shown in my book about Rosenberg, he is the first author to have made the connection between the Golem, R. Löw, and the blood libel. His book is also the first to present the myth of the Golem to the general public—non-Jews as well as Jews, developing the legend from an esoteric tradition intended for the few to a familiar part of the common culture of society at large.[22]

R. Löw creates the Golem only when the number of blood libels begins to increase in Prague, and even then, after many reservations. The Maharal uses the Golem only for normative purposes: to rescue members of the Jewish community, especially persons against whom the blood libel was invoked. That is why the Golem never endangers the Maharal or the community of Prague, and he never gets out of control. The instant the threat of the blood libel disappears, R. Löw returns his creation to dust. We have learned from different examples that control of the Golem is limited to the purpose for which it was created.

In one of the most charming versions for children, Isaac Bashevis Singer's *The Golem*, one of the *lamed vavniks*, the thirty-six anonymous righteous men for whom the world exists, appears before the Maharal, instructs him about the creation of the Golem, and warns him: "Make use of the Golem only for helping the Jews, and for no other purpose." As long as the Maharal uses him to combat the blood libel, the Golem functions as expected; however, when R. Löw's wife lusts for the treasure hidden under a big rock and persuades her husband to use the Golem to retrieve it, he loses control over it.

It would appear that Bashevis Singer, with his sensitive artistic intuition, has pointed correctly to the core of the ancient myth: the creation of the Golem, as *Imitatio Dei,* must be a moral deed, not an intellectual or utilitarian one. If it is done for a moral-normative cause, it can succeed. But when done to imitate the deeds of God, or for a personal or immoral cause, it endangers the whole of creation.

Thus although there have been variations of the myth over time, as well as differing specifications imposed by particular periods, underlying the myth of the Golem is the theme of creativity: every creation is basically an imitation of the acts of God (or in profane terms, of nature—the Platonic concept of mimesis). The unconscious claim expressed through the myth is that creation for the sake of creation, or "art for art's sake," emerges only out of the egotistical drives of its creator and endangers, or destroys, the only true creation—that of God. The only kind of creation in which man can legitimately be involved is the moral one, whose orientation is the wellbeing and safety of man.

It seems to me, after a comprehensive examination of the myth in all the three categories in which it has been presented—scholarly, popular, and folk—that the real theme of the Golem tradition is the act of creation. The Golem represents the pinnacle, the highest achievement of man-made creation; therefore we must concentrate on the question of the motive for this act. Since ancient times, the Golem has been regarded as a creation either for the sake of art, or for the advancement of knowledge. The myth of the Golem in all its variations strongly rejects these claims: there is no justifiable aesthetic or scientific creation without moral purpose. Without such a motive, any creation would be, as the Hebrew proverb has it, "like the Golem that destroyed its creator." These seminal questions of the legitimacy and morality of creating something out of nothing or out of formless matter, of producing it in the "real" world and not only in the imagination, are posed in new guises in every age and concern every level of society. To my mind, the mystery of the survival and vitality of the Golem myth throughout the ages lies exactly here, in its deep meaning.

The contribution of twentieth-century Jewish folklore to the long history of the Golem myth was the presentation of a fighting Golem whose raison d'etre was the protection of the Jewish community and the defeat of its enemies. This aspect of the myth is the main characteristic of the best known Golem, the one created by R. Löw, the Maharal of Prague. As I have already suggested elsewhere, it was introduced by Judl Rosenberg in the first decade of the twentieth-century as a reaction to the wave of pogroms in Russia and Poland and to the new Jewish idea of active defense, which was one of the characteristics of the new Zionism.[23] This new activism was one of the outstanding mental and physical elements that propelled the "creation" of the new movement, which in turn "created" the new Israel. The well known objections of the radical religious Jewish movements to the creation of the State of Israel—that it was an interference with the deeds of God[24]—remind us of the objections to the creation of the Golem. As a Jew is prohibited to imitate God by creating another man, so is he prohibited to "create" the sacred State, which is also to be the sole creation of God. The ancient dispute over the legitimacy of the creation of a Golem became, in modern Jewish culture, the symbol of the dispute over the legitimacy of the creation of a man-made state. Therefore the deep meaning of the ancient myth is merged with the most crucial question of modern Jewish history. The man-as-creator dilemma, which is the core of the ancient myth, as we have seen, gives the modern phenomena their real meaning. It is also another proof of what we have tried to indicate here, that there can be no study of modern myths without consideration of their traditional significance.

1. I will refer here only to some of the recent publications on myth, which have relevance to questions raised in this paper: A. Dundes, ed., *Sacred Narrative: Readings in the Theory of Myth* (Berkeley and Los Angeles, 1984); M. Detienne, *The Creation of Mythology* (Chicago, 1986); I. Strenski, *Four Theories of Myth in Twentieth Century History* (Iowa, 1987); N. Austin, *Meaning and Being in Myth* (University Park & London, 1989).

2. R. Jakobson and P. Bogatyrev, "Die Folklore als eine besondere Form des Schaffens," *Donum Natalicium Schrijnen* (Nijmegen-Utrecht, 1929), pp. 900–913; F.L. Utley, "Folk Literature: An Operational Definition," in A. Dundes, ed., *The Study of Folklore* (Englewood Cliffs, 1965), pp. 7–24.

3. See, for example, S. Eidelberg, "The Origins of Germanic Jewry: Reality and Legend," G. Hirschler, ed.; *Ashkenaz: The German Jewish Heritage* (New York, 1988), pp. 5–7; J. Shatzmiller, "Politics and the Myth of Origins: The Case of the Medieval Jews," in G. Dahan, ed.; *Les Juifs au Regard de L'histoire. Mélange en l'honneur de B. Blumenkranz* (Paris, 1985), pp. 49–61; S. Zfatman, *The Jewish Tale in the Middle Ages. Between Ashkenaz and Sepharad* (Jerusalem, 1993), pp. 111–58 [in Hebrew].

4. J. Katz, *Between Jews and Gentiles* (Jerusalem, 1960) [Hebrew]; D. Noy, "Between Jews and Gentiles in Folk-Legends of the Jews of Yemen," S. Morag and I. Ben-Ami, eds., *Meḥkerei edot u-geniza* (Jerusalem, 1981), pp. 229–95 [Hebrew].

5. Compare, for example, H.W. Surkau, *Martyrium in jüdischer und früchristlicher Zeit* (Göttingen, 1938); E. Tcherikover, "Jewish Martyrology and Jewish Historiography," *Yivo Annual of Jewish Social Science* 1(1946): 9–23; G.W.E. Nickelsburg, *Resurrection, Immortality, and Eternal Life in Intertestamental Judaism* (Cambridge, Mass., 1972).

6. The tension between body and spirit in ancient Jewish sources is described in some studies presented in H. Eilberg-Schwartz, ed., *People of the Body. Jews and Judaism from an Embodied Perspective* (Albany, 1992).

7. This is the preferred approach of modern myths in general. Cf. R. Samuel and P. Thompson, eds., *The Myths we Live By* (London and New York, 1990); M. Warner, *Managing Monsters: Six Myths of Our Time* [The 1994 Reith Lectures] (London, 1994).

8. G. Scholem, "The Idea of the Golem," *On the Kabbalah and its Symbolism*, trans. R. Manheim (New York, 1965, 1977), pp. 158–204; B. L. Sherwin, *The Legend of the Golem: Origins and Implications* (New York, 1985); A. Goldsmith, *The Golem Remembered, 1909–1980* (Detroit, 1981); M. Idel, *Golem: Jewish Magical and Mystical Traditions on the Artificial Anthropoid* (Albany, 1990).

9. On these three categories see E. Yassif, "What is a Folk-Book?" *International Folklore Review* 5 (1987): 20–27.

10. On the expression of the myth in literature see B. Rosenfeld, *Die Golemsage und ihre verwertung in der deutchen Literatur* (Breslau, 1934); S. Mayer, *Golem: Die literarische Rezeption eines Stoffes* (Bern, 1975); idem., "Der Golem Stoff in den Vereinigten Staten. Elemente der Literatur," *Elizabeth Franzel Festschrift*, vol.I (Stuttgart, 1981), pp. 155–74; A. Scheiber, "Die Golem-Sage in der ungarischen Literatur," in his *Essays on Jewish Folklore and Comparative Literature* (Budapest, 1985), pp. 156–60.

11. For an overview of their works and ideas concerning the Golem see Idel, op. cit.

12. For examples of the reflection of the myth in popular culture and art, see Goldsmith, op. cit. and Sherwin, op. cit.

13. Translated by Idel from an unpublished Hebrew Kabbalistic work from Poland. See Idel, op. cit., p. 208.

14. On these legends and beliefs in European context see H.L. Held, *Das Gespenst des Golem. Eine studie aus hebräischen mystic mit einem exkurs über das wesen des doppelgängers* (München, 1927); K.Völker, ed., *Kunstlische Menschen. Dichtungen und Documente über Golems, Homunculi* (München, 1971).

15. Tractate Sanhedrin 65b. For discussion of these sources, see Idel, op. cit., pp. 27–43.

16. The important collection *Sippurim* (Tales of the Jews of Prague) bears evidence of this process. See *Sippurim. Eine Sammlung jüdischer Volkssagen, Erzählungen, Mythen, Chroniken, Denkwürdigkeiten und Biographien berühmter Juden,* herausgegeben von W. Pascheles (Prague, 1847–1864), 5 Sammlung; and K. Krejci, "Les legends juives pragoises," *Judaica Bohemiae* 4 (1968): 3–19.

17. The vast literature on the subject has been discussed in P. Schäffer, "Jewish Magic Literature in Late Antiquity and the Early Middle Ages," *Journal of Jewish Studies* 41 (1990): 75–91; E.Yassif, *The Hebrew Folktale: History, Genre, Meaning* (Jerusalem, 1985), pp. 161–85 [Hebrew].

18. Rabbinic attitudes to magical beliefs are described by E.E. Urbach, *The Sages—Their Concepts and Beliefs* (Jerusalem, 1969), pp. 81–102 [Hebrew].

19. J. Dan, "The Beginnings of Hebrew Hagiographical Literature," *Jerusalem Studies in Jewish Folklore* 1 (1981): 82–100.

20. On the social function of late medieval Jewish hagiographical literature see Yassif, *The Hebrew Folktale,* pp. 350–71.

21. Examples for this widespread narrative model are discussed in Völker, *Kunstlische Menschen.* Mary Shelley's Frankenstein was the literary model that was followed throughout nineteenth- and twentieth-century literature and cinema. On these works, compare the studies mentioned in n. 9 above.

22. E.Yassif, *Yehuda Judl Rosenberg, The Golem of Prague and Other Tales of Wonder* (Jerusalem, 1991) [Hebrew].

23. Yassif, *Judl Rosenberg,* pp. 48–59.

24. On the history of the debate and its development see A. Ravitzky, *The Messianic Idea and the Jewish State* (Tel Aviv, 1993) [Hebrew].

Sylvie Anne Goldberg

The Myth of Life's Supremacy Over Death:

Was Judaism Always More Concerned with Life than with Death?

Death is grim, harsh, cruel, a source of infinite grief. Our first reaction is consternation. We are stunned and distraught. Slowly, our sense of dismay is followed by a sense of mystery. Suddenly, a whole life has veiled itself in secrecy. Our speech stops, our understanding fails. In the presence of death, there is only silence, and a sense of awe (. . .) The view of death is affected by our understanding of life. If life is sensed as a surprise, as a gift, defying explanation, then death ceases to be a radical, absolute negation of what life stands for. For both life and death are aspects of a greater mystery, the mystery of being, the mystery of creation. Death, then, is not simply man's coming to an end. It is also entering a beginning.

So wrote Abraham J. Heschel in H.J. Riemer's *Jewish Reflections on Death*, a book intended for a broad public.[1] Towards the conclusion of his article, he goes on to say:

The greatest problem is not how to continue but how to exalt our existence (. . .) Eternity is not perpetual future, but perpetual presence. He has planted in us the seed of eternal life. The world to come is not only a hereafter, but also a herenow.[2]

In 1626, Aaron Berachiah of Modena wrote in the introduction to his *Ma'avar Yabbok*, the most popular Jewish book in the mortuary literature:

May the blessed day come, the day of the Redemption, for with its
coming, death will disappear forever (. . .) all Israel will be redeemed (. . .) and on that day [will be proclaimed] God, one and
indivisible in the higher union [of the divinity] and his Name, one
and indivisible in the lower union.[3]

Only a few centuries separate these two quotations. Yet, clearly, they express two differing conceptions of the universe. The question they raise is
this: Does Judaism indeed affirm the supremacy of life or is that only a
myth, developed and transmitted by tradition? To those who say, like the
Midrash *Kohelet,* that there is "nothing new under the sun" and that the
essence of Judaism is by definition invariable, I suggest we test the validity
of such a view by going for a stroll through the history of Jewish mortuary practices. The intent of this volume is to spark a reflection on the production of mythologies usable or adaptable by contemporary Judaism. I
will therefore attempt an analysis of Jewish relationships with regard to
death, with particular emphasis on the notions of "tradition" and "myth"
and on the conditions that produce mythologies about death in the
framework of Jewish society.

Nowadays, we tend to equate tradition with Orthodoxy. We view the
two as synonymous or at least as intimately linked. My own use of "tradition" is a little more historical and anthropological. By "traditional society" I mean not one in which Orthodoxy reigns, but one in which Jewish
laws and customs had the force of civil law and legal jurisprudence—that
is to say, Jewish society before the Emancipation. The so-called "tradition"
that the common parlance refers to stems far more from contemporary
interpretation. As for death, since the work of Philippe Aries, historians
have understood how some notions that seem to be the most enshrined
in tradition are really quite recent, and how our so-called "common
sense" can itself produce myths of antiquity in its own support. To
demonstrate, I will take the "discourse on death" as it appears in contemporary works or in Jewish bioethics, and contrast it with sources from
traditional Jewish society.

In seeking to understand how traditional beliefs are maintained in a
given society—and the kinds of implicit tensions and explicit questionings
to which the various beliefs about society (or natural phenomena) are
subjected—we can, as G. Lloyd writes, seize the moments of passage from

the metaphorical to the literal sense[4] or, in other words, evaluate the changes in the discourse on the formation of beliefs.

I would like to attempt such an exercise. To begin with, let us consider the notion of *pikuah nefesh*. As commonly used, it means: permission to waive religious interdictions whenever human life is at stake. However, its imperatives must surely have varied over time and with changing interpretations. Understood at one time as meaning the saving of the soul (as in *kiddush ha-shem*), at another time it meant the saving of the individual (in cases of illness, when it is permitted to light a fire or prepare food on the Sabbath). Still, the term *nefesh* can be taken as a metaphor for the way in which the concept of the human body is understood in different epochs. Today the expression *pikuah nefesh* clearly means that saving human life prevails over any other consideration, based on the biblical injunction: "Neither shalt thou stand idly by the blood of they neighbor" (Lev. 19:16), and reinforced by the Talmud: *pikuah nefesh doheh et ha-shabbat* ("The saving of a life may postpone the sabbath," Yomah 85a). Based on such statements from the source books of Judaism, and accompanied, if necessary, by other appropriate excerpts and quotations on life, such as "He who observes the commandments increases the days of his life," the reward for obedience to God, according to Rashi, "will be health to thy body and marrow to thy bones" (Prov. 3:8).[5]

Thus presented, Judaism sees itself as a source and way of life, with its religious and ethical components focused on earthly human life in this world rather than on the perspective of a future redemption in the other world. This sort of interpretation obviously relegates the approach of death to a background so distant as to be practically absent. However, it conforms so closely to the most common conceptions of our end-of-the-twentieth-century Western world that it seems it could not possibly have been valid "for all time" and "in all epochs." The changing meaning of the word *nefesh* is a good illustration of the point I want to make. In setting out to examine whether the supremacy given to life in Judaism is a constant, I will now comment on the most distinctive institution in Jewish society of the past: the *hevrah kaddisha*.

Although the Jewish burial society is an institution that has persisted over time, its present nature does not begin to suggest the power it once wielded over the communities. The *hevrah kaddisha* of Prague, founded in

1564, was the first to be established in the Ashkenazi region. It was approved by the Maharal, the Great Rabbi Loew, who ratified the earliest body of rules. This "state within a state"[6] was then exported from Prague to Frankfurt in 1597 and subsequently to all the great European communities. By vocation, the *ḥevrah kaddisha* was responsible only for the management of burial, cemeteries, and last rites, but it was not long before it also took charge of caring for the sick, the organization of *sandakim* for circumcisions, and the study of the Mishnah for the dead. It even concerned itself with matchmaking and dowries for fiancees. Also authorized to lend money, it became the precursor to an insurance fund. Having gradually taken over most of the social and religious life of the communities, in addition to its authority over death, it certainly exercised authority over life.

In the year of the creation of the world 5324 (1564), the Holy Community of Prague decided to put a stop to the improper behavior of two gravediggers "who (. . .) did not conduct themselves with the respect owed to the dead. They cavorted and amused themselves on the way to the grave." In so doing, the Community based its action on the commandment of *imitatio dei*, which states, "I am the Lord who buries the dead. . . ." Yet the institution had been created to correspond to the social norms of the urban environment in which its members lived. As instituted in Ashkenazi Jewish society of the sixteenth century, the *ḥevrah kaddisha* was quite in line with other institutions existing in the West, be they guilds or charitable brotherhoods, that fulfilled the social functions of philanthropy and assistance.

However, instead of claiming inspiration from a model that existed around them and whose effects were easily visible, the notables of the Prague community chose rather to stress the continuity of filiation, using phraseology taken from talmudic sources to strengthen the legitimacy of creating a new body within the community. This new body had to be recognized not only as performing a function, but existing by divine right. Its religious status had to be consonant with the holiest elements in the day to day regulation of the management of group life. This organization, whose vocation was to administer last rites, was conceived from the outset to exercise its prerogatives over Jewish society without any question or dispute. Over what did this Burial Society exercise its exclusive rule? Over Jewish attitudes toward death!

The importance of what anthropologists call "rites of passage" in traditional societies is directly proportional to the influence accorded to the divine in daily life. The greater the part taken by the divine in accomplishing its will through human beings, the more everything having to do with birth, procreation, and death belongs to its sphere. These crucial moments in human life are consecrated by rituals that stamp them with the seal of the divine. By elevating the practice of last rites to the level of a holy commandment and imposing a fixed series of ritual funeral tasks to be carried out henceforth by an organization specially entrusted with this function, the organization in question acquires a particular status in administering the rites of passage and the funeral rite itself. It is, by the same token, elevated to a particular rank in the scale of the sacred.

The workings of this process can be examined from the following excerpt from a preliminary paragraph added in 1754 to the original copy of the founding charter of the Prague *ḥevrah kaddisha*:

> As our former masters have said, the just and cherished commandment must be kept by the members of the Holy Brotherhood, *gomlei ḥasadim,* toward the living and the dead from time immemorial, from the lineage of Eli—eminent, exceptional persons who have displayed their generosity in order to maintain the purity of this commandment. The leaders of the generation, treasurers of the community, (. . .) have signed with their own hands the list of statutes, new and old, passed on from generation to generation, as well as the practices ordained by the masters: the different records and acts. And they all answered unanimously that it is good to follow the well-trodden path: "in the house of mourning rather than the house of marriage." And the sons will walk in the ways of the fathers . . .[7]

The entire text of the founding charter is too long to be reproduced here in its entirety or its total information analyzed. What is particularly noteworthy about it is the skillful way in which the past is integrated into the present and innovation turned into tradition by repeated quotations from the Mishnah *(Mo'ed Katan).* It is also clear that its members wished to institutionalize the Holy Brotherhood for all eternity, to ensure that it would pass from generation to generation within the pattern of Jewish community life.

Above all, we should note that if they chose to put their founding charter into writing, it is because it acted as a guarantee of authenticity and thereby the formation of a tradition. The reference to the past (in this case, not biblical or mishnaic times but the past immediately preceding the creation of the *ḥevrah*), would nevertheless open the way for future generations. To insure its transmission, "all memory, any oral culture, must reserve a place for the representation of a before, for a series of successive stages and for temporal landmarks" in the words of Marcel Detienne.[8] This makes it possible to confer on the past the role of affecting the present by giving it the status of tradition, or else by turning it into history.[9] The act of putting it into writing begins to transform a cultural phenomenon into an effect of historicity, enabling it to integrate into the heritage and to become a vehicle for the transmission of tradition and of antiquity.

Once the myth was consigned to writing, it could defy the antiquity of the account without being affected by it. Indeed, between the sixteenth and eighteenth centuries, the *ḥevrah kaddisha* spread from Prague to the rest of the Ashkenazi Jewish world and became the most representative institution in the community, the one that ruled supreme over the heart of daily life. Thus to the commandment of "Lord who buries the dead," the members of the *ḥevrah* added the one that said: "I am the Lord that healeth thee" (Exodus 16:26). Listening to Nahmanides, who said, "God buries the dead, visits the sick and consoles the afflicted," it also took charge of hospices and the care of the sick.

In the end, it supervised not only funeral rites but nearly all the community's collective structures. In fact, the responsibilities held by the Holy Brotherhood may be defined as those ritual acts linked to the rites of passage: birth, marriage and death, all of which became in time the exclusive right of a body originally created only as a provider of funeral ritual. In view of this, how can we imagine that today's commonly accepted notion of a Judaism essentially preoccupied with preserving human life could have coexisted with the immense power granted to an organization based on relations with the beyond?

Attitudes toward death that particular societies develop often shed much light on the beliefs of the living, on their social relations, and on their conceptions of the universe. These attitudes invoke key concepts that define and determine the individual as a being endowed with reason—in other words, able to create and apply notions with respect to the infinite that allow him to act and to perceive himself as a human being in everyday life. The belief in a form of life beyond our earthly finitude implies a series of practices whose daily exercise influences the nature of religion as well as of social relations.

The attitudes that a given society develops toward death stem in great part from the meaning that society gives to eschatological time: Christians, Muslims, and Jews all look to the end of time, but their behavior will differ depending on whether they await the Second Coming, the Apocalypse, the coming of the Messiah, or the Last Judgment. Thus, the place the Burial Society carved out for itself in pre-Emancipation Jewish society can be understood as an indicator of the importance given to the place of death in daily life. This was further clarified by Isaiah Horowitz, the *Shelah*, when he said in the seventeenth century that the human being is constantly subjected to the divine will, "giver of life and death," and that he must therefore think all the time of his death "as if he were on his deathbed."[10]

The system of rotation, by which the community notables took turns volunteering to perform the daily, monthly, or yearly tasks, is both a permanent reminder of the importance of the mortuary event and a proof of their belonging to the community elite. Being part of the Brotherhood was an honor one had to apply for. It was granted only after the applicant had overcome numerous obstacles, including a public examination. Membership in the Brotherhood was strictly reserved, sometimes even limited in number, and thus opened the way to social status. The last rites became the first steps to power in the community.

For Jews, the relationship to death was dictated by beliefs specifically linked to their conception of it at different periods. In Ashkenaz, the main body of sources was in part composed of classical texts: the Bible and the tractate *Semaḥot* serve as a basis for comparative analysis and the identification of changes that occurred over the course of time; Nahmanides' *Torat Ha-adam* and the *Shulḥan Arukh* serve as general temporal indicators. But the real tools of analysis are provided by the mortuary literature, which evolved from the seventeenth century in the wake of the *Ma'avar Yabbok* and spread throughout the Ashkenazi communities along with the new social structures promoted by the *ḥevrah kaddisha*. The emergence of a new kind of religious literature within a society suggests that deep transformations had begun to take place.

Considering that Ashkenazi Jews lived mainly in a Christian world, it is hardly surprising that they did not escape the changes that affected their neighbors, both in attitudes and in mental constructs. However, from the *Artes Moriendi* they made the *Sefer Ha-ḥayyim*, thereby transforming the Art of Dying into the Book of Life.

What P. Aries—like Maurice Halbwachs before him—called the "collective unconscious" refers to a system of coherent representation common to an entire society during a given period.[11] Can we then conclude that the Jews were part of the same mental world as the Christians? And if not, how can we explain that despite extremely different attitudes toward corporality, the sacred, holiness, and even the divine, not to mention conjugal, kinship, and educational structures, certain universal elements cut across these distinctions and can be found at the heart of Jewish attitudes, either simultaneously or after a lapse of time?

Today, when Jews are integrated into the larger social world, we find that death remains the last, if not the only, reference to a form of traditional Judaism. Even those who are not observant in everyday life rarely hesitate to call upon the *ḥevrah kaddisha* at a time of death, if only to carry out a rite they no longer know. Why accord to death alone such a privilege? Why cling in death to a distinction one may have rejected in life?

To answer this question, we now turn to a comparison of Jewish and Christian attitudes toward the cemetery, an analysis that shows the singularity of Ashkenazi Jewry during the Middle Ages. During this same period Christians prayed, calmly kneeling on the flagstone that covered collective graves, wandered through the potter's field where animals peacefully grazed, and held dances in the cemetery. But this differentiation of medieval Jewish attitudes toward death is not transposable to all other times and places. It corresponds more to a specific moment in Christian attitudes than to any desire for differentiation stemming from Judaism. Indeed, the main themes of the Jewish relationship to funerary places seem to have been codified with the writing of the tractate *Evel Rabbati* in the third century. From earliest antiquity, Jewish mortuary literature has been concerned first with caring for the sick, and afterwards with the funerary acts themselves, followed next by mourning rites, anniversaries, and cemetery visits. How then can we situate the changing interpretations in the Jewish approach, changes that show it was indeed influenced by the "spirit of the age"?

Where Western civilization is concerned, specialists have hotly debated the exact time, somewhere between the eleventh and thirteenth centuries, when purgatory appeared in Christian eschatological imagery.[12] With regard to Jewish eschatology, the debate could not be based on the same criteria, for lack of pictorial sources, obviously, but also for lack of written dogma on the subject. The idea of an intermediate territory emerged from the biblical *she'ol,* and when (between the period of the Maccabees and Bar Kochba) Judaism introduced the notion of retribution in the other world, a place of punishment also appeared. Does the Western Gehenna have an originally Jewish spatial context? The advent of the mourner's Kaddish is useful as a temporal index to situate the beginning of the notion that redemption is possible for the souls of the dead. We find it mentioned in the *Sefer Ḥasidim* as well as codified in the thirteenth-century siddurim. So it seems then that the essential turning point in Jewish attitudes toward death occurred around the time of the Crusades. It was clearly linked to changes in the historical conditions of Jews in the Christian world, but also to mental modifications of the period historiographers call the "second Middle Ages." From this period on, the elements gradually came into play that would become an inherent part of mortuary rituals or rituals that determined Jewish attitudes towards death.

With the writing of the *Memorbuch,* the rites of *Hazkarot neshamot,* the recitation of the *El maleh raḥamin,* as well as the *Kiddush ha-shem* and the *U-netaneh tokef,* the place death gradually assumed in everyday life became more apparent, and the possibility of acting on and for the other world became more palpable. This Jewish specificity is due, of course, to a context of tragedies, but how then are we to account for the fact that Christians picture death in the same terms? And how can we avoid comparing Ashkenazi penitential practices with those of their Christian contemporaries?

From the year one thousand until the Emancipation in the eighteenth century, a number of transformations affected Jewish attitudes toward death, but very few rituals were actually severed from the main body established at the time. The most remarkable changes were those introduced by the spread of the Kabbalah, which redesigned in its own way the contours of eschatological space and territory. However contemporary researchers may judge the work of Gershom Scholem, he emphasized the way in which rites of passage can confer on mystical elements a ritual value that is usable in everyday life. Without ever examining questions of historical anthropology, he wrote: "Death, repentance, and rebirth were the three great events of human life by which the new Kabbalah sought to bring man into a blissful union with God."[13] If we study the *Ma'avar Yabbok* and the period in which it was the most popular mortuary work, we can see that for at least a century, the Kabbalah cannot be isolated from the general body of Jewish religious norms. This background certainly contributed to the position that the *ḥevrah kaddisha* gradually attained within the fabric of the community. It acquired the status of an intermediary between human beings and their future (redemption), a fate perceived as collective, involving all of *klal yisrael*, and for which each individual had a share of responsibility.

The eighteenth century saw the implosion of the Jewish world, caught as it was between contradictory aspirations that drew it outward and at the same time pulled it back into a religious revivalism. Both were expressions of its internal break-up. In the end, the Jewish world sifted through its heritage to find those strands that would serve as supports for fidelity to Judaism in the modern world of emancipation. The process of revelation of the designated norms that would henceforth bear the tradition led to increased conflict with the community oligarchy. The community structure, the first target of the juridical reforms of the Emancipation, was affected in its ruling function, but the weight of its law would continue to influence its members, even if its power was now essentially a moral one.

Giving the past only a distracted glance, it might seem that the *ḥevrah kaddisha* was but a besieged remnant of a former authority that ought to have been content with its original vocation, the carrying out of mortuary and funerary services. Yet, before the *ḥevrah* became an agent of Orthodoxy, the centralized power of the notables in the *ḥevrah* was fought by the proliferation of dissident *ḥevrot*, each of which demanded the right to bury its own as it saw fit. Thus the transformation brought about by relegating the *ḥevrah* to a space of "ritual services" raises another, broader question on the place occupied in contemporary Judaism by resurrection, redemption, and messianic times. To a Judaism that proclaimed "Be fruitful and multiply" (Genesis 1:28), the Kabbalah had replied by proclaiming belief in the *gilgul*, the permanent reincarnation of the scattered fragments of the single soul that would be assembled at the time of redemption, and which, in the meantime, kept the links of the group inexorably united.

The fear of purgatory that once induced people to recite the mourner's

Kaddish all year long has been replaced in modern Judaism by paying a substitute to do it for them. Stripped of the cohorts of demons that once lay in wait for human souls, the earthly world has evacuated its terror of death. The funeral procession in which the whole community accompanied the deceased to the fenced-in cemetery and there implored his pardon has been replaced by ceremonies in which survivors march through burial grounds where crosses and stars of David stand side by side in an effort to preserve the memory of the martyrs of the Second World War. In a universe where the fear of hell had yielded to the fear of dying, mortuary literature has been transformed into bioethics.

Rewriting the past and coming to terms with the present in the sense proposed by Hannah Arendt,[14] the daily life of the traditional society, ordered by the rhythm of the *hevrah kaddisha*, has been supplanted by a dissociation from the ancient model in a dual exercise of adaptation or invention of traditions. Roland Barthes[15] posed as a postulate that "myth is a word" and as such does not enter into the categories of concept, idea, or object, but rather presents itself as a message and also as a value. Thus, when Emanuel Feldman has to explain to contemporary readers the extreme ritualization of the various stages of mourning, he says: "The rigorous halakhah of mourning thus underscores, paradoxically, the heavy Judaic stress on life." Quoting from the 115th Psalm "The dead do not praise the Lord," he postulates that "the dynamic interaction with God can take place only in the context of life."[16] Like A.J. Heschel, whom I quoted in my introduction, Feldman stresses the exaltation of existence in the "herenow" and relegates to some far-off time the emphasis that A. Berachia had put on waiting for redemption.

It would be vain to note the changes in Jewish approaches to attitudes toward death without resituating them in the context of changes in the matter that affected the entire Western world. Jews and Christians alike have redrawn their eschatological maps, and the space reserved for the world to come has been reduced, in common sense terms, to a metaphor rather than an eternal truth. To conclude as a proper French scholar should, I would suggest you meditate with Michel Foucault on the displacement that has occurred in present-day societies in relation to death, which make them neglect it in daily life:

The care we take to elude death is related not so much to a new anxiety that renders it unbearable in our societies as to the fact that the powers that be have never ceased to turn away from it. With the passage from one world to another, death represented a change from an earthly sovereignty to another, far more powerful one: (. . .) Now the earthly power has its hold through all of life; death is its boundary, the one moment that escapes from it; this is what makes death the most secret, the most private point of existence.[17]

Nowadays, when we have occasion to carry out a rite at those great events that punctuate the course of human life, the way in which we remain faithful to those rites nevertheless calls for gradual reinterpretation. The ceremonies that accompany circumcisions, bar-mitzvot, marriages, and funerals are far more social acts than the expression of clearly-defined religious beliefs. In being faithful to contemporary Judaism, the passage from myth to tradition, passing by Orthodoxy, has accomplished a mutation in theological space: in order to evoke one's belonging to Judaism, be it intellectual, filial, or as an affirmation of identity, we do not hesitate to define ourselves as traditionalists, meaning we observe a few rites and celebrate a few family holidays. In the same way, why not accept Maurice Lamm's affirmation among the new Jewish mythologies that "Judaism is a faith that embraces all of life"? [18] In the end, such an affirmation, by naturally integrating death into life, reduces it practically to a minor event, but it also reminds us of that process of euphemization that once transformed the tractate on mourning, *Evel Rabbati*, into *Semaḥot* ("rejoicings") and the cemetery into the *beit ḥayyim* ("House of the Living").

---

1. Abraham Joshua Heschel, "Death as Homecoming," in Jack Riemer, ed., *Jewish Reflections on Death* (New York: Shocken Books, 1976), pp. 58–59.

2. Heschel, op. cit. p. 73.

3. Aaron Berachiah de Modene, "Hakdamat ha-meḥaber," in *Ma'avar Yabbok* (Mantoue, 1626). I am using the facsimile from the Vilna edition, 1860, Jerusalem, 1989.

4. Geoffrey Lloyd, *Demystifying Mentalities* (Cambridge University Press, 1990). French translation by Franz Regnot, *Pour en finir avec les mentalités* (Paris: La Decouverte, 1993), p. 49.

5. Fred Rosner & David Bleich, eds., *Jewish Bioethics* (New York, London: Sanhedrin Press, 1979), p. 47.

6. H. Flesch "Aus der Statuten dem der Mahrischen Beerdigung Bruderschaften," in *JGJC* VII(1933): 157–73.

7. For the whole text, see S.A. Goldberg, *Crossing the Jabbok: Illness and Death in Ashkenazi Judaism*

in Sixteenth- through Nineteenth-Century Prague, trans. Carol Cosman (Berkeley: University of California Press, 1995).

8. Marcel Detienne, "Ouvertures," in *Transcrire les mythologies* (Paris: Albin Michel, 1994), p. 16.

9. Jean Lenclud, in Detienne, p. 26.

10. Isaiah Horowitz, "Ner mitzvah," in *Shnei Luḥot Ha-brit* (Amsterdam, 1649).

11. Philippe Aries, *Essais de mémoires*, assembled texts by R. Chartier (Paris: Seuil, 1993), p. 35.

12. The discussion was held mainly between Aries, Aaron Gurewitch, Pierre Chaunu, and Jacques Le Goff about the emergence of the "troisieme lieu," located within the here and now and the hereafter.

13. G. Scholem, *Major Trends in Jewish Mysticism* (New York, 1961, chap.7, p. 249.

14. For example, in *Between Past and Future*, 1954; in French, *La crise de la culture* (Paris: Gallimard, Folio- Essais, 1972).

15. Roland Barthes, "Le mythe, aujourd'hui," in *Mythologies* (Paris: Seuil, 1957), p. 193.

16. Emanuel Feldman, "Death as Estrangement" in Jack Riemer, ed., *Jewish Reflections on Death* (New York: Shocken Books, 1976), p. 91.

17. Michel Foucault, *La volonté de savoir* (Paris: Gallimard, 1976), p. 189.

18. Maurice Lamm, *The Jewish Way in Death and Mourning* (New York: Jonathan David Publishers, 1979), p.2.

Franz Kafka:
The Unsinging Singer

The failed transmission of wisdom could be said to be the central preoccupation of Franz Kafka's fiction, the fatal misunderstanding his favorite plot. That the imperiled wisdom happens to be Jewish wisdom is considerably less obvious, especially in the novels, which all but erase the Jewish face of the problem. The reader's eye must be sharp to detect the faint outlines of Jewishness, but they remain. Consider *The Trial*, with its alternate system of law grounded in inaccessible mystery; Joseph K.'s exegetical speculations about his case; the delivery of the capital sentence at the end of the book as a form of ritual slaughter.

But these are subtleties. For an explicit account of Kafka's attitude towards his Jewish inheritance, the reader may turn to Kafka's "Letter to His Father." In that famously undelivered letter,[1] in devastating, dispassionate prose, Kafka wanders the ruins of his relationship with his father, lamenting, among other failures, the fact that father and son never managed to find a common ground in Judaism, a rapprochement made impossible, in Franz's opinion, by the father's debased faith. The problem, he writes, was that there was too little in that faith to be handed down; it "dribbled away" while the father was passing it on.

> How one could do anything better with that material than get rid
> of it as fast as possible, I could not understand; precisely the getting
> rid of it seemed to be the devoutest action.[2]

If the "devoutest action" was to reject the father's assimilationist legacy, what then was the next step in recovering an authentic Judaism? Kafka sought that Judaism first among his friends from the Yiddish theater; in his tutelage, as a grown man, in the Hebrew language; and even in his fleeting interest in Zionism. His search for Judaism found its deepest expression, however, in his own fiction, which rose up like a labyrinth around his metaphysical investigations.

An insidious double doubt haunts Kafka's fiction: first, that the key to his ancestral tradition might be unrecoverable; worse yet, that his own literary attempt to recover it might somehow be responsible for the blockage. In *The Trial*, this anxiety finds expression in Joseph K.'s gradual realization that, no matter what course of action he follows, the result will be folly, if only for the fact that a course of action is followed. *The Castle* takes up this theme of self-induced blockage in the character of K., whose persistent demands to be acknowledged by the local authorities seem themselves to seal off access to the reaches of power.

In the novels, the protagonists worry the question of their unconscious complicity in their misfortune. The shorter works occasionally take up the question explicitly, shifting the burden of that complicity onto the shoulders of the author himself. Nowhere is this clearer than in the "parables," such as "The Tower of Babel," "Mount Sinai," and "The Coming of the Messiah," which take an unmistakably hostile attitude towards Jewish tradition by rewriting—essentially unwriting—the Hebrew myths themselves.

One of Kafka's literary inventions in particular encapsulates this deep ambivalence towards the tradition of the past. Ranging across the landscape of the shorter works, cast variously as a performing mouse in "Josephine the Singer, or the Mouse Folk;" a canine angel in "Investigations of a Dog"; and a Homeric Siren in "The Silence of the Sirens," is a mythological figure for our times: the paradoxical, self-negating, unsinging singer. We will read these three works closely, with an eye to the interwoven characteristics that define each encounter: singing as a metaphor for the transmission of Jewish tradition as Kafka interpreted it; and the antinomian impulse—on the part of both the singer and the listener—to block that transmission.

"Josephine the Singer"

"Josephine the Singer, or the Mouse Folk," which Kafka wrote virtually on his deathbed, comes as close as any of his short stories to announcing the world of its characters as Jewish. It seems almost painfully obvious that Kafka means the mouse folk to be a metaphor for the Jewish people, although taking the story this way means to read into Kafka the absorption and deployment of some antisemitic stereotypes—in the broadest stroke, the Jew as rodent. A quick catalogue of the characteristics of the mouse folk should suffice to illustrate the point: the mouse folk suffer from the loss of tradition (which for them means their music); their life is constantly subject to external threats, including massacres; in spite of this endless siege, or because of it, they have become inured to the hardness of their lives. They are prolific despite the hostile world around them, but they age prematurely; their children are denied a real childhood; generally speaking, they ignore historical research; they live in dispersal, hungry for the appearance of a savior.

Against this backdrop, enter Josephine, a performer whose art seems to transcend its performance, for what Josephine does cannot really be described as singing. In his efforts to understand Josephine's art, the narrator invokes a bygone era when the mouse people could still sing:

> Although we are unmusical we have a tradition of singing; in the
> old days our people did sing; this is mentioned in legends and some
> songs have actually survived, which, it is true, no one can now sing.
> Thus we have an inkling of what singing is, and Josephine's art does
> not really correspond
> to it.[3]

Josephine doesn't sing so much as she pipes, and even that not very virtuosically. In fact, what she does in front of an audience is something every mouse does. Every mouse is a piper; Josephine's art is to remove piping from its daily context, and by doing so, waken the community to intrinsic artistic possibilities of piping. This common piping, which bears the faint stamp of tradition, is elevated to an art almost purely by an act of Josephine's will.[4]

> Josephine's quirks of personality aside, she does provide a vital ser-
> vice for the community. Josephine . . . has a love for music and
> knows too how to transmit it; she is the only one; when she dies,
> music—who knows for how long—will vanish from our lives.
> (*KCSS,* p.360)

The mouse singer serves as the vital link between the tradition of the past and the forgetful community; her art represents the transmission—perhaps even the transmissibility—of the traditional culture of the mouse folk. And the mouse folk seem to recognize that. They hear in Josephine's piping a music that helps them transcend their difficult lives. Josephine's concerts are occasions for public communion. She is wildly popular, a fact the narrator treats as the great mystery of her art.

But as popular as Josephine is, she is never as popular as she wants to be. The narrator details Josephine's strategies for achieving the special status in the eyes of the community that she feels she has earned with her art. Frustrated in these attempts, Josephine begins to withhold her art from the community. By the end of the story, she has completely disappeared; but the narrator accepts her disappearance with ease, almost with disdain. It is not in the nature of the mouse people to receive gifts easily, even the gift of their own heritage:

> She hides herself and does not sing, but our people, quietly, without
> visible disappointment, a self-confident mass in perfect equilibrium,
> so constituted, even though appearances are misleading, that they
> can only bestow gifts and not receive them, even from Josephine,
> our people continue on their way.
> (*KCSS*, p. 376)

Equally at issue in Josephine's disappearance, and, by extension, the disappearance of the transmitted tradition, is the short memory of the mouse folk, a condition suffered upon a race that shuns history. Singers, not historians, are the stewards of the mouse folk's collective mind; the semi-permeability of the audience to its musical artists and the fitful commitment of the artist to her work are jointly responsible for an irreplaceable cultural loss. The story ends with the suggestion of Josephine's ironic apotheosis, an ascent to oblivion:

> So perhaps we shall not miss her so very much after all, while
> Josephine, redeemed from the earthly sorrows which to her think-
> ing lay in wait for all chosen spirits, will happily lose herself in the
> numberless throng of the heroes of our people, and soon, since we

are no historians, will rise to the heights of redemption and be forgotten like all her brothers. (*KCSS*, p.376)

Kafka's encounter with a Yiddish theater troupe in 1911 may shed some
light on Josephine. The diary entries from 1911 are filled with notes from
Kafka's research into Jewish history, excited observations of the Yiddish
theater, and evidence of the spell cast by the charismatic Yiddish actor
Isaac Loewy and the actress Mrs. Tschissik, who seemed to embody the
very possibilities of Jewishness that would later recede from Kafka's grasp.
The account of his first meeting with the troupe at the Café Savoy, with
its penetrating analysis of the role of Yiddish performers in the Jewish
community, could almost be taken as a brief on Josephine:

> If I wanted to explain them to someone to whom I didn't want to
> confess my ignorance, I should find that I consider them sextons,
> employees of the temple, notorious lazybones with whom the com-
> munity has come to terms, privileged shnorrers for some religious
> reason, people who, precisely as a result of their being set apart, are
> very close to the centre of the community's life, know many songs
> as a result of their useless wandering around and spying, see clearly
> to the core the relationships of all the members of the community,
> but as a result of their lack of relatedness to the workaday world
> don't know what to do with this knowledge, people who see Jews
> in an especially pure form because they live only in the religion,
> but live in it without effort, understanding, or distress.[5]

Of all the troupe, the most Josephine-like is Mrs. Tschissik, whose face, according to Kafka, ". . . sometimes looked like the face of a girl out of the
past."(*Diaries*, p. 84) Mrs. Tschissik's voice, like Josephine's, is transcendent:

> . . . the soft voice, that, without being raised, mounts heroically in
> even, short ascents aided only by a great inner resonance, the joy
> that spreads through her face across her high forehead into her hair;
> the self-sufficiency and independence of all other means when she
> sings solos . . . (*Diaries*, p. 85)

The Jewish community of Prague, however, takes these Yiddish performances for granted, just as the mouse folk take Josephine's:

> The sympathy we have for these actors who are so good, who earn nothing and who do not get nearly enough gratitude and fame is really only sympathy for the sad fate of many noble strivings, above all of our own. (*Diaries*, p. 85)

At the end of "Josephine, the Singer," the narrator observes that the mouse folk have moved too far away from the singing of legend to be bothered much by Josephine's disappearance. Ten years before he wrote that passage, Kafka came to a similar conclusion about the Yiddish theater; namely, that the Jewishness it transmitted, while initially comforting, could not be the foundation for his own Judaism, whatever that might ultimately be:

> My receptivity to the Jewishness in these plays deserts because they are too monotonous and degenerate into a wailing that prides itself on isolated, violent, outbreaks. When I first saw the plays it was possible for me to think that I had come upon a Judaism on which the beginnings of my own rested . . . instead, it moves farther away from me the more I hear of it. The people remain, of course, and I hold fast to them. (*Diaries*, p. 167)

"Investigations of a Dog"

Dogdom in "Investigations of a Dog," like mousedom in "Josephine the Singer," can be read as Judaism; the following are a few of the canine community's characteristics: its members are subject to divine revelation; its institutions are grounded in a tribal history; there is nostalgia for the days of the founding fathers, when the Word had mystical power; "uncovering one's nakedness" is a taboo; no other creatures live in such a wide dispersal; the community paradoxically holds firmly to laws that are not those of the dog world, but are actually directed against it. Here again, as in the case of the Jew as mouse, we must put it to Kafka: why paint the Jew as dog?[6] Allegorizing the Jewish community as mouse folk, huddled together in fear of the hostile world, makes possible an exploration of the communal aspect of Jewish life, with a focus on audience; the canine world, comprised of creatures in a sort of transition, half wild, half domesticated,[7] allows for an investigation into the Jew's limitations as he moves away from the world of tradition. The dog is a creature frozen in metamorphosis—one of Kafka's crossbreeds—whose domestication is constantly threatened by an underlying wildness. The dog, eager for submission, but also at war with the demands of its nature, is a powerful metaphor for the Jew in transition, measuring the sacrifice of its traditions against the security of living in the larger world. The dog is happy to surrender its freedom and live in the illusory security of forgetfulness; so too the Prague Jew.

"Investigations of a Dog" parodies many of the forms of divine encounter familiar to Jewish tradition: sudden, terrifying revelation, conversion to a life of questioning, the appearance of angels. But unlike the mysteries of Josephine's singing, the cosmic secret so earnestly sought by the canine narrator in "Investigations of a Dog" is made known to the reader. We are given more insight into the narrator's research than he will ever have: it becomes clear early in the story that the divine agency the dog seeks is actually a human hand. Why, the narrator asks, does food come down from above? The simple answer is that a human hand provides it, but that idea is beyond the conceptual grasp of the dog, whose deadpan insistence on the most rigorous "scientific" method for his investigations is the straight man in the story's comedy. It is in this gap between the dog's comically serious, life-or-death investigations into the hidden causes of the world, and our awareness that the "divine" powers are simply human ones, that the comedy of the story exists, and also its horror. As hilarious as the dog's investigation may be, we cannot fail to recognize the parallels to human investigations of the divine.

The idea of human agency plays constantly at the edges of the narration; even so, it is difficult to read "Investigations of a Dog" without some sympathy for the narrator, whose piety, if misplaced, is at least authentic. Early in his investigations, the narrator encounters a troupe of dogs in the midst of a stupefying performance. Particularly mysterious is the overwhelming music generated by the dogs' performance, which the narrator describes with religious awe:

They did not speak, they did not sing, they remained generally silent, almost determinedly silent; but from the empty air they conjured music.
(*KCSS*, p. 281)

He struggles to preserve himself in the face of such a song

. . . my mind could attend to nothing but this blast of music which seemed to come from all sides, from the heights, from the deeps, from everywhere, surrounding the listener, overwhelming him, crushing him, and over his swooning body still blowing fanfares so near that they seemed far away and almost inaudible . . . (*KCSS*, p. 282)

The only refuge from the music's "annulling" force is in a strange encircling labyrinth:

. . . the music started again, robbed me of my wits, whirled me around in circles as if I myself were one of the musicians instead of being only their victim, cast me hither and thither, no matter how much I begged for mercy, and rescued me finally from its own violence by driving me into a labyrinth of wooden bars which rose around that place, though I had not noticed it before, but which now firmly caught me, kept my head pressed to the ground, and though the music still resounded in the open space behind me, gave me a little time to get my breath back . . . (*KCSS*, p. 282)

The music has all of the force of divine revelation, yet the dogs who generate it indulge in the greatest taboo of the canine world by "uncovering their nakedness." The bewildering ambiguity of the encounter initiates the narrator's lifelong metaphysical search, a quest that ultimately isolates him from the rest of the canine community. After a lonely life of searching, the narrator decides that his most powerful research tool is fasting. "The way," he pronounces, "goes through fasting; the highest, if it is attainable, is attainable only by the highest effort, and the highest effort among us is voluntary fasting." (*KCSS*, p. 309)

He does fast, and his prophetic comportment is rewarded with an encounter with a canine angel in the form of a strange and beautiful hunting hound. The hound orders the feverish narrator—whose hallucinatory state of mind throws the entire encounter into doubt—to leave the fasting ground. The narrator quibbles, but soon makes a disturbing observation: the angelic hound is about to raise a song:

> "You're going to sing," I said. "Yes," he replied gravely, "I'm going to sing, soon, but not yet." "You're beginning already," I said. "No," he said, "not yet, but be prepared." "I can hear it already, though you deny it," I said, trembling. (*KCSS,* p. 314)

The culmination of the encounter is the angelic hound's unsung song:

> He was silent, and then I thought I saw something such as no dog before me had ever seen, at least there is no hint of it in our tradition, and I hastily bowed my head in infinite fear and shame in the pool of blood lying before me. I thought I saw that the hound was already singing without knowing it, nay, more, that the melody, separated from him, was floating on the air in accordance with its own laws, and, as though he had no part in it, was moving toward me, toward me alone. (*KCSS,* p. 314)

The most awful feature of the divine music is that it is meant for an audience of one:

> But the worst was that it seemed to exist solely for my sake, this voice before whose sublimity the woods fell silent, to exist for my sake; who was I, that I could dare to remain here . . . (*KCSS,* p. 314)[8]

Dazed and spiritually wounded by the encounter, the narrator reluctantly turns his research to music: music is the starting and ending point of the canine narrator's investigations. Looking back on his career, he observes: "I felt myself less attracted to the science of music than to any other until I heard that voice in the forest."(*KCSS,* p. 315)

"Investigations of a Dog" finishes with the narrator musing about his failure in the realm of science, and particularly the science of music, which is emblematic of the general failure of his theological investigation: "Here again it is very much against me that I have never seriously tackled the science of music and in this sphere cannot even count myself among the half-educated . . ."(*KCSS*, p. 315)

On Being Unmusical

As a young man, Franz Kafka also spent considerable energy trying to appreciate music, without much luck. In a diary entry from 1911, he describes the problem as a feeling of intermittent connection with music, and, like the young canine narrator of "Investigations of a Dog," a kind of encirclement by it:

> The essence of my unmusicalness consists in my inability to enjoy music connectedly, it only now and then has an effect on me, and how seldom it is a musical one. The natural effect of music on me is to circumscribe me with a wall, and its only constant influence on me is that, confined in this way, I am different from what I am when free. (*Diaries*, p. 137)

A year later, Kafka attributes his inability to enjoy music to the concentration of his energies into writing. Note the ascendant position of music in the list of life's joys lost to writing:

> When it became clear in my organism that writing was the most productive direction for my being to take, everything rushed in that direction and left empty all those abilities which were directed towards the joys of sex, eating, drinking, philosophical reflection, and above all music.[9]

A few months later, however, there was a breakthrough:

> Max's concert Sunday. My almost unconscious listening. From now on I can no longer be bored by music. I no longer seek, as I did in vain, in the past, to penetrate this impenetrable circle which immediately forms about me together with the music. (*Diaries*, p. 198)

The secret of music is to find in it a refuge from one's self. From the same entry:

> I am also careful not to jump over it, which I probably could do, but instead I remain calmly in my thoughts that develop and subside in this narrowed space without it being possible for disturbing self-observations to step into their slow swarm. (*Diaries*, p. 198)

The unmusical music in "Josephine, the Singer" and "Investigations of a Dog," with its tunelessness and its simultaneously transcendent and self-negating properties, is linked to a primal song, mystical in nature; listening to it is a matter of finding a way to exist within an "impenetrable circle," a search for self-preservation that is paradoxically bound up with the search for community. Much more dangerous than failing to hear the music in ritual piping is lending one's ear to the unintelligible song of the divine, which carries with it the risk of a wholesale annihilation.

"The Silence of the Sirens"

As if to make the point that all received wisdom, not just Jewish wisdom, is endangered in the modern era, Kafka unwrote Hellenic myths as well as Hebrew ones. Kafka conjures a new Poseidon, a bored administrator of the waters, trapped at a desk doing figures, daydreaming about a different job; a new Prometheus, impotent, it seems, to command an authoritative legend about himself, erasing himself by pressing his body into the rock.

Perhaps the most pessimistic account of the modern fate of wisdom can be found in "The Silence of the Sirens." We have already mentioned Kafka's "parables," his openly blasphemous retellings of myths and canonical legends. The adulteration of the original stories in these parables is accomplished by the insertion of what Walter Benjamin called "a little trick,"[10] often a single word, dropped so casually as to resist detection, but that nevertheless radically alters the meaning of the story. Robert Alter discusses this mechanism in fine detail in his reading of "The City Coat of Arms," Kafka's subversive retelling of the Tower of Babel story from Genesis 11.[11]

"The Silence of the Sirens" undermines the Homeric narrative in a similar way. The parable opens with a wholly unmythological statement of purpose: "Proof that inadequate, even childish measures, may serve to rescue one from peril."[12]

This kind of narrative commentary is typical of Kafka's parables. It is as if myths no longer have the power to speak for themselves, and the intervention of a narrator—whether it be in the form of a preface, an exegetical interruption, or a moralistic coda—is required to reinforce the flagging power of the story to dictate its own meanings. The precise nature of those "inadequate, even childish measures" is immediately spelled out: "To protect himself from the Sirens Odysseus[13] stopped his ears with wax and had himself bound to the mast of the ship." (*Parables and Paradoxes*, p. 89) Just as in the rewritten Hebrew myths, we find ourselves far from the original text almost immediately. In *The Odyssey*, Odysseus does use wax as a form of protection from the Sirens, but the wax is for his crew, not himself. Homer's Odysseus leaves his ears open to the Sirens' song; his protection from it is twofold: the ropes that bind him to the mast and his injunction to his crew not to relent and loosen the ropes, even if he should beg them to do so.

Kafka's Odysseus, by contrast, seeks not to hear the song, but to block it, an effort which the narrator openly mocks:

> Naturally any and every traveller before him could have done the same, except those whom the Sirens allured even from a great distance; but it was known to all the world that such things were of no help whatever. (*Parables and Paradoxes*, p. 89)

The invocation here of what is "known to all the world" is particularly interesting, since myths have historically concerned themselves with precisely what is not generally knowable. But even more striking than the sudden grounding of the story in general knowledge is Kafka's erasure of the witch Kirkê, one of the main figures in the Homeric version. We will recall that it is Kirkê who instructs Odysseus on the oceanic perils he will face; it is she who suggests the prophylaxes of wax and rope. Yet Kafka has removed her as a mediator between the mortal and divine.

The omission of Kirkê is significant. As the witch who transforms half of Odysseus' crew into swine—a transformation that leaves the consciousness of the men brutally intact—Kirkê provides perhaps the earliest narrative model of Kafka's own man/beast metamorphoses. In *The Odyssey*,

Kirkê's power over Odysseus and his men is such that the intervention of Hermes is required. Overpowering Kirkê, the disguised Hermes tells Odysseus, is a matter of resisting her magic; in that way, Kirkê's story is bound up with that of the Sirens. In both cases, the key to the enjoyment of dangerous pleasures—whether it is Kirkê's "flawless bed of love," which Odysseus enters, having successfully disarmed her; or the irresistible song of the Sirens, which Kirkê herself encourages Odysseus to hear—is a divinely inspired tactic.

But Kafka's Odysseus has invented his own tactics:

> The song of the Sirens could pierce through everything and the longing of those they seduced would have broken far stronger bonds than chains and masts. But Odysseus did not think of that, although he had probably heard of it. He trusted absolutely to his handful of wax and his fathom of chain, and in innocent elation over his little stratagem sailed out to meet the Sirens. (*Parables and Paradoxes*, p. 89)

Kafka's most radical departure from his Homeric source is, as the title suggests, in his Sirens' capacity for silence:

> Now the Sirens have a still more fatal weapon than their song, namely their silence. And though admittedly such a thing has never happened, still it is conceivable that something might possibly have escaped from their singing; but from their silence certainly never. (*Parables and Paradoxes*, p. 89)

Here again, it is useful to read Kafka's version against the Homeric text. In The Odyssey, Kirkê warns Odysseus with the following description:

> Square in your ship's path are Sirens, crying beauty to bewitch men coasting by; woe to the innocent who hears that sound! He will not see his lady nor his children in joy, crowding about him, home from sea; the Sirens will sing his mind away . . .)[14]

What is so beguiling about the Sirens' song becomes clear only in Odysseus' encounter with it: the Sirens offer up the story of the Trojan War, which is also, by extension, the story of Odysseus' own recent past:

> Sea rovers here take joy
> Voyaging onward,
> As from our song of Troy
> Greybeard and rower-boy
> Goeth more learned.
> All feats on that great field
> In the long warfare,
> Dark days the bright gods willed,
> Wounds you bore there,
> Argos' old soldiery
> On Troy beach teeming,
> Charmed out of time we see.
> No life on earth can be
> Hid from our dreaming.[15]

The mind-emptying seduction of the Sirens is their promise to mythologize the hero's past: What hero could resist the song of his exploits on those timeless lips?

Kafka transmutes Odysseus' hunger for the song of his past into the exhilarating possibility of silencing that past. Although the narrator asserts that an escape from the silence of the Sirens is "inconceivable," the reward for the hero who could manage it would be equally inconceivable, a sort of divine exaltation:

> Against the feeling of having triumphed over them by one's own strength, and the consequent exaltation that bears down everything before it, no earthly powers could have remained intact. (*Parables and Paradoxes,* p. 89)

In the end, Kafka's Odysseus resists the Sirens by concentrating fully on his own invention, his self-imposed blockage of wax and chains. Odysseus, hearing nothing, assumes that he has succeeded in blocking their song. Kafka could have stopped there, in a narrative moment roughly analogous to the end of the Sirens episode in *The Odyssey,* but instead he drives the parable right up to the symbolic annihilation of the Sirens. Kafka does not relent until he has utterly reversed the polarity of the legend: his Sirens, impotent even to attract the hero's attention, much less to seduce him to their shores, are overcome by the hero's blissful invulnerability. They have been seduced themselves and would happily perish in the radiance of Odysseus' oblivious eyes.

There is a final codicil to "The Silence of the Sirens," written in Kafka's best bureaucratic fashion, which quietly eviscerates the newly minted parable. Perhaps, the narrator suggests, Odysseus really did notice that the Sirens were silent and used the pretense of not hearing as a shield. In this interpretation, the hero's self-imposed blockage is no barrier at all, merely a pretense of one—just as the song of the Sirens is no song at all, just an unsung silence. The narrator considers this equation: on the one hand, the listening unlistener; on the other, the unsinging singer, and concludes that ". . . here the human understanding is beyond its depths." With that pronouncement Kafka's parable has finally reached its destination.

Conclusion

Gershom Scholem cast Kafka as a latter-day mystic in the venerable tradition of the Kabbalists, whose antinomian interpretations of Jewish scripture often served to reinvigorate the very Judaism they threatened to undermine. Scholem considered Kafka's collected writings to be canonical; he read them side by side with the Hebrew Bible and the Zohar.[16]

Kafka's own assessment of the possibility of a modern Kabbalah was less sanguine. In a diary entry from January 16, 1922, reeling from the aftershocks of an episode he interprets first as madness and then possibly as divine encounter, Kafka describes the act of writing as a kind of assault, and considers whether the assault was "launched from below" or "aimed" at him "from above." At one point he openly considers a new Kabbalah; the very thought of it seems to trigger a self-deprecating reproach to the modern artist.

> All such writing is an assault on the frontiers; if Zionism had not intervened, it might have easily developed into a new secret doctrine, a Kabbalah. There are intimations of this. Though of course it

would require genius of an unimaginable kind to strike root again in the old centuries, or create the old centuries anew and not spend itself withal, but only then begin to flower forth. (*Diaries,* p. 399)

In seeking the strains of a divine song still capable of penetrating the twentieth century's thickening ear, Kafka weighed the terrors and exaltations of a message aimed at him "from above" against the terrors and exaltations of blocking that message with his own fictional stratagem. He gave this paradox the figure of the angelic, self-negating unsinging singer, poised on the narrow stage between two abysses, equally capable of preserving tradition and annihilating it.

Kafka's unsinging singer—the performing mouse who selfishly abandons her role as the link to her community's traditions; the canine angel whose unsung song carries an indecipherable, annihilating message; and the Siren whose silence is even more seductive than her song—can be read as a metaphor for Kafka's unfulfilled metaphysical search, and, in a broader sense, as a metaphor for the dilemma of the modern Jewish artist: how to balance the antagonistic impulses to sing—and silence—the songs of the past.

1. In an account attributed to Max Brod, the letter was intercepted by Franz's mother and returned, undelivered, to the author. If true, the irony of the miscommunication is purely Kafkan.

2. Franz Kafka, *Letter to His Father*, trans. Ernst Kaiser and Eithne Wilkins (New York: Schocken Books, 1966), p. 79.

3. Kafka, *The Complete Short Stories*, ed. Nahum Glatzer (London: Minerva, 1996) p. 361. Hereafter, *KCSS*.

4. While the story is ostensibly about what it means to gather an audience and give a live artistic performance, there are hints that Kafka intends some connections to his own art of writing, particularly in the description of Josephine's artistic medium, "piping." Piping is common to the entire community: every mouse pipes. Just so, every human being uses language in his/her daily life; what separates fiction from common discourse is the occasion of storytelling, not the medium, which in either case is language.

5. Franz Kafka; *Diaries, 1910–1923*, ed. Max Brod (New York: Schocken Books, 1976), p. 64.

6. *The Letter to His Father* is an interesting source for the reader searching for the root of Kafka's animal metamorphoses. Kafka, in painting a portrait of his father's hostility to his friends, has his father calling them variously "vermin" and "pig," and being "automatically ready with the proverb of the dog and its fleas." The father threatens to tear little Franz apart "like a fish"; he labels a sick employee "a mangy dog." The association of his father's rage with animals could be a reasonable basis for the transformations in Kafka's animal stories, which do seem to bear the mark of the father's curse.

7. For his thoughts on the transitional nature of dogs, I am indebted to Dr. Alun David of Corpus Christi College, Oxford.

8. Compare this with another terrible singling-out, the final sentences of the parable "Before the Law," from *The Trial*:

> *The doorkeeper recognizes that the man has reached his end, and, to let his failing senses catch the words, roars in his ear: "No one else could ever be admitted here, since this gate was made only for you. I am now going to shut it." (KCSS, p. 4)*

9. *Diaries*, p. 163. Note the similarity between this diary entry and the following passage from "Josephine the Singer: ". . . it is as if she has concentrated all of her strength on her song, as if from everything in her that does not directly subserve her singing all strength has been withdrawn, almost all power of life. . . ." (*KCSS*, p. 363)

10. Walter Benjamin, *Illuminations* (N.Y.: Schocken Books, 1969), p.117.

11. Robert Alter, *Necessary Angels* (Cambridge: Harvard University Press, 1991), p. 54.

12. Franz Kafka, *Parables and Paradoxes* (New York: Schocken Books), p. 89.

13. I have taken the liberty of changing the hero's name from the Latin "Ulysses," as translators Willa and Edwin Muir have rendered it, to the Greek "Odysseus," which is the form Kafka used.

14. Book XII, lines 48–53, Homer, *The Odyssey*, trans. Robert Fitzgerald (New York: Random House, 1990), p. 210.

15. Book XII, lines 232–45, p. 215.

16. Robert Alter, *Necessary Angels*, p. 69.

Authors

Glenda Abramson is Cowley Lecturer in Post-Biblical Hebrew at the University of Oxford, Schreiber Fellow in Modern Jewish Studies at the Oxford Centre for Hebrew and Jewish Studies, and Fellow at St. Cross College, University of Oxford. Among her publications: *Modern Hebrew Drama* (1978); *The Writing of Yehuda Amichai: A Thematic Approach* (1989); *Hebrew in Three Months* (1993, 1999); and *Drama and Ideology in Modern Israel* (1998). She is the editor of *The Blackwell Companion to Jewish Culture—from the Eighteenth Century to the Present* (1989); *The Oxford Book of Hebrew Short Stories* (1996); and *The Experienced Soul: Studies in Amichai* (1997).

David Cesarani is Parkes-Wiener Professor of Twentieth-Century Jewish History and Culture at Southampton University and Director of the Institute of Contemporary History and the Wiener Library, London. He has written and edited several books on British-Jewish history and the history of the Holocaust. These include *The Making of Modern Anglo-Jewry* (1990); *Justice Delayed* (1992), a study of how Nazi war criminals entered the U.K. after the war; The Final *Solution: Origins and Implementations* (1994); *The Jewish Chronicle and Anglo-Jewry 1841–1991* (1994); *Citizenship, Nationality, and Migration in Europe* (1996) (edited with Mary Fulbrook); and *Genocide and Rescue: The Holocaust in Hungary, 1944* (1997). His most recent publication is *Arthur Koestler: The Homeless Mind* (1998).

Sally Frankental, the first Director of the Isaac and Jessie Kaplan Centre for Jewish Studies and Research at the University of Cape Town, now lectures in the Department of Social Anthropology at U.C.T. and teaches a course in contemporary Jewry in the Department of Hebrew and Jewish Studies. Her early work focused on kinship among Tamil Indians in Cape Town and on urban (white) aging. Her current research examines the Jewish identity of Israeli migrants in South Africa.

Nurith Gertz is Professor of Literature and Cinema at the Open University of Israel. Among her recent publications are *Motion Fiction: Literature and Cinema* (1994); *Captive of a Dream: National Myths in Israeli Culture* (1995); *Not From Here: A Biography of a Century* (1997).

Sylvie Ann Goldberg is Associate Professor at the Ecole des Hautes Etudes en Sciences Sociales. She is a historian of Ashkenazi societies and author of *Crossing the Jabbok: Illness and Death in Ashkenazi Judaism in Sixteenth-through Nineteenth-Century Prague,* translated by Carol Cosman, with an introduction by T. Laqueur (1996). She is the editor of *Histoire juive, Histoire des Juifs: d'autres approches* (1994); *Dictionnaire Encyclopédique du Judaïsme; Esquisse de l'histoire du Peuple Juif* (1993, 1996), and of a special issue of *Annales: Histoire, Sciences, Sociales* [HSS 5, September–October 1994].

Matthew Olshan is a writer and teacher of writing in Baltimore, Maryland. His paper grew out of a dissertation written at the Oxford Centre for Hebrew and Jewish Studies. Mr. Olshan was educated at Harvard, Johns Hopkins, and the Oxford Centre. This is his first academic publication.

Tudor Parfitt is Reader in Modern Jewish Studies at the School of Oriental and African Studies, University of London, where he is also Chair of the Centre for Near and Middle Eastern Studies and Director of the Centre for Jewish Studies. He has published widely on Hebrew language and literature and on Judaizing sects and Jews in the Islamic world. Among his publications are *The Jews of Palestine 1800–1882* (1987) and *The Road to Redemption* (1996).

Milton Shain is Professor of Modern Jewish History in the Department of Hebrew and Jewish Studies at the University of Cape Town, where he is also Director of the Isaac and Jessie Kaplan Centre for Jewish Studies and Research. He has published numerous scholarly articles, chapters in books, and encyclopedia entries and is the author of *Jewry and Cape Society: The Origins and Activities of the Jewish Board of Deputies for the Cape Colony* (1983), *The Roots of Antisemitism in South Africa* (1994), which was awarded the University of Cape Town Book Prize for 1996, and *Antisemitism* (1998).

Anita Shapira was born in Poland and emigrated to Israel in 1947. She is Professor in the Department of Jewish History, Tel Aviv University, where since 1996 she has been the incumbent of the Ruben Merenfeld Chair on the Study of Zionism. Professor Shapira is currently Head of the Yitzhak Rabin Center for Israel Studies, the national commemoration project on behalf of the late Prime Minister. Her research focuses on the history of

Zionism and the Jewish community in Palestine since 1882 and her recent works concentrate on questions of identity and culture in Israel. Among her publications: *Berl Katznelson, A Biography of a Socialist Zionist* (Hebrew, 1980), a shortened version of the Hebrew edition, in English (1984) and in German (*Berl Katznelson, Ein Sozialistischer Zionist* (1988); *The Army Controversy*, 1948 (Hebrew, 1985); *Land and Power, the Zionist Resort to Force, 1881–1948* (Hebrew and English, 1992); *New Jews, Old Jews,* with Yehuda Reinharz, ed. (Hebrew 1997); and *Essential Papers on Zionism* (1996).

Dan Urian is Associate Professor in the Theatre Department at Tel Aviv University. He is the author of *Drama and Theatre* (1988); *The Judaic Nature of Israeli Theatre* (Hebrew, 1999); *The Arab in Israeli Drama and Theatre* (English, 1997); and the editor of *Contemporary Theatre Review* (1995), published in the U.K. by Harwood Academic Press. Many of his works have been published in English translation.

Jonathan Webber is a social anthropologist and, since 1983, has been the Fellow in Jewish Social Studies at the Oxford Centre for Hebrew and Jewish Studies; Hebrew Centre Lecturer in Social Anthropology at Oxford University; and since 1980, Research Fellow, Wolfson College, Oxford. His principal research interests are identity and ethnicity; the anthropological study of contemporary diaspora Jewish society; and Polish-Jewish relations, with particular reference to the Holocaust. Dr. Webber is a Founding Member of the International Auschwitz Council, a Polish government advisory body, and Chair of its standing committee for education. Among his publications are *Auschwitz: A History in Photographs* (with Connie Wilsack, 1993) and an edited volume on *Jewish Identities in the New Europe* (1994). He is currently working on an illustrated volume entitled *Traces of Memory: The Ruins of Jewish Civilization in Polish Galicia.*

Eli Yassif is Professor of Hebrew Literature and Jewish folklore at Tel Aviv University. He is also the founder of Folklore Studies at Ben-Gurion University, and has taught as Visiting Professor at the University of London, the University of California at Berkeley and the University of Chicago. He has published books and articles on the study of Jewish folklore and medieval Jewish narratives. His latest publication is *Hebrew Folktale: History, Genre, Meaning* to be published by the University of Indiana Press (1999).

Index